Stwertka, Eve

Genetic engineering

DATE DUE

GENETIC ENGINEERING

GENETIC ENGINEERING

REVISED EDITION

BY
EVE
AND
ALBERT
STWERTKA

Franklin Watts
New York | London | Toronto | Sydney | 1989
Revised Edition | An Impact Book

Library of Congress Cataloging-in-Publication Data

Stwertka, Eve.
Genetic engineering / by Eve and Albert Stwertka. —
Rev. ed., 2nd ed.
p.   cm.—(An Impact book)
Bibliography: p.
Includes index.
Summary: Discusses recombinant DNA techniques; the application of
this technology including amniocentesis, genetic counseling, and
test-tube parenthood; and the ethical-moral questions raised by
genetic engineering.
ISBN 0-531-10775-2
1. Genetic engineering—Juvenile literature.   [1. Genetic
engineering.]   I. Stwertka, Albert.   II. Title.
QH442.S78 1989   89-5808   CIP   AC
660'.65—dc20

CONTENTS

Illustrations by: Vantage Art

Photographs courtesy of:
Photo Researchers: pp. 10 (Dr. Tony Brain/SPL),
16 (Farrell Grehan), 20 (Biophoto Associates/
Science Source), 26, 37 (Biophoto Associates), 45
(Dr. Jeremy Burgess/SPL), 73 (Philippe Plailly/
SPL), 78 (Sinclair Stamers/SPL), 100, 122
(Petit Format); UPI/Bettmann: pp. 12, 88;
Rijksmuseum voor de Geschiedenis de Natuur-
wetenschappen, Leiden: p. 17; Cold Spring
Harbor Laboratory: pp 28, 83; Dave Meeklas:
p. 47; Taurus: pp. 49 (L.I.T. Rhodes), 70
(Tim McCabe), 105 (Grace Moore); JB
Pictures: p. 54 (John Nordell, Cambridge,
MA); Wide World: p. 89

GENETIC ENGINEERING

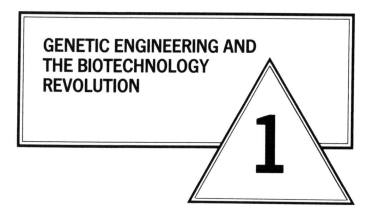

GENETIC ENGINEERING AND THE BIOTECHNOLOGY REVOLUTION

1

In 1982, scientists took the gene that produces human insulin and inserted it into *E. coli*, a microorganism that lives in the intestines of human beings. Within days they had produced insulin. Today, insulin produced this way is used by diabetics around the world.

The production of insulin in this manner is a striking example of the biotechnology revolution, possibly the most significant revolution in science since the discovery, four hundred years ago, by Copernicus that the earth revolves around the sun and not the other way around.

Biotechnology includes all those techniques that use living cells to produce commercial products. Wine and beer making are biotechnology, since microorganisms are used to transform sugar into alcohol. Using bacteria to eat up oil spills is also biotechnology, as is using bacteria to clean up sewage and extract metals from rocks.

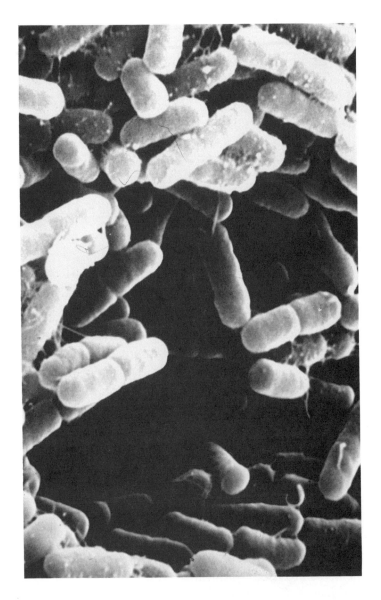

E. coli (Escherichia coli), *a generally harmless microorganism that colonizes the human intestine, is one of the workhorses of biotechnology.*

Microorganisms are the workhorses and unsung heroes of the biotechnological revolution. They are essential for hundreds of different jobs. In medicine, they help make antibiotics, vaccines, and hormones. In industry, they make chemicals, gases, and fuels. In agriculture, they produce cattle medicines and new plant varieties. Grown by the billions in big vats, they provide a solid protein-rich animal food.

Biotechnology has existed for thousands of years. For instance, the first known beer recipe is 4,000 years old. Throughout the centuries these tiny creatures we now call microorganisms or bacteria have helped us. Their mysterious presence enabled people to make a soft, springy bread, turn milk into delicious cheese, and ferment grape juice into wine for celebrating happy occasions. But it is the application of the techniques of genetic engineering that is at the heart of the new biotechnological revolution. Genetic engineering is what was used to produce insulin.

Genetic engineering involves the manipulation of the molecules that make up the innermost structure of living matter. These molecules control the hereditary information carried by cells. Genetic engineering is a totally new process and is based on the science of molecular biology, which came into being barely forty years ago.

The idea of scientists manipulating organisms in the interests of either research or industry has both positive and negative aspects. On the one hand, the new technology represents a significant advance in our ability to use microorganisms to improve life. On the other hand, it can change the very forms of life as we know them, possibly resulting in harm to the environment.

With the techniques of genetic engineering, these four scientists—(L to R) Keiichi Itakura, Arthur D. Riggs, David V. Goeddel and Roberto Crea—were able to artifically produce human insulin.

The biotechnological revolution has led to the creation of more than a hundred new biotechnology companies. Some of the leading companies—such as Cetus Corporation in Emeryville, California; Genentech in San Francisco; Biogen Corporation in Geneva, Switzerland; and Molecular Genetics in Minnetonka, Minnesota—have already invested more than $3 billion in research and development.

At the same time questions have been raised about the safety, necessity, and morality of the entire enterprise. Already, biotechnologists have used human growth hormones to engineer a "supermouse" twice the size of its twin brother.[1] Companies such as Amgen in Thousand Oaks, California, are developing cattle and poultry growth hormones that are expected to yield larger, firmer, meatier animals and birds. New technologies often have dangerous implications. It's important that these technologies are used only by responsible people in responsible ways.

Suppose science were to develop a pill that could make children grow 7 feet high or even taller. Should such a pill be sold or should it be banned? How would you prevent some misguided parent with dreams of future glory from trying to turn a normal youngster into a monster-sized athletic colossus?

Actually, a substance that helps children grow taller is already available to doctors for experimental use. Engineered by biotechnologists at Genentech and called Protropin, this artificial growth hormone was designed to help children who do not produce enough of their own natural growth hormone due to injury or birth defect.

In order to better understand genetic engineering and make the right decisions concerning it, we need to understand more about the functioning of the cell.

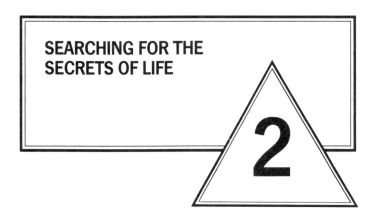

SEARCHING FOR THE SECRETS OF LIFE

Life has existed on earth for hundreds of millions of years. Scientists believe that life began in the oceans, in the form of simple organisms similar to bacteria, amoebas, and algae. Over time, these organisms developed into more complex organisms, including plants, reptiles, fish, and mammals. Eventually, the various species as we know them today developed. This developmental process is called *evolution*.

All living organisms exhibit certain features that characterize them as being living. The ability to reproduce is one of the most important of these traits. All organisms have a way of reproducing themselves, whether it is by budding, dividing in half, or joining with another organism to produce an offspring.

In reproduction, some features of the parent organism or organisms are transmitted to the offspring, while others are not. Some new features are introduced in the reproduction process. The reproduction process is behind the continuation of species and also behind their evolution and extinction.

For thousands of years, people have witnessed the process of reproduction and continuation, both in human beings and in plants and animals. They have known, too, that beans from one crop give rise to more beans when planted.

People probably didn't know exactly why elephants always gave birth to elephants and not to giraffes or other animals. However, it was known that by careful breeding one could change the characteristics of offspring. One could select horses with particularly long legs, allow them to mate, and pick only the longest-legged foals for mating again. In this way, new generations of racehorses might be created, looking rather different from their early ancestors. Selective breeding has long been practiced to give farmers cows that produced more milk or hogs that were meaty rather than fatty. Gardeners, too, have been aware for centuries that crossbreeding certain plants produces new forms.

Despite this knowledge, no one really understood the mechanisms of life, reproduction, and heredity. No one could answer: How does the human body grow? What happens during human conception? Why don't offspring always share the same physical traits as their parents?

Dominant and Recessive Traits

In 1866, the Austrian monk Gregor Mendel published the results of his five-year study of heredity in garden peas. He sorted, mixed, and counted thousands of wrinkled peas and smooth peas, yellow ones and green ones, tall plants and short plants. Contrary to popular expectation, the first generations of hybrids

*Techniques of selective breeding have been
followed for centuries by vineyardists, orchardists,
ranchers, and others.*

did not show a blending of their parents' traits. A tall
plant crossed with a short one did not produce a me-
dium-sized hybrid. Instead, one characteristic asserted
itself, while the other seemed to disappear. Hybrids
of tall and dwarf plants were all tall; hybrids of yellow-
seeded and green-seeded plants all bore yellow seeds.
As Mendel termed it, one trait was *dominant*, the
other *recessive*.

What happened in the next generation of pea
plants was even more surprising. The plants grown

Gregor Mendel, an Austrian botanist and
Augustinian monk, developed his theories about
heredity through breeding experiments with
peas in the monastery garden.

from yellow hybrid seeds did not breed true; that is, they were not all the same color as their parental stock. Approximately one of every four seeds produced by these new plants was not yellow but green.

These observations led to Mendel's discovery that each plant inherits two genes (Mendel called them *factors*) for a trait such as seed color: one from the male parent and one from the female parent. If each parent carries both dominant and recessive characteristics, then four possible combinations can be passed down to the next generation. In Figure 1, we are assuming that both parents are like Mendel's first-generation hybrids, each carrying one Y and one g

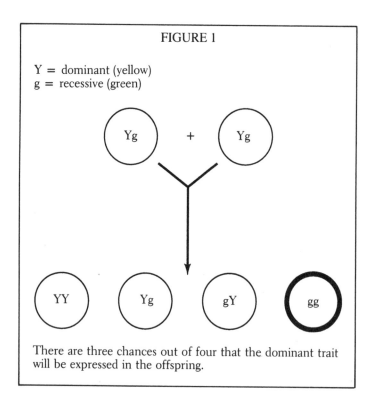

FIGURE 1

Y = dominant (yellow)
g = recessive (green)

Yg + Yg

YY   Yg   gY   gg

There are three chances out of four that the dominant trait will be expressed in the offspring.

factor. (We use a capital Y because yellow is dominant, and a small *g* for the recessive green.)

Plants whose makeup is YY have yellow seeds, of course. But, because yellow is dominant, plants whose makeup is Yg or gY will also have yellow seeds. Two g genes coming together (gg), though, will result in only green seeds. You can see that there are three chances out of four that the dominant gene will be expressed in the offspring, but only one chance out of four that the recessive gene will be expressed.

Today, Mendel's insights are still valid, although we know that inheritance works by a combination of many complex factors. Skin color in humans, for example, is determined by several genes, not by just one.

In 1903, an American graduate student named Walter Sutton and the German zoologist Theodor Boveri independently discovered that *chromosomes*, which are long, threadlike structures present in the nuclei of all cells, separate and pair off during cell division. The next major developments in genetics were due chiefly to the work of the American geneticist Thomas Hunt Morgan. His discovery that genetic material consisted essentially of genes strung along a chromosome, with each gene controlling a separate characteristic of the organism, won him the Nobel Prize in physiology in 1933. But what were genes made of, and how could they reproduce themselves?

The Discovery of DNA

Only three years after the publication of Mendel's study, an apparently unrelated discovery that proved to be the key to the problem was made in Switzer-

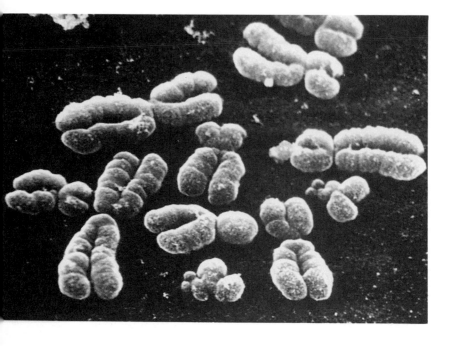

*The human chromosomes shown here have been
tilted to show their cylindrical shape.*

land. A young chemist named Johann Friedrich
Miescher was experimenting with white blood cells,
which he had obtained from the pus on used hospital
bandages. Interested in the chemistry of the cell nucleus, he analyzed the cells and found an unusual
compound, which was rich in phosphorous and made
up of molecules that were very long. What Miescher
had discovered was a complex form of DNA *(deoxyribonucleic acid)*. He later proceeded to isolate a pure
form of DNA. Neither Miescher nor his contempo-
raries understood just how nucleic acid functioned in
the cell. However, it was suspected that it exerted some
influence on hereditary processes.

Although chemists did not know the precise structure of DNA, by the beginning of this century they knew that it was a very long molecule made up of three important constitutents. The first was a sugar called ribose. The second, a phosphorous atom surrounded by four oxygen atoms, was called a phosphate. The third was called a base and was built up mainly of nitrogen and carbon atoms. There were four bases of importance: guanine, adenine, cytosine, and thymine, usually represented by the initials G, A, C, and T. Chemists also knew that the sugar molecules were linked together in pairs by the phosphate molecules to form a long, thin, threadlike chain. The bases were attached at regular intervals to the sugar molecules in the backbone of the long chain.

Was DNA the basic substance of heredity? And if so, how and where did it store its information?

DNA and Heredity

In 1944, Oswald Avery and his associates, working at Rockefeller University in New York City, presented convincing proof that the gene is made up of DNA. The group was studying the properties of two different strains of pneumococcus bacteria, with the goal of developing serums that could treat severe cases of pneumonia. One strain looked rough (R) under the microscope, and the other smooth (S). The S forms were known to be virulent (dangerous), while the R forms were benign (harmless).

It was known that when mice were injected with a mixture of live R-form bacteria and killed S-form bacteria, they soon died of pneumonia. When the blood of the dead mice was examined, live S-form bacteria were discovered. Where did the smooth virulent forms come from?

Avery repeated these experiments, but instead of adding dead S-form bacteria along with the R forms, he simply added highly purified DNA that he had extracted from the S form. Much to his astonishment, the DNA produced the same result as the S-form bacteria. The DNA had transformed the benign bacteria into a different strain of bacteria, one that was virulent. Avery, a very careful and conservative scientist, finally convinced himself and his colleagues that DNA played a key role in influencing the heredity of a cell. He referred to DNA as the fundamental unit of what he called a "transformation principle."

DNA and Viruses

Scientists were still not clear about the role that DNA played in heredity, but more evidence came from studies of a family of organisms called bacteriophage, tiny viruses that invade and infect bacteria. These organisms had been observed and studied as early as 1915 by the French biologist Félix d'Hérelle, who also named them. (The word *bacteriophage* is based on a Greek root and means "bacteria-eaters.")

Phage, as they are commonly called, are such relatively simple life-forms that they hover on the margin between lifeless chemical molecules and live organisms. Like all viruses, they are dormant outside a living cell but multiply to form duplicate copies of themselves when they have infected a cell. Similar to an invading army, they take over the chemical- and energy-producing machinery of the cell to make all the vital biological molecules needed for their own reproduction.

In 1945, in an attempt to understand the mechanism of viral reproduction, a group of biologists called the Phage Group began concentrated research on bacteriophages. Led by Max Delbrück of the California Institute of Technology and his associates Salvador Luria and Alfred Hershey, the group established that viruses were composed essentially of DNA or occasionally a closely related nucleic acid called *ribonucleic acid*, or RNA. The DNA was enclosed in a protective shell made of protein, very much like a hat within a hatbox. To complete the structure there was a tail and some tail fibers with which the phage attached themselves to their bacterial prey. The researchers demonstrated that the DNA finds its way into the bacteria through the tail, which acts like a hypodermic needle. Once inside the cell the DNA takes over the chemical-making machinery of the cell. The viral DNA carries the genetic message that permits the virus to reproduce itself inside the cell it invades. The DNA serves as a template—a model or pattern—for the formation of other phage.

| A New Way to
| Study Biology

Now that scientists understood that heredity was governed by DNA carried in the genes, in turn carried on the chromosomes, they were ready to try to understand the nature of DNA itself. What was its structure? Was it involved in growth or only in heredity? Once scientists understood the structure of DNA and the mechanism by which DNA participates in reproduction, they would be able to understand fully the mechanism of heredity. Finally they would know why elephants breed elephants and people breed people. And once this was known, it would be possible to artificially alter known life-forms and create new ones.

Tackling these questions required scientists to revolutionize their approach to the study of biology. Until the early 1940s, most biology was descriptive, involved with classifying and describing. It was about this time that biologists began to apply advanced chemical theory and techniques to the study of life-forms. Many of the ideas of atomic physics, developed by scientists studying the properties of atomic structure, also began playing a major role in the study of biology.

A slender volume published in 1944 focused the scientific community's attention on an ancient, basic question. *What Is Life?* was the book's title. The author was Erwin Schrödinger, one of the founders of a branch of physics known as quantum mechanics and a physicist of great renown. He suggested that the time had come to describe biological phenomena on an atomic and molecular basis. Physicists, with their new mathematical methods that had been developed to describe atoms and molecules, should join biologists and chemists in the study of life.

James Watson, one of the codiscoverers of the three-dimensional structure of DNA, has often stated that this work had a decisive influence in his life. He said that after reading this book, "I became polarized towards finding out the secret of the gene."[1] Francis Crick, the other discoverer of the double-helix structure of DNA, and Max Delbrück were among the physicists whose interest was thus drawn to biology. Some years later, summing up changes that had occurred in the field, Crick stated that the ultimate aim of the modern movement in biology is, in fact, to explain all biology in terms of physics and chemistry.

The Chemical Bond

The fusion of modern chemistry with the more traditional forms of biology eventually led to the discovery of the structure of DNA. One of the chief architects of *molecular biology*, as the fusion came to be called, was the American scientist Linus Pauling. Pauling is one of only three people to receive two Nobel prizes. He was awarded the Nobel Prize for chemistry in 1954, "for his work on the nature of the chemical bond and its application to the elucidation of the structure of complex substances." Pauling's second Nobel Prize was for peace, in 1962.

Pauling's book *The Nature of the Chemical Bond*, published in 1939, changed the way scientists thought about biological molecules. What Pauling did was to demonstrate that both the size of atoms and the chemical bond, or force, holding atoms together determined how the atoms arranged themselves into molecules. Size was important because atoms have to fit snugly together in a molecule. The type of bond was important because it determined whether the atoms that were held together were free to rotate freely or were restricted and held rigidly in one position only.

Pauling was also a pioneer in using *X-ray diffraction* to study the structure of molecules. X-ray diffraction is a technique usually used by physicists to determine the structure of a crystal. Physicists can deduce how atoms are arranged in a crystal by studying the way X rays are diffracted, that is, bent, by the

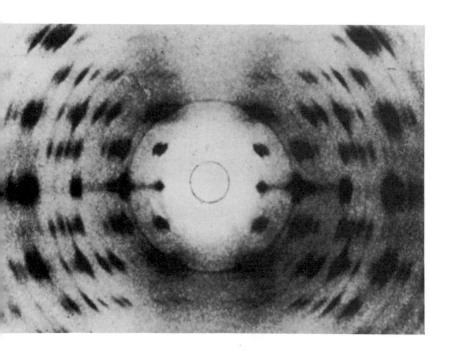

*By X-ray diffraction, the structure of this
DNA molecule can be determined.*

atoms that make up the crystal. Using the work of
Pauling, the chemist John Desmond Bernal influ-
enced a generation of biologists by showing that giant
molecules such as proteins could be studied by X-ray
diffraction methods.

The Structure of the DNA Molecule

In the late 1940s, many scientists began to feel that
finding the structure of DNA and unraveling the way
it directs heredity would be the most important scientific goal ever undertaken. Unlocking the secrets

would enable scientists to understand life and they would then be able to create or alter it.

In several labs around the world, teams of scientists devoted themselves to unlocking these secrets. In Pasadena, California, at the California Institute of Technology, there was one group led by Pauling. At the Cavendish Laboratory of Cambridge University in England, there were Watson and Crick. In London, at King's College, there were Maurice Wilkins and Rosalind Franklin, both specialists in the X-ray diffraction analysis of biological molecules.

As described by Watson in his book *The Double Helix*, the contest was often frantic, at times taking on the trappings of a full-blown thriller. In the end, Watson and Crick won. In a letter that appeared in 1953 in the April 25th issue of the scientific journal *Nature*, they announced their now-famous double-helix model of the DNA molecule.

It was a close race. Crick, writing of the events that led to the discovery, said, "Watson and I always thought that Linus Pauling would be bound to have another shot at the structure once he had seen the King's College X-ray data. Rosalind Franklin was only two steps away from the solution, and Maurice Wilkins announced to us just before he knew of our structure, that he was going to work full time on the problem."[2]

The final breakthrough for Watson and Crick came when they used a technique developed by Pauling. Pauling's method for understanding molecules was to build models with precisely scaled representations of the atoms. Like a three-dimensional puzzle, the atoms had to fit together for the model to be valid.

Watson and Crick deduced much of DNA's structure from an analysis of X-ray diffraction pic-

James Watson and Francis Crick present their double-helix model of the DNA molecule.

tures—pictures taken by Wilkins and Franklin. Instead of relying entirely on chemical analysis and X-ray observation, they tried making a large model of the DNA molecule. With sheet-metal cutouts and wire they attempted to work out a structure that would accommodate all the physical restraints they saw in the X-ray photos, and all the chemical elements of which DNA was known to be composed.

After several false starts, they suddenly realized that DNA must consist of not one but two long, thin molecules twisted about each other in the form of a double helix, much like a ladder twisted to fit into a circular staircase. Along this structure, the chemical groups called bases are arranged in pairs to form the rungs of the ladder, as shown in Figure 2.

The bases attached to the chains are on the inside of the helix and face each other across the center of the helix. In order to fit inside the helix, however, the bases on the two chains are always paired in exactly the same fashion. Adenine always pairs with thymine; guanine always pairs with cytosine. The paired bases are called *complementary bases* and fit inside the helical coil, binding the two strands together. The sequence of the base pairs spells out the particular code for the growth and reproduction of each living cell and organism. Each sequence of bases that spells out a complete message is called a *gene.*

Semiconservative Replication

A month after the publication of their original paper on the structure of DNA, Watson and Crick presented a model of how DNA copies itself. The sci-

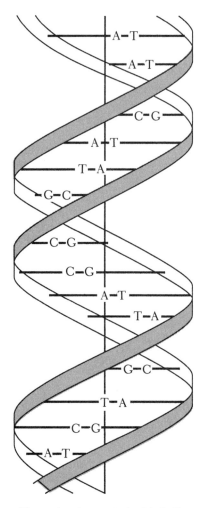

Figure 2: The DNA double helix.

The DNA molecule is a double helix composed of two strands. The sugar-phosphate backbones twist around the outside, with the paired bases on the inside serving to hold the chains together. Adenine (A) pairs with Thymine (T); Guanine (G) pairs with Cystosine (C).

entific term is *replication*. Their idea was that if the two chains were to unwind and separate, each chain would act as a template or pattern for the construction of its complementary chain (see Figure 3). The idea of complementarity was often compared to a lock and key. Given the key, one could construct a lock that would fit the key.

A critical feature of this new model was that the sequence of base pairs in the original double helix be exactly duplicated in the "daughter." Each new daughter double helix that was formed would have one strand from its parent and one newly synthesized strand that was exactly complementary. Biologists call this form of replication, where one strand of the double helix is always derived from a previously existing double helix, *semiconservative replication*.

Proteins

Scientists knew at last how a DNA molecule made an exact duplicate of itself. But how does a cell reproduce itself? Cells are much more complicated than DNA. They contain, among other things, hundreds of different kinds of proteins. How does the DNA contained in a cell reproduce proteins?

Proteins play a crucial role in almost all biological processes. They make up more than half of the solid substances in the tissues of the human body. There are thousands of different kinds of proteins, all of them long and complicated molecules. Some contain as many as 50,000 atoms. But the astonishing fact is that they are all constructed from just twenty kinds of building blocks called *amino acids*. The dif-

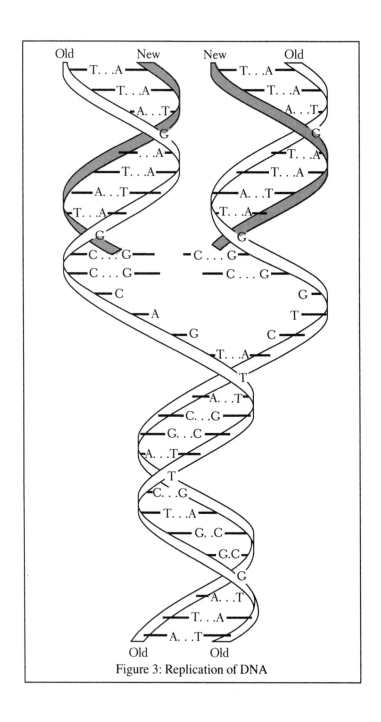

Figure 3: Replication of DNA

ferences between proteins depend on which amino acids are used and how they are arranged and sequenced in the molecule.

Each kind of protein has a unique amino-acid sequence. The change of a single amino acid in a protein can cause it to malfunction and produce disease in the entire organism. Sickle-cell anemia, for example, is caused by the substitution of just one amino acid for another in the hundreds of amino acids that make up hemoglobin in the blood.

The Flow of Information— The Central Dogma

Scientists were convinced that the main function of DNA was to manufacture proteins. They believed that the sequence of bases on the DNA molecule must be a simple code for the amino-acid sequence of a particular protein. In cells, almost all the DNA is found in the genes, which are strung out in a row along the thin, threadlike chromosomes. The chromosomes are found in the nucleus of the cell. But the manufacture of proteins occurs in the body of the cell, outside the nucleus. How does the information get from the nucleus to the protein-manufacturing sites? The answer is that a "messenger" carries the DNA instructions out of the nucleus.

The messenger was identified as a slightly modified form of nucleic acid called *messenger RNA*, or mRNA. Aside from the lack of a hydroxyl group on each sugar in the sugar backbone of the molecule, it differs from DNA in also having a base called uracil (U) substituted for thymine in its set of four bases.

Described as simply as possible, the DNA in the

gene first constructs a molecule called mRNA, which contains all the information needed to manufacture a given protein. This is called *transcription*. The mRNA then leaves the nucleus of the cell and carries its information to other locations in the body of the cell. The information is then "translated" into protein. This flow of information from DNA to RNA to protein is diagrammed below.

DNA → RNA → PROTEIN
TRANSCRIPTION → TRANSLATION

Crick went one step further. He stated what has been called the central dogma of molecular biology: Once information has passed into protein, it cannot get out again. The transfer of information from protein to protein or from protein to nucleic acid is impossible. This explained why characteristics acquired by an organism during its life cannot be inherited by its offspring.

The Genetic Code

The information carried by DNA is determined by the sequence of its four bases. A typical protein, however, is made up of a specific arrangement of a group of amino acids taken from a set of twenty different amino acids. How does the base sequence determine the amino-acid sequence? Through the genetic code.

Experimental evidence has established that a sequence of three bases, called a *codon*, represents one amino acid. The triplet of bases AGU followed by the triplet AUU on a DNA molecule, for example, means that a protein will be constructed that has an amino acid called serine followed by an amino acid called isoleucine. The cell constructs proteins by reading one codon after the next. There is even punctuation in the code. The codon UAG, for example, functions as a period. It is a signal to stop or terminate the manufacture of the protein. The genetic code is shown in Figure 4.

There are sixty-four different codons. Since there are only twenty amino acids, many of the acids are designated by more than one codon. This built-in redundancy is thought to be important in minimizing the accidental exchanges that might occur in the base sequence. Changes such as the substitution of one base for another, or a base being left out of the sequence, are the major causes of mutations. Mutations result in offspring having different and inheritable characteristics than their parents.

The genetic code represents a universal language. It is essentially the same in plants, viruses, bacteria, and humans. There is strong evidence, furthermore, that it has remained essentially the same throughout billions of years of evolution.

| Translation and | the Ribosome |

How does a cell actually manufacture proteins? If you examine a cell under an electron microscope you will see a scattering of tiny black dots. These are the *ribosomes*, the "factories" that translate the genetic code and create the proteins.

The manufacture of proteins begins with the ribosome attaching itself to an mRNA molecule. You

FIGURE 4: THE GENETIC CODE

AAU
AAC } Asparagine

AAA
AAG } Lysine

AGU
AGC } Serine
AGA
AGG } Arginine

AUU
AUC } Isoleucine
AUA
AUG — Methionine

ACU
ACC
ACA } Threonine
ACG

GAU
GAC } Aspartic acid

GAA
GAG } Glutamic acid

GGU
GGC
GGA } Glycine
GGG

GUU
GUC
GUA } Valine
GUG

GCU
GCC
GCA } Alanine
GCG

CAU
CAC } Histidine

CAA
CAG } Glutamine

CGU
CGC
CGA } Arginine
CGG

CUU
CUC
CUA } Leucine
CUG

CCU
CCC
CCA } Proline
CCG

UAU
UAC } Tyrosine

UAA
UAG } Stop signals

UGU
UGC } Cysteine
UGA — Stop signal
UGG — Tryptophan

UUU
UUC } Phenylalanine
UUA
UUG } Leucine

UCU
UCC
UCA } Serine
UCG

Each amino acid is represented by one or more base-triplets,
and each base-triplet stands for one specific amino acid.

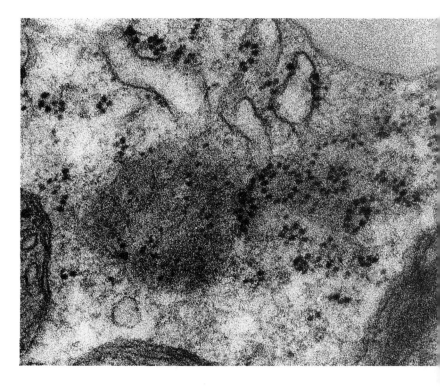

The black dots seen scattered through the cell are ribosomes, which manufacture proteins.

will remember that mRNA carries information that was given to it by the genes in the nucleus. The ribosome then moves along the mRNA from codon to codon. It is often compared to a film moving across a ratchet in a camera. At each stage, one codon is made visible. This is shown in Figure 5.

Another group of molecules, called *transfer RNA,* or tRNA, then "transfer" the amino acid specified by the exposed codon to the construction site. Here it is linked into the growing protein chain. The ribosome

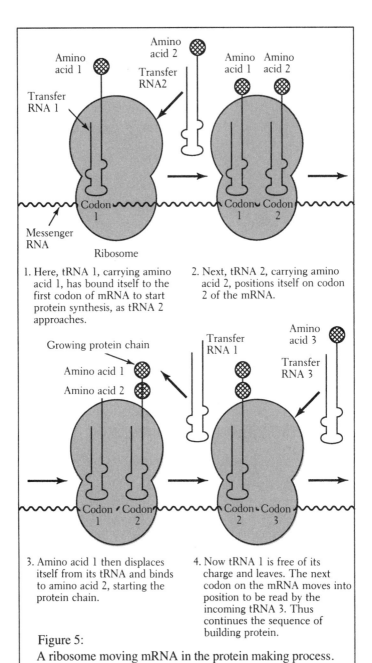

1. Here, tRNA 1, carrying amino acid 1, has bound itself to the first codon of mRNA to start protein synthesis, as tRNA 2 approaches.

2. Next, tRNA 2, carrying amino acid 2, positions itself on codon 2 of the mRNA.

3. Amino acid 1 then displaces itself from its tRNA and binds to amino acid 2, starting the protein chain.

4. Now tRNA 1 is free of its charge and leaves. The next codon on the mRNA moves into position to be read by the incoming tRNA 3. Thus continues the sequence of building protein.

Figure 5:
A ribosome moving mRNA in the protein making process.

then moves on to the next codon, and so the process continues to form the protein coded by the mRNA.

The discovery of the genetic code was one of the most remarkable achievements in the history of science. As Crick has suggested, "Once you got the idea of the code, and that the ribosome was a reading head, then the whole world changed. You see."[3]

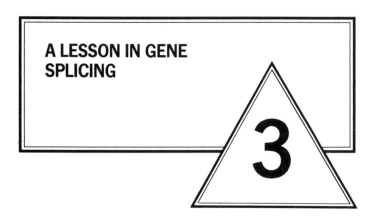

A LESSON IN GENE SPLICING

3

In the early 1970s, scientists learned how to manipulate and change the structure of genes. They developed techniques to split the DNA of a given gene, remove certain parts, and add, or splice, them to the DNA of other genes. The result of this so-called gene splicing was called *recombinant DNA*.

The new gene could be programmed to produce biological substances quite foreign to its original nature. Bacterial colonies could be used almost like farms to produce useful and scarce products such as insulin and interferon.

Genetic Engineering

The process of introducing genetic material from one organism into another is fairly straightforward.

First, you have to remove the piece of genetic material to be transferred. Let's say it's the gene for making insulin. The cells with the gene are placed in a solution containing a restriction enzyme. This is an enzyme that recognizes a specific base sequence on a DNA molecule and causes the DNA molecule to split or cleave at this site. There are more than 400 such restriction enzymes and each recognizes a different base sequence. The restriction enzyme separates the gene from the rest of the chromosome (see Figure 6).

At the same time, you take a circular piece of DNA called a *plasmid* from another cell (usually *E. coli*) and use another restriction enzyme to break off a piece of it, as shown in Figure 7.

You then combine the gene and the broken plas-

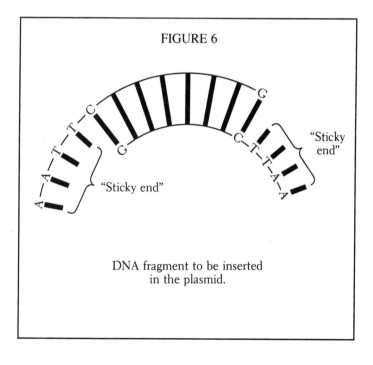

FIGURE 6

DNA fragment to be inserted
in the plasmid.

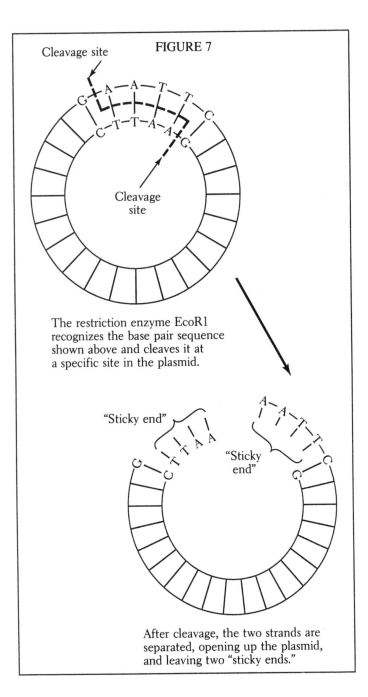

FIGURE 7

Cleavage site

Cleavage site

The restriction enzyme EcoR1 recognizes the base pair sequence shown above and cleaves it at a specific site in the plasmid.

"Sticky end"

"Sticky end"

After cleavage, the two strands are separated, opening up the plasmid, and leaving two "sticky ends."

mid with a substance called *ligase*, which "glues" the gene into the space left in the plasmid. The gene attaches to the "sticky ends" of the broken plasmid (see Figure 8). The resulting plasmid, often called a *hybrid*, is then injected into a solution containing *E. coli* cells. Most laboratories use *E. coli* as a host cell because it is a common type of bacteria found in the human intestines and is quite harmless. It is usually necessary to first treat the *E. coli* with a calcium salt. The salt makes it easier for the plasmids to flow through the bacterial membrane.

When the modified *E. coli*—those cells that contain the hybrid plasmids—reproduce, they pro-

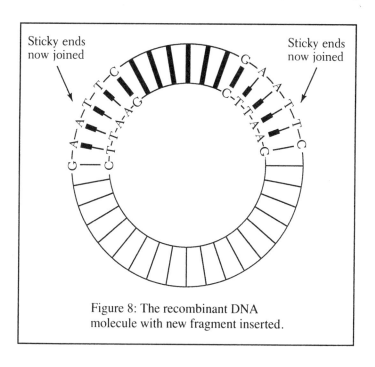

Figure 8: The recombinant DNA molecule with new fragment inserted.

duce cells that contain the altered plasmid. All of these cells are genetically identical and are called *clones*. The fragment of DNA we wanted copied will have been cloned to make millions of copies of itself. Since the gene directs the bacteria to produce insulin, these *E. coli* may end up manufacturing insulin in significant quantities.

Other Genetic Engineering Techniques

The process just described is the one most commonly used by scientists and technicians, whether doing basic research or working on a new product. Other processes are used in special situations. One of the most important involves *monoclonal antibodies*.

Here, genetic engineers use a technique of fusing together two cells whose outer membranes have been modified. The fused cell is called a *hybridoma*. The hybridoma cell contains the chromosomes of both parent cells and therefore takes on the characteristics of both.

If a cancer cell is fused with a cell that produces a particular antibody, for example, the hybridoma takes on the characteristics of both parents. It will be a fast-growing cell and also produce the antibody. Unlike most antibodies, such as those induced by vaccination, the monoclonal antibody is produced by a single molecular species. Monoclonal antibodies have been shown to be of great value in diagnosing diseases and offer great prospects for their treatment.

In the field of medicine, scientists are now introducing new combinations of genes directly into animal cells in an attempt to cure some of the diseases known to be caused by defective gene structure. By

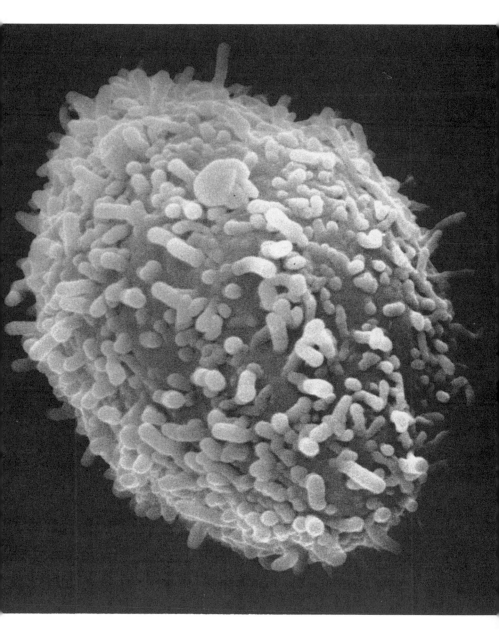

An electron microscope view of a hybridoma
cell producing a monoclonal antibody

transferring a functioning gene into the cell to correct the faulty gene, it is hoped that a cure for such human genetic disorders as sickle-cell anemia and dwarfism will be found.

Scientists sometimes use a technique called *microinjection* to insert genes into the nucleus of the defective cell. This is a very delicate procedure in which the researcher, working with a powerful microscope, guides a long and very thin tube, called a capillary tube, into the cell. The gene to be implanted is then fed in through the tube.

Another important way of introducing genes into cells is by means of viruses. Scientists usually call any mechanism for implanting genes a *vector*. Virus vectors have become an important tool for genetic therapy. One of the most effective vectors is a virus called a lambda phage. Like all phages, the lambda phage attacks bacteria. But the lambda phage is remarkable because it incorporates its own DNA into the chromosome of the bacteria and then lies dormant for several generations. When the bacteria replicates itself, so does the virus. Eventually, the virus becomes virulent, usually after being triggered by certain chemicals or X rays, and detaches itself from the host chromosome. While doing so, however, it carries some of the host's genes along with it. When it then reinfects another cell, the new genes are carried along with it and become incorporated in the genes of the new host.

Inside a Molecular Biology Lab

The laboratories involved with genetic engineering are very careful to guard the health and well-being of their research scientists. They also take elaborate precautions to prevent any newly created hybrid form of life from escaping the laboratory and contaminating the environment.

The Cold Spring Harbor Laboratory complex on Long Island, New York, is justly famous for its DNA research. It was here that Max Delbrück and his group held their pioneering seminars on bacteriophages. Scientists interested in doing research in molecular biology come here from all over the world. Its current director of research is Nobel laureate James Watson.

Right now, for example, the work of the James Laboratory, the Tumor Virus Division of the com-

Cold Spring Harbor Laboratory, on Long Island, New York, is a center of DNA research.

plex, is focused on viruses that cause breast tumors in rats. One of the ongoing projects is to study how these viruses change the cells they infect and how these changes relate to the growth of cancerous tumors.

It is known that specific viruses produce breast tumors in live rats. To find out exactly how this happens, the researchers use gene splicing to induce small changes in the DNA of the cells and observe how the cells are affected. The cells are not observed in the live animals but *in vitro*, that is, in isolated cells in the controlled environment of laboratory glassware.

A visitor walking through the corridors of this laboratory might notice the flasks of rose-colored liquid shelved in glass cabinets. These contain human cells suspended in a nutrient solution of amino acids and vitamins. In every room, researchers lean over laboratory benches, intent on their tasks.

In a black-walled cubicle, a young woman in a lab coat concentrates on a high-powered microscope in front of her. She is microinjecting pieces of DNA into a single rat cell. She must insert the tip of the long, needlelike tube, called a pipette, into the cell nucleus, which has an inner diameter of 0.5 micrometers, or 5/10,000ths of a millimeter.

Rows of warming cabinets hold a thick soup of cell-growing material kept moving by automatic stirrers. Outside the Cold Room, which looks very much like a butcher's refrigerator, stand blue, thick-necked, large vacuum bottles called Dewar flasks. Near these are gleaming steel vats of liquid nitrogen. Assorted cells that have been carefully frozen are stored in these vats, sometimes for as long as a decade.

In a corner of each lab section, a small lead-shielded area is set aside to contain materials that have

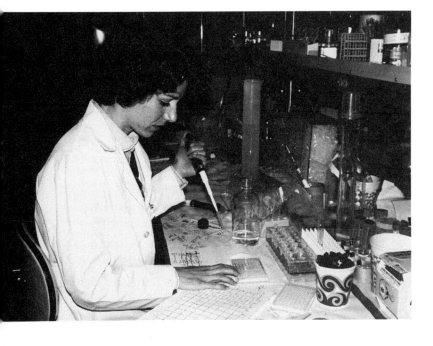

*A genetics research scientist inserts an
automatic pipette into a cell nucleus.*

been made radioactive for observation. A darkroom is
available for developing X-ray and other film. Vital
to the lab is a sterilizer for laboratory garments and
equipment. It is set in the wall like a huge laundry
dryer.

Most of the equipment molecular biologists use
is simple and inexpensive compared to that needed by
other branches of science. There are exceptions,
however, and Cold Spring Harbor owns three electron microscopes. Aside from this costly research apparatus, the rest of the equipment is standard gear in
any biological laboratory.

The scientists carry out many of their manipulations at hooded benches. With their hands they can reach under the curved glass hood and do their work while looking through the transparent surface that protects them from inhaling any chemicals or microorganisms. The hood also protects the microorganisms from contamination.

Research at this lab requires strict controls. To prevent the accidental meeting of cultured viruses and cultured cells, the two are put on separate floors. Cells grow upstairs, viruses downstairs. Upstairs, containment hoods are mainly important in keeping foreign organisms out; while downstairs, the hoods are needed to keep the viruses in. When the cells on the upper floor are ready, a researcher brings them down a flight to be infected under supervision.

All laboratories involved with gene splicing are very aware of the possible danger of releasing a genetically engineered bacterium or virus into the environment. They fear that both plantlife and animals as they have evolved over the years might not be able to defend themselves against a new form of microorganism. According to government regulations, experiments are classified by the level of physical containment required. Levels range from BL1 (low risk) to BL4 (high risk); BL refers to biosafety levels. The higher the risk, the more precautions the laboratory must take to prevent possible contamination of the environment or the scientist.

James Lab is rated BL2. Few facilities in the United States are engaged in B4 research. One of them is Plum Island, the Department of Agriculture's Animal Disease Center, in Long Island Sound. James Lab does have a small B3 room at the back of the building. Access is restricted to the few people who work there. Workers wear protective gowns in the lab. The gowns are left in the lab to be sterilized later. At the entry to the high-containment room is a negative air curtain, a space closed off by two doors, in which the air pressure is kept slightly lower than outside. This causes air to move in rather than out, preventing bacteria from being carried out of the room.

Scientists hope the information gained from experiments in these laboratories will eventually yield a more basic understanding of our genetic makeup as well as contributing to improved methods of dealing with inherited diseases.

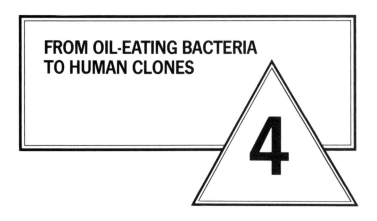

FROM OIL-EATING BACTERIA TO HUMAN CLONES

4

In 1972, the U.S. Patent Office received a surprising request. General Electric wanted to patent a new form of life, an organism created in the company's laboratories. Its creator, Ananda M. Chakrabarty, took plasmids from three bacteria known for their ability to break up hydrocarbons and transferred them to a pseudomonas bacterium. The brand-new pseudomonas would have the power to clean up oil spills and would die off after having no more petroleum to devour.

Patent officials were at a loss. Could a live organism be patented? Crossbred plant or animal strains such as racehorses and hybrid tomatoes had never been protected by patenting. The officials concluded that their legal mandate did not extend to granting patents on living bacteria.

General Electric took its case to the courts. In June 1980, the Supreme Court voted 5 to 4 in favor of granting patents on life created in the laboratory.

In the words of Chief Justice Warren Burger, the issue was "not between living and inanimate things, but between products of nature—whether living or not—and human-made inventions."

The first American patent on a living organism was granted in February 1981, while G.E.'s patent was still pending. This patent was awarded to Bristol Myers and three of its staff scientists.

The microorganism *Streptosporangium,* as their creation is called, produces carminomycin, an antibiotic and antitumor agent. The patent for the pure cultured organism was added to an earlier patent for the process by which the drug is made. Since then, more than two hundred new microorganisms have been patented.

This was just the beginning, though. On April 16, 1987, the U.S. Patent and Trademark Office announced an unprecedented decision: America would be the first country in the world to grant patents on animals created through gene splicing or other novel reproductive techniques.[1] Included would be custom-designed "transgenic" mixtures of all kinds and innovative types of livestock. For the moment, the Patent Office would not consider patents for novelty traits in humans but was processing the first fifteen applications received for patenting new animals.

Another historic event took place on April 12, 1988, when the world's first patent for a higher form of life was issued to Harvard University for a specially prepared mouse developed by Dr. Philip Leder of the Harvard Medical School and by Dr. Timothy A. Stewart, a genetic scientist at Genentech.[2] The two researchers isolated a gene that causes cancer in humans, spliced it into mouse eggs, and developed a

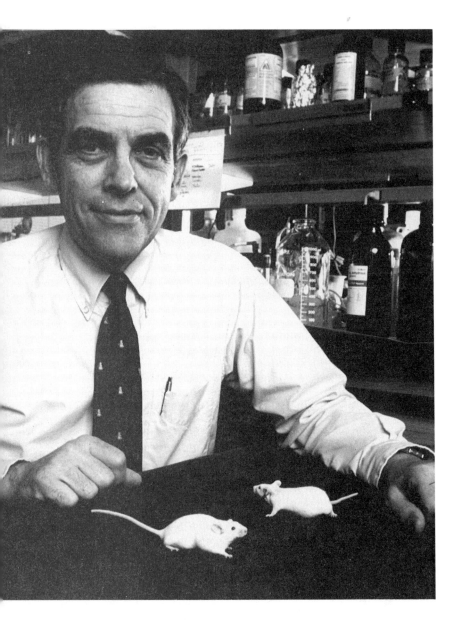

*Dr. Philip Leder of the Harvard Medical School,
with transgenic mice*

new breed of mice. Most of the genetically altered female mice develop breast cancer, and scientists hope to use the mice to understand how genes contribute to cancer in humans and hopefully hasten the development of treatments for breast cancer.

Many members of Congress, however, protested the issuance of the patent. They asked that a moratorium be placed on all patents for genetically altered animals (there are now twenty-one patent applications pending) until Congress had considered all the moral and economic issues raised by religious leaders, animal welfare organizations, and environmental groups.

The Biotechnical Pharmacy

By rearranging the genetic makeup of a microorganism, scientists can reprogram the organism to produce any number of different compounds needed for the treatment of human disease. Pharmaceuticals of this sort were the first recombinant DNA products actually available to the public.

In the past, chemists usually developed a new drug by first manufacturing hundreds of compounds called *analogs* that resembled a drug they knew to be effective in curing a particular disease or symptom. These analogs were then screened, one by one, to see if they could also cure the disease or perhaps do it better or faster. Another common technique was to extract chemicals from various plants and check to see if the chemicals had any therapeutic properties.

The major disadvantage of these methods, aside from the hit-and-miss character of much of the research, was that the chemicals developed were usually foreign to the human body. In addition, they often produced side effects that were worse than the disease they cured.

Gene splicing allows scientists to extract from human cells genes known to combat disease. These genes express proteins that can control infections and injuries, fight harmful viruses and bacteria, and kill cancer cells. Since these proteins already exist in human cells, they are generally safe and nontoxic. The genes can be transferred to *E. coli,* and the proteins manufactured in large quantities as the cells multiply to form clones.

A recent development known as protein engineering promises to extend the ability of scientists to create new proteins to meet human needs.[3] By changing the genetic instructions in the DNA molecule using gene-splicing techniques, scientists can also create artificial proteins by controlling the sequence of amino acids that make up the protein. They hope to use this new technique to tailor proteins for drugs with improved properties and for industrial enzymes that last longer than natural ones.

Hormones

Some essential human bodily functions such as growth and muscle development are regulated by the proteins called hormones. Secreted by various glands, hormones circulate with body fluids, leaving chemical calling cards that trigger important reactions in organs and tissues. An imbalance in the secretion of a hormone can cause serious illness.

The first hormones derived from genetically manipulated bacteria were insulin and growth hormone. Insulin is normally secreted by the pancreas to regulate the amount of sugar in the body. More than a million Americans, though, suffer from diabetes, an insulin deficiency, and require daily supplementary injections. Until recently, pharmaceutical insulin was extracted from pig, beef, and sheep pancreas and occasionally caused undesirable side effects. The new product is less likely to do so.

Growth hormone is designed for children suffering from growth hormone deficiency, or GHD. Growth is regulated by the pituitary gland located at the base of the brain. Children whose pituitary gland is underdeveloped, either as a result of injury or from birth, usually start out as normal-size babies but grow slowly and are doomed to remain far below average height.

A normal pituitary gland produces minuscule quantities of growth hormone. To treat one child's deficiency for one year, the product of fifty human pituitary glands is needed. Until recently, this product had to be gathered from human cadavers and was therefore expensive and hard to obtain. Not every GHD child's family could afford the hormone. Only about a third of the children who could have benefited from it were treated. Even worse, in 1985 a rare but deadly virus was discovered to reside in the brain tissue of some human victims, and doctors feared the risk of contaminating the hormone product. Distribution of human growth hormone was therefore stopped.

Genentech, one of America's first and best-known biotechnology companies, came to the rescue. In 1981 the company had received permission to test Protropin, a human growth hormone, in clinical trials under hospital conditions. The results were promising, and by 1986 the Food and Drug Administration approved Protropin as safe and effective for treating children with GHD. According to Dr. Selma Kaplan, professor of pediatrics at the University of California School of Medicine, injections of Protropin "tripled the average growth rate of children with growth hormone deficiency during the first year, and more than doubled growth rates in years two and three."

| How Drugs | | Are Made |

The method used by Genentech to produce Protropin is similar to the protein-clone-factory method we have already described. First, scientists identify the desired protein. From the sequence of its amino acids they can deduce and isolate the corresponding DNA blueprint in the gene. Next they prepare the host cell plasmids taken from *E. coli* and the isolated genes for recombination. They then add control signals before and after the gene to instruct the host cell to make the desired protein. Finally, they insert the recombined DNA into the host for reproduction.

When the host microorganism is ready to do its new job, it is given a temporary home in a mechanically stirred flask filled with a medium of sugar, water, and other nutrients. Here the organisms greatly expand and multiply. But to make industrial quantities of the new protein, the organisms must be further amplified through fermentation. They pass through a series of fermenters until they go through a final population explosion in large, gleaming, stainless steel vessels. The last manufacturing steps are purifying, drying, testing, and packaging the protein product.

The New
Biocompanies

Genentech was started in 1975 by a handful of young scientists and entrepreneurs working out of a renovated San Francisco warehouse. Actually, they were comparative latecomers to the scene, having been preceded by Cetus Corporation, in Emeryville, California, begun in 1971 by a small group of adventurous scientists and daring investors. In those days, recombinant DNA technology was still the newborn infant of the research laboratory, and its commercial possibilities were only beginning to be realized. By the early 1980s, though, these two companies led the recognized "big four" of biotechnology, together with Genex (now defunct) and Biogen.

Today, the picture is constantly changing. Many other companies have sprung up, and large chemical and drug conglomerates as diverse as Monsanto, Johnson & Johnson, and Eastman Kodak now recognize that the new biology has opened a bonanza of desirable products.

Genentech has racked up an impressive record of firsts in its brief existence. It was first to apply recombinant techniques to making interferon, a rare protein promising success in fighting cancer and viral infections; first to engineer a blood clot–dissolving agent (under the trademark Activase) to be used in treating heart attacks; and first with a blood-clotting agent, Factor VIII, for treating hemophilia, a disorder whose victims suffer from uncontrolled bleeding because their own blood lacks this clotting factor.

Amgen, another company new on the scene, is known for its genetically engineered vaccine against hepatitis B, a widespread and often lethal virus-induced liver infection. Among other important pharmaceuticals Amgen has developed are interferon and other anticancer drugs, as well as several different types of growth factors to be used in wound healing and tissue growth. In particular, Amgen is in the forefront of producing animal hormones and vaccines to preserve the health and improve the meat yield of farm animals.

State governments are playing an increasingly important role in financing biotechnical research and helping newly formed companies develop. According to the U.S. Office of Technology Assessment, some thirty states spent approximately $160 million in 1988 to aid both university and industrial research.[4] State officials hope that investment in genetic engineering will aid employment and contribute to new production techniques in agriculture, mining, and fishing.

| Vaccines |

When the first Salk vaccine against polio came on the market in the 1950s, doctors injected it into thousands of children before discovering that monkey cells used for growing the vaccine carried undesirable viruses, including a monkey tumor virus. Luckily, as far as we know, no one got sick or developed any tumors as a result of the injection. Still, cultured vaccines always carry risks, and virus contamination is only one of them. Each vaccine contains dead or weakened viruses for the disease it is meant to defeat. On entering the body, the viral protein stimulates the patient's immune system to produce the antibodies that confer immunity to this particular disease. Unfortunately, even though weak or disabled, a virus occasionally triggers a serious or even deadly reaction.

Genetically engineered vaccines eliminate most such risks. Using recombinant DNA, scientists can now bypass the process of culturing live bacteria and then disabling them. Instead, they clone only the proteins that stimulate a system to make specific antibodies.

| Controlling |
| Rabies |

One such vaccine being genetically engineered by French researchers[5] gives hope of wiping out rabies, a disease that kills thousands of animals as well as a few people each year. Attempts to culture a laboratory-weakened virus were never successful. Rabies tends to spread from wildlife such as raccoons and foxes to dogs and cats and then to people. To contain rabies, large numbers of animals often had to be destroyed. But the new vaccine can be administered in bait to animals in the wild. Scientists hope that it will make so many woodland creatures immune to rabies that the deadly virus may eventually be eliminated.

| Antibodies |

Bioengineering may eventually produce every type of vaccine more safely and cheaply than older methods. Using similar basic principles, scientists have forged yet another sort of "magic bullet" for diagnosing and treating disease. These are the monoclonal antibodies, introduced in Chapter Three. Just as the new vaccines copy the proteins of microorganisms that attack the body, so monoclonal antibodies copy the proteins that defend the body.

Millions of antibody types are assumed to exist, each capable of striking one specific target. Monoclonal antibodies are so pure and so specialized that they can even distinguish, for example, among the six different forms of measles virus or among the proteins on the surface of red blood cells that specify different blood types. They can be used as probes and tracers to map parts of the body, as well as to attack particular diseases.

Injected into a patient's bloodstream, specific antibodies can head straight for the cells of a cancerous tumor. By tagging the antibody with a tracing material, doctors can locate the position of a cancer cell. By tagging the antibody with an antitumor drug or a radioactive element, doctors hope to kill the cancer cell, as with a poisoned bullet.

The technique used to make monoclonal antibodies is cell fusion. An organism, usually a mouse, is injected with an *antigen,* a substance that stimulates the production of a specific antibody. The cells that produce the antibody are removed from the animal's spleen and fused with a fast-growing cancer cell. The resultant fused cells are grown in tissue culture. They possess the capacity both for rapid growth and for producing the antibody originally stimulated by the antigen. Continuous "harvesting" of such a culture permits the collection of specific antibodies as needed. Cloned antibodies may eventually replace vaccines to provide immunity against a host of infectious illnesses.

There are many scientific problems still to be solved before bioengineered vaccines replace the more conventional vaccines. Although it is possible to clone the genes involved, turning the single protein produced by the bacteria into an effective vaccine is still difficult.

Lymphokines

An early contender for the miracle drug of the decade was interferon. Interferon is a family of certain rare proteins that stimulate the body's natural defenses. Unfortunately, two types of interferon—alpha and beta—showed only moderate success against cancer. A third type—gamma interferon—is still in the testing stage but seems to be giving better results. Interferon may ultimately find its true role in fighting viral infections, including such elusive ones as the common cold, hepatitis, and herpes.

The interferons belong to a group of proteins called *lymphokines*, which carry the immune system's chemical messages. At Cetus, researchers manufacture lymphokines by recombinant DNA techniques. One of Cetus's products, Interleukin-2 (IL-2), is designed to stimulate cells to seek out and kill cancer cells that have spread throughout a patient's body.

Interleukin-2 enters a cancer patient's system and binds to receptor sites on certain white blood cells called T cells. This causes the T cells to multiply and actually produce lymphokine-activated killer (LAK) cells. LAK cells ignore normal cells and make straight for a cancerous cell, destroying it. Interleukin-2 has proved successful in experiments with mice and is now undergoing clinical trials at the National Cancer Institute and many other sites, with encouraging results.

Late in 1984, a team of researchers headed by Dr. Steven A. Rosenberg at the National Cancer Institute in Bethesda, Maryland, started using IL-2 to treat patients with cancers so far advanced they no longer responded to chemotherapy or radiation. In this experimental treatment, the team removed some of a cancer patient's white blood cells, mixed them with IL-2, and injected the mixture back into the patient. A year later, Dr. Rosenberg was able to report in the *New England Journal of Medicine* that in eleven of twenty-five patients this treatment had reduced the size of tumors by more than 50 percent. Four types of cancer responded, though not in every case, to the treatment: melanoma (an extremely serious skin cancer), cancers of the colon and rectum, kidney cancer, and lung cancer. Such victories may not sound monumental, but because cancer is so complicated and evasive, they are encouraging.

DNA Probes

Cetus is also developing DNA probes to provide simple diagnostic tests for diseases such as cancer and AIDS, to be made not only in laboratories and hospitals but even in doctors' offices.

DNA probes are pieces of "tagged" DNA that will attach to a specific gene sequence in the sample to be tested. Often, though, the looked-for gene in the patient's sample is present in such small quantities that the probe can't detect it. This is where Cetus's new DNA amplification technology comes in. By this method, scientists are able to amplify the number of target DNA sequences in the sample a millionfold.

Detecting the AIDS Virus

Cetus's DNA probe and amplification technique may soon provide a more effective test for the AIDS virus, called human immunodeficiency virus, or HIV. Identifying individuals who are infected with HIV is important, so they can be warned and stopped from passing the disease on to others. Current tests of blood samples detect only the antibodies the immune system forms in response to HIV. However, some people who have antibodies may no longer have the virus, and others who have the virus may not yet have formed antibodies. The new DNA-probe–based test would be more reliable because it is designed to zoom in directly on the genetic material of HIV itself.

Mail-Order Genes

If you wish to buy a testtube full of viral DNA, a few cubic centimeters of restriction enzymes, or a research kit containing live human skin cells, you can order all these and more from a specialized supply house such as New England Biolabs or Bethesda Research Laboratories.

Mail-order biological products have greatly facilitated recombinant DNA technology. Even more important in speeding up biotechnology, though, are the computerized, automated processing machines. Gene recombination by hand is difficult and slow. In the early days, the time and expense involved created bottlenecks in new research and industrial development.

Today, equipment developed in the early 1980s by companies such as Applied Biosystems in Foster City, California, makes the basic manipulations quick and easy. Already a leader in manufacturing protein sequencers and DNA synthesizers, Applied Biosystems is hard at work developing apparatus for protein synthesis and DNA sequencing.

Polynucleotide assembly machines controlled by microprocessors can make chains of genetic fragments to exact specifications. The short strands thus assembled are used as probes for finding the corresponding genes in large collections of genetic material.

"Gene machines" add one nucleotide after another onto a rigid column of support material in the order dictated by a programming card. Because they can add a subunit every thirty minutes or so, the machines finish in a few hours what used to take months to accomplish.

Instruments of this kind can find, snip, and reassemble genes, change their hereditary messages, and redesign them to order, all under the supervision of an operator who needs relatively little training.

The Range of Products

In nonpharmaceutical fields, scientists are attempting to make a whole range of useful chemicals by manipulating bacterial genes.

One scientist, J. Herbert Waits of the University of Connecticut Medical School in Farmington, became fascinated by the way mussels are able to "glue"

themselves to rocks.[6] He unraveled the chemical secrets of their adhesive, and researchers at Genex Corporation (now defunct) were able to map the genetic
structure of this remarkable substance. Soon, scientists may be able to program bacteria or yeast cells to
copy the mussels' sticky excretion and make it in
quantity. Within a year or two, the new "superglue"
could be ready for clinical trials in dental schools and
hospitals. Because mussel glue can retain its hold in
a wet and salty environment, dentists expect it to be
tough enough to reattach broken teeth and orthopedic
surgeons hope to use it for reassembling fractured bone
splinters without pins or screws.

Biomethods are also likely to become important
in making such chemicals as ethanol and liquid and
gaseous fuels. One such attempt by scientists at
Genentech hopes to use bacteria specifically designed
to convert municipal garbage and human waste into
combustible fuels.

Bacteria are already being used as "cleanup
squads" for oil spills, chemical dumps, and waste
streams. Other mineral-dissolving strains are at work
"mining" rare metals such as uranium and copper.
The bacteria leach the metals out of the soil by a kind
of digestive action. One long-range project is to use
microbes as catalysts in converting natural substances
such as glucose into raw material for textile fibers.
Some companies are also planning to use genetically
engineered microorganisms for such diverse purposes
as making natural fructose (a sweetener), propylene
oxide (a chemical used to manufacture plastics), gas-
ohol (a fuel composed of gasoline and ethyl alcohol),
fertilizers, insecticides, and many other compounds.

However, many scientists are pessimistic about

the abilities of biocompanies to produce these commodities economically. Most of these new processes can't really financially compete with conventional production methods at the present time. Initial research costs are high. The process of "scaling up" to commercial quantities and trial tests can cost as much as $10 million. The followup clinical and field tests are usually estimated to cost from $30 million to $60 million. Many scientific and financial experts feel that most of the hundred or so new companies now operating will not survive the next few years.

| The Human | Genome |

One of the most exciting possibilities of modern bioengineering is that of improving the quality of life by manipulating human genes. The complete set of genetic instructions on human DNA (called the human *genome*) is enormous. Several organizations are now attempting to map the human genome by compiling decoded gene sequences from research labs all over the world. Mapping the human genome means finding the precise location of all the genes on one or another of the forty-six human genes. The identity and sequence of all the DNA subunits on the genes must also be defined. A map of all the gene sequences in the human body will be a valuable aid to medicine and medical research. But what a job! The human genome consists of 3 billion DNA base pairs. With diligent work scientists have thus far managed to decode the base sequence of only about five hundred human genes, less than 1 percent of the total.

The effort is expensive and highly competitive. In Japan, a group of powerful corporations plans to pool resources in order to sequence one million base pairs per day. At this rate they should actually be done with the task in about ten years.

Early in 1987, Dr. Walter Gilbert, Nobel laureate in biology, announced that he was forming a new company called the Genome Corporation, whose sole objective would be to decipher the human genome and sell the information.[7] Many scientists objected on the grounds that it was immoral to "own" the human genome and exploit it for private gain. Dr. Gilbert's argument is that if it's proper for a hospital to make a profit, it's proper for a company to make a profit by selling knowledge of the sequencing of the human genome, which could revolutionize medicine.

The U.S. government has embarked on a genome project of its own. In October 1988, Nobel laureate James Watson was named associate director of the National Institutes of Health for genome research. His task will be to head an effort to define all the roughly 50,000 to 100,000 human genes. The research team also hopes to work out the genomes of other species that have been important for genetic research, such as *E.coli* bacteria, yeast, and mice. The effort is expected to take fifteen years and cost several billion dollars.

The benefits of this research would be enormous. Not only are genetic factors important in diseases such as cancer, mental illness, and heart disease, but more than three thousand other diseases, most of them rare, are known to be caused by a mal-

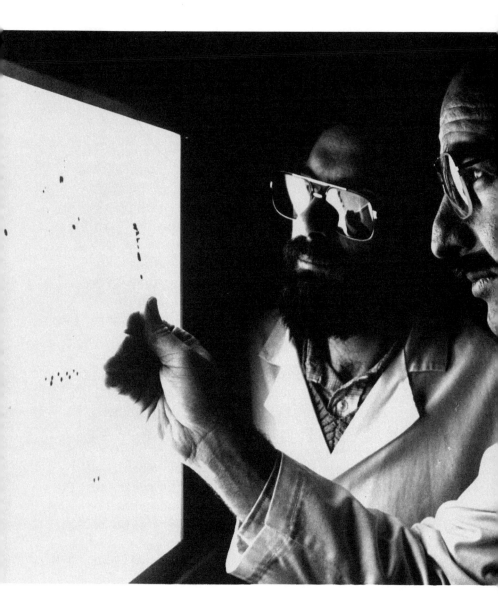

*Scientists at Tufts University view an
X-ray scan of defective genes.*

functioning or faulty gene. The genetic knowledge gained will be used to seek new ways of coping with or curing these diseases.

Cloning—in Fact and Fiction

The philosophical and ethical questions that would stem from having an exact blueprint of the human genome are similar to those that would stem from cloning a human being. Making a human clone would be such a sensational feat that one might think every molecular biologist must be trying to accomplish it. In reality, this is not so at all. Cloning—the asexual reproduction of an organism in which the offspring is the result of a single parental cell—is primarily used as a research tool.

Asexual reproduction is not uncommon in nature. It is found in plants that grow from cuttings, in single-celled organisms that reproduce by dividing, and in certain jellyfish that reproduce by budding. The phenomenon in which offspring develop from the nucleus of an unfertilized egg is called parthenogenesis, from the Greek *parthenos*, meaning "virgin," and *genesis*, meaning "origin." Worker bees, for example, are formed this way. They are the offspring of the queen bee alone. Parthenogenesis sometimes occurs in birds and occasionally in mammals such as hamsters and mice. This kind of accidental mammalian parthenogenesis, though, results in only a few rudimentary cells and never goes far enough to produce a complete animal.

Several dozen plants can now be propagated by

cloning. That is, they are regenerated from single cells in tissue culture. Among them are strawberries, asparagus, and pineapple, as well as African violets and carnations.

To clone plants, growers place minute slivers of a parent plant in nutrient broth for several months. Eventually, the cells multiply, and when these cells are transplanted they put down roots. Commercial growers find this cultivating method practical. A stock of tissue culture 2 feet (0.6 m) square can turn out 20,000 plants. Another advantage of this method is the rapid rate at which seedlings grow. This is due to the hormones surrounding the tissues as they lie in the culture bath. In the future, this method may be widely applied in forestry as well as in agriculture.

Three Cloned Mice

Cloning a mammal differs from parthenogenesis. It does not begin with the nucleus of an egg cell but with the nucleus of a single body cell. An egg cell is used, but only as a carrier or incubator for a foreign cell nucleus.

In 1981, the first successful mouse cloning experiments were reported from Switzerland and the United States. Cell nuclei were taken from a gray mouse embryo at an early stage of fetal development. One of these nuclei was inserted into each of a group of freshly fertilized eggs of a black mouse. The original nuclear material was then removed from the eggs to leave only the new material. After culturing the eggs for a few days, researchers transferred them to

A young grapevine seedling grows in a liquid
culture medium in a test tube. This is an example
of a tissue culture used in cloning plants.

the wombs of white mice made ready for pregnancy by treatment with hormones.

In one experimental setup, 542 transplants were performed. From these, only three mice resulted that could be recognized as true clones. Two were female, one male. They were, of course, gray like their parent. Studies of cultured tissue samples and enzyme analysis showed that they were in all respects just like the donor of the nuclei and not at all like the donor of the egg or the surrogate mother who carried them in her womb.

Cloning the cell nuclei of a young embryo works because such cells have hardly begun to differentiate. That is, they have not started to form legs or eyes or fur. The nuclei of these embryonic cells are identical, and all contain the full complement of genetic instructions to form a new animal.

In 1988, the Granada Corporation, a cattle-breeding company based in Houston, Texas, announced that it had successfully applied a technique developed by Dr. Steen M. Willadsen, a researcher at the University of Calgary, to clone livestock.[8] The technique promises to revolutionize the way the finest breeding cows and bulls are produced. Using micro-surgical tools, Granada scientists removed the genetic material from the embryo of a prize cow and inserted it into unfertilized bovine eggs whose nuclei had been removed in a separate procedure. When the genetically altered eggs were transplanted into surrogate mothers, the surrogate cows gave birth to eight identical coal-black calves. Theoretically, the cloning process can be repeated using the same genes so that thousands of identical calves could be produced.

Unfortunately, the rate of success is still only 10 to 30 percent, and each attempt costs thousands of dollars. But within two or three years it is expected that this technique will become more reliable and dominate the reproductive technology of prize cattle.

Human Cloning

In the future, similar cloning techniques might be devised for humans. A book published in 1978, David Rorvik's *In His Image—The Cloning of a Man*, falsely claimed to be a factual report on the genetic copying of a baby boy, an exact duplicate of his millionaire father. In fact, it describes all the steps of mouse cloning, from nuclear transfer to gestation in a surrogate womb, except that the cell donor is a human adult. Though interesting reading, the book is fiction. Of all the obstacles in the way of this enormous undertaking, the lack of knowledge of human embryonic development is the most formidable.

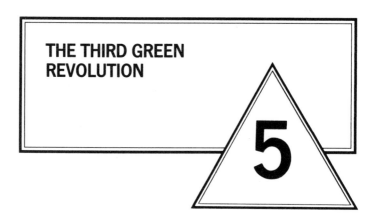

THE THIRD GREEN REVOLUTION

5

Twentieth-century science has given us three green revolutions. The first occurred when farmers first turned from using animal power to motors and machines. The second came after World War II, with the use of new chemical pesticides and fertilizers. The third green revolution has been brought about by genetically engineered grains, produce, and animal medicines.

Plant Genetics

To learn more about the scientific basis for the technology of the new green revolution, let's return once more to Cold Spring Harbor Laboratory, this time to a building named after Max Delbrück.

The work of the lab is chiefly involved with manipulating the genetic potential of plants. Plants are usually divided into two categories—the dicots and the monocots. Dicots start their sprouting life with two cotyledons (seed leaves), while monocots sprout only one. Dicots consist of such common plants as tomatoes, broccoli, and tobacco.

Most of the research done in this laboratory uses the tobacco plant. The characteristic most interesting about dicots in general and tobacco in particular is that under the right hormonal conditions you can regenerate the plant from a single cell. This is a special and important property. Only about a dozen plants, such as petunias, carrots, tobacco, asparagus, and broccoli, can be reliably regenerated from a single cell. The ease with which the tobacco plant can be taken through its entire cell culture cycle makes it ideal for experimentation. You can start with a plant in a pot, take some cells from it, transform the cells, and let them grow into a new plant. Since the cells also grow nicely as a suspension in a liquid, biochemical analysis is made especially convenient.

Dicots have another important property that makes them ideal for research. It is relatively easy to introduce a sequence of foreign DNA into these plants. This means that scientists can control the plant's genetics in a direct, straightforward way. The ideal tool for this transformation has proven to be a soil microbe called *Agrobacterium tumefaciens*.

If a plant is wounded, or if any kind of damage occurs to the cell wall, the cell releases a small molecule that acts as a signal for the *Agrobacterium*. This remarkable microbe enters the plant and acts like a virus by injecting some of its DNA into the plant. The injected DNA takes the form of a small loop called the Ti (for tumor-inducing) plasmid. The plasmid eventually gets integrated into the cell's nuclear DNA, where its genes tell the plant to produce a variety of

A young, genetically engineered tobacco plant
is part of the technology of the new green revolution.

chemicals and hormones that the plant cell ordinarily never manufactures. The presence of these foreign materials generally results in a crown gall, a characteristic bulbous, cancerlike growth on the tissues of the plant.

To be useful in genetic engineering, the Ti plasmid must first be stripped of its harmful genes. These genes produce the hormones and other substances that cause the abnormal growth and tumor in the plant. Scientists discovered that even after cutting out all the harmful genes, they could still transfer the little plasmid circles from the microbe to the plant nucleus. The "disarmed" Ti plasmids have proven to be a most effective tool for transforming plants.

Scientists at Cold Spring Harbor use genetically altered Ti plasmids to study the effects of different genes on plants. They often jokingly refer to the gene substituted in place of the excised gene as the YFG gene, for Your Favorite Gene. One gene of particular interest is a mammalian (mouse) gene that produces a group of chemicals called polyamines. Polyamines are absolutely essential for all living organisms, whether animals or plants. They seem to control certain developmental processes and appear to be critical, for example, in the sexual development of plants. When polyamine production is inhibited, strange-looking plants are produced—in particular, sexual transformations called developmental switches, where the male part of the flower acts as if it's the female part and the female acts as if it's the male. The stamen (the male part of the flower) will often be found inside the ovaries in place of the ovules, or the tip of the ovary will suddenly develop a petal. The integration of polyamine-producing mouse genes into plant DNA is being used to try to understand why the metabolism of polyamines is so critical for the sexual development of plants.

In the laboratory of Dr. Andrew Hiatt, the young biologist in charge of the plant genetics research team, there is a purposeful clutter of bottles, tubes, beakers, covered petri dishes, meters, and microscopes. In a small adjoining room, rows and rows of cell culture flasks stand neatly arranged on shelves. They contain cells of tobacco, yeast, and corn, floating in various growth regulators for shoot formation or root development. Some are still in the undifferentiated form called callus—an unpromising-looking greenish-yellowish slime. Others are beginning to regenerate into small shoots, roots, and leaves. The tobacco is doing well, but the corn seems to be stagnating. The corn needs special treatment to regenerate successfully in cell cultures.

In the hall, a white cabinet resembling a huge refrigerator has dials for adjusting not only the temperature but also the light inside, to simulate the cycle of night and day at any season of the year. Inside is a leafy array of potted tobacco plants at several stages of growth. The tallest, about 4 feet (1.2 m) high, is just about to flower. It seems extraordinary that its only parent was a mere snippet of another plant. What's even more impressive is that the tiniest cutting of this fine offspring, given the proper growing conditions, will regenerate into a new plant and run true to form.

The Monocot Barrier

The microbe A. *tumefaciens* does not interact with monocots. Unfortunately, some of our most important grains—corn, wheat, and rice—are monocots. A new technique called *electroporation* has recently been developed and is being used at the Cold Spring Harbor Laboratory. It substitutes electric currents for plasmids.

The technique consists of taking a section of a corn cell and a small piece of DNA and subjecting the cell wall to a high voltage. This makes the cell wall more porous and enables the DNA to enter the cell. Once the DNA is in the cell, it gets integrated into the nucleus, and the plant cell does the rest. Many researchers feel that this technique offers a glimmer of hope for altering the genes of cereals and other monocots.

The genetic engineering of corn, rice, and other cereals could make toxic pesticides and other harmful chemicals obsolete. Recently, for example, Agracetus, a company in Middleton, Wisconsin, developed a gene transfer technique for cotton plants that will eventually help produce cotton poisonous to certain leaf-eating insects such as the boll weevil. Until now, cotton growers had to control these pests by spending about $300 million a year on insecticide-spraying programs. Aside from being expensive, some chemical insecticides are toxic to humans and wildlife. That's what makes a built-in protective system for the cotton plant so desirable. It would be cheaper and less damaging to the environment.

Early in 1987 two separate European research centers claimed to have introduced foreign DNA into corn.[1] Scientists working at these two research centers eventually hope to be able to improve the strains of many crop plants by making them resistant to drought or disease.

Jumping Genes

One of the most famous scientists at Cold Spring Harbor is Barbara McClintock. Dr. McClintock has devoted her lifetime to research on the genetics of corn, specifically the sort that has bright-colored kernels and is commonly called Indian corn. In 1983, Dr. McClintock received the Nobel Prize in physiology and medicine. An independent and diligent scientist who likes to keep out of the public limelight, she was eighty-one years old at the time of the prize.

According to traditional Mendelian theory,[2] such characteristics of corn kernels as color should always be passed on to future generations in certain predictable ways. Dr. McClintock noted, however, that in corn this is often not the case. It occurred to her that perhaps corn genes do not always follow each other in the exact same sequence in the genome when they are inherited. This was quite a revolutionary idea when she first proposed it, in the 1940s.[3] But her painstaking work did indeed confirm what she had suspected. There are genes that change their position, transposons as she called them, in the genome of corn.

To everyone's surprise, moreover, in recent years such "jumping genes"—bits of DNA that unaccountably change their place in the chromosome chain—have been identified in every other kind of organism that has been examined, including bacteria, worms, and fruit flies.[4]

For the moment, the discovery of transposons is unlikely to have a direct impact on agriculture or industry. Its significance is not well understood, but scientists hope that it will eventually help us to better understand the process of evolution in all species.

For her research on Indian corn genes,
Dr. Barbara McClintock won the Nobel prize.

The Ti technique used at Cold Spring Harbor has been refined and is being used in other genetic engineering laboratories. One of the best known companies doing work in this field is Agrigenetics, in Madison, Wisconsin. Scientists at Agrigenetics have managed to transfer a gene for phaseolin, a major protein of the French bean, into sunflower cells. They called their creation a sunbean, although unfortunately it looks like a slimy piece of cauliflower. The final product is not attractive, but the researchers did manage to produce a sunflower that can make bean protein. Researchers have also successfully transferred the French bean gene into a tobacco plant and formed a new plant now called a Tobean.

A group working at the Monsanto Corporation Laboratories has inserted a bacterial gene that confers resistance to the antibiotic kanamycin into petunia cells. Another group, working at the Calgene Corporation, has transferred a bacterial gene that confers resistance to the herbicide glycoside into tobacco. Giving free rein to their imaginations, many scientists now talk of plants tailor-made to produce a variety of useful products such as fats, oils, steroids, and codeine. Researchers also hope to identify the genes that confer resistance to various herbicides and transfer them to important commercially grown plants.

| Self-Fertilizing |
| Plants |

Most dramatic of all is the possible development of self-fertilizing plant strains, which experts envision in the not-too-distant future. Contemporary agriculture uses enormous quantities of nitrogen-based fertilizers to increase crop yields. Not only are these fertilizers costly, but they also tend to pollute streams and ground water. Nitrogen, an essential substance for all growing plants, is a gas freely available in the atmosphere. Plants only absorb it, though, when it has been changed to ammonia by nitrogen-fixing bacteria in the soil.

Scientists at Cornell University have isolated the group of genes in bacteria that enable them to fix nitrogen and have spliced these into yeast cells. The genes remain stable during many divisions of their host cells and resume nitrogen-fixing activity when they are spliced back again into their native bacteria. Until now, though, experimenters have not induced yeast to fix nitrogen. A cluster of as many as seventeen genes directs this process in bacteria, and more could be needed to direct nitrogen fixation in plants. Research is pushing ahead, though, toward the day when recombinant techniques will produce nitrogen-fixing strains of wheat, corn, and other food plants.

| Photosynthesis |

The use of genetic engineering to modify the process of photosynthesis is another target for scientists using Ti plasmids. During photosynthesis, plants use chlorophyll to produce chemical energy by absorbing sunlight. This energy is then used to convert carbon dioxide and water into carbohydrates. The mechanism for useful photosynthesis depends on an enzyme known as ribulose 1,5-biphosphate carboxylase, or Rubisco. This enzyme is probably the most abundant protein on earth. Recently, a group of scientists at

Plant Genetic Systems has developed a technique for introducing Ti plasmids into chlorophyll-rich plant cells. They hope to remodel the Rubisco molecule so that it can increase the efficiency of photosynthesis.

| Modifying
Frost Damage |

Rather than directly influencing the genetics of plants, some scientists have taken a different path in their desire to improve certain plant characteristics. Since more is known about the genetics of bacteria than of plants, their plan is to modify the plant's behavior by redesigning the bacteria known to support the plant in some way. A group of scientists at the Advanced Genetics Sciences Corporation in Berkeley, California, has been trying to reduce the frost damage to crops by producing genetically engineered bacteria.

Frost damage is caused by ice crystals. The ice usually requires a nucleus or seed of some kind to start the crystal growing. This phenomenon is similar to the well-known seeding of clouds that causes liquid drops of rain to form. Certain plant bacteria, such as *Pseudomonas syringae*, are known to be "coated" with a protein that acts as such a nucleus and initiates the growth of ice crystals. Scientists have made bacteria lacking this protein. Preliminary tests conducted in greenhouses have shown such engineered bacteria to have a "smooth coat" and to be of great value in preventing frost damage.

Outdoor tests began in April 1987 when a judge of the California Supreme Court cleared the way to allow such bacteria to be released in field experiments. Researchers sprayed a gene-altered microorganism called Frostban over an experimental strawberry plot in Brentwood, California, about 50 miles (80 km) east of San Francisco. At a remote field station belonging to the University of California, another group of scientists planted potato seeds treated with the modified *P. syringae*. The tests showed that the altered bacteria could survive in nature despite competition from their natural relatives. Researchers also determined that plants sprayed with Frostban exhibited less damage at lower temperatures than plants that had not been sprayed.

Making Plants Healthy and Hardy

Even more important, perhaps, than damage caused by weather is the ability to free a crop strain of viral disease or adjust it to a new environment by altering its genetic makeup. Early in May 1986 Agracetus launched the first outdoor field test in the United States of a plant altered by recombinant DNA techniques.[5] The company received permission from the National Institutes of Health to plant a garden plot in Wisconsin with two hundred 4-inch (10-cm) gene-altered tobacco seedlings containing an added gene to make them disease-resistant. Special precautions were taken, such as placing bags over the buds of the plants, to eliminate the chance of pollen transfer.

Such tests are closely watched by environmentalists and citizens' groups. Will this new life-form pose an unforeseen threat of some kind? In this case, scientists at the National Institutes of Health didn't think so. Jeremy Rifkin disagreed with the scientists. President of the Foundation on Economic Trends lo-

An experimental strawberry patch is sprayed with Frostban, a gene-altered microorganism whose use is controversial.

*Jeremy Rifkin explains to an audience
his opposition to field tests
using genetically modified bacteria.*

cated in Washington, D.C., Rifkin has been a prominent critic of such tests. Several field tests involving
genetically modified bacteria have been postponed
because of his opposition or lawsuits he has brought.

Animal Farming

Dairy farmers as well as cattle and sheep breeders are
likely to benefit from genetic engineering in many

different ways. For instance, Australian scientists are hoping to raise wool production by as much as 100 percent by feeding sheep a new form of alfalfa into which they have inserted pea genes.[6] To grow thick and abundant wool, sheep need plenty of sulfur, and this is what the added pea gene will provide in the new alfalfa diet.

Other aids to the farmer are more direct. Companies such as Agracetus and Amgen manufacture pharmaceuticals for animals as well as for people. Vaccines and hormones create healthier, stronger herds and poultry, assure a greater yield of milk, more and bigger eggs, and better meat.

A vaccine against hoof-and-mouth disease is an important priority for international dairy, cattle, sheep, and hog farmers. This highly contagious disease produces sores in the mouths and on the hooves of the animals, weakening the animals severely enough so that they become agriculturally useless. Many biotechnology companies are busy working to develop a vaccine which they hope will be effective against the disease.

Growth hormones have been used effectively in raising cattle. Experiments show that beef cattle treated with growth hormones grow meatier and that dairy cows grow more productive. In a study done at Cornell University, a Holstein cow treated with daily injections of bovine growth hormone gave up to 40 quarts (38 l) of milk a day rather than the usual 30 quarts (28 l).[7]

Actually, farmers have used growth-promoting drugs and chemicals on animals for years. But these additives are not altogether desirable because they tend to leave residues in the meat that comes to our table. Since the genetically engineered product is a natural protein from an animal gene, raising meat and milk yields may be possible without leaving traces of substances harmful to human consumers.

| A Patent for |
| the Geep |

The most radical way to produce more productive farm animals is to produce entirely new kinds of livestock. Recombinant DNA techniques can mix genes from different species of animals, or mix plant or microbe genes into animal embryos to produce custom-designed animals—cows that give more milk, or pigs that are leaner.

For example, scientists at the Department of Agriculture's station in Beltsville, Maryland, have inserted a human growth hormone into pig embryos to make them grow faster. The genetically altered pigs produced offspring that also had the human hormone. Although these pigs are generally leaner and therefore more desirable, they have arthritis and increased susceptibility to disease.

Scientists at Colorado State University are developing methods to clone cattle, pigs, and goats. A cattle embryo about a week old is collected in a glass dish and cut in half with a microsurgical blade. The pieces are then implanted into surrogate mother cows. Eventually, the cows will give birth to two perfectly healthy identical twin calves.

By fusing together a goat embryo and a sheep embryo, researchers at the University of California at Davis have obtained a live novelty animal, which they call a geep. This living biological monster has little to recommend it. It is very frail and cannot reproduce itself, but it is a prophesy of things to come.

The U.S Patent Office announced in April 1987 that it was getting ready to issue patents to inventors of new types of animal life.[8] This made the United States the only country in the world granting patents on animals. No doubt it will encourage more experiments and greater investment in cross-splicing of genetic material to obtain any number of desirable traits in livestock and other farm-bred animals. But many critics oppose this step and are trying to prevent it.

A coalition led by the Humane Society of the United States and the Foundation on Economic Trends was formed to block the policy. Jeremy Rifkin, the vocal critic of genetic research, summarized his opposition by saying, "In literally one stroke, the Patent Office has moved society into a commercialized brave new world. Living things are to be considered no differently than chemical products or automobiles or tennis balls."

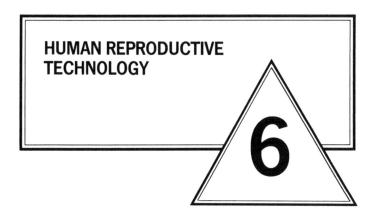

HUMAN REPRODUCTIVE TECHNOLOGY

6

Can human genes be engineered like those of micro-organisms? Can scientists cure inherited illnesses by replacing "bad" genes with "good" genes? Some people hope for this possibility, while others fear it. Those who fear it disapprove of meddling with the basic processes of heredity. They consider all such experiments dangerous and believe that they diminish the value of human life. Those who welcome the possibility look forward to a better understanding of hereditary disorders as well as to their prevention and possible cure.

We are lucky to live in an age when vaccines have brought many killing and crippling childhood diseases under control. Unfortunately, though, thousands of different genetic defects still take a heavy toll. Each year, their impact brings sadness and hardship to many families.

Until recently, there was little help for the accidents of biological inheritance. People had no influence over the great genetic lottery. But now, medicine is developing new options for prospective parents. Many birth defects can be prevented. Some can be diagnosed in the unborn fetus. Others can even be treated successfully—before or after birth.

| A Genetic Accident |

Some years ago, Susan and David M. were pleased to discover that they were about to become parents. They were in their late thirties, a time of life when many of their friends' children were already entering high school.

Unfortunately, the child born was gravely ill. The baby girl's eyes were fused together, her nose flattened, her palate cleft. She had difficulty breathing, her kidneys were in the wrong place, and she was unable to urinate. One week later, the baby died. During her short life, teams of doctors attempted to save her life by various surgical techniques. Had she lived, she would have been mentally retarded and physically disabled.

Today, a couple like Susan and David M. is less likely to suffer the same catastrophe. The attending physician would point out that a woman close to forty runs nearly a three percent risk of giving birth to a child with chromosomal abnormalities. The doctor would undoubtedly tell the expectant parents about several possible tests that might reveal abnormalities in the baby. One of these tests, a procedure called amniocentesis, allows experts to examine the amniotic fluid surrounding the fetus in the womb. Analysis of this fluid will reveal many genetic disorders if they are present. Usually, the test is conducted between the fourteenth and twentieth weeks of pregnancy. Recently, doctors developed a new test called chorionic villus biopsy that can be done even earlier, some time between the tenth and twelfth week.

If Susan had undergone these tests, a chromosome count would have revealed that the cells of the expectant baby carried forty-seven instead of forty-six chromosomes. Specifically, there were three number thirteen chromosomes instead of the usual pair. Although such abnormalities cannot yet be cured, prenatal testing would have offered the parents a chance to decide whether to go through with the pregnancy.

Human Gene Structure

To understand the many causes of birth defects, it is helpful to review the mechanism of human heredity. Each kind of plant and animal has its own specific number of chromosomes in all its cells. Humans have forty-six chromosomes, or, rather, twenty-three pairs. Of each pair, one chromosome has been inherited from the mother and one from the father.

Although chromosomes can be seen under a powerful microscope, the genes that direct the cells' behavior are far too small to be visible. Their existence can only be inferred by their activities and by certain chemical probes. Scientists are still uncertain how many genes are located within our twenty-three pairs of chromosomes. Estimates range from 500,000 to over a million. Even though all our cells, with rare exceptions, contain the same number of chromosomes, the cells vary widely in function. Some cells make up the brain, others the intestine, still others function as skin or as blood. Just how this differentiation begins, during the embryo's development, and just how it is maintained, remains a mystery.

Sexual Reproduction

To start a new human life, twenty-three chromosomes from a man must join twenty-three chromosomes from a woman. How is this accomplished when each individual's cells contain twice that number? The reproductive cells, also called *germ cells,* produced by the testes in men and the ovaries in women, undergo a special process called *meiosis.* In meiosis, the cell divides twice, but the chromosomes duplicate only once. As a result, the male and female germ cells contain half the usual number of chromosomes.

The basic genetic makeup of men and women differs in only one chromosome. Twenty-two pairs, the so-called *autosomes,* are identical in the cells of both sexes. The twenty-third pair, the sex chromosomes, consist of two X chromosomes in females (XX) and of one X and one Y in males (XY). Genetic disorders in any of the twenty-two autosomes are called *autosomal disorders.* Those residing in the sex chromosomes are called X-*linked* disorders. No Y-linked disorders have been discovered.

Any accident, however slight, in germ cell division of one parent may result in a severe birth defect. If division is not completely equal—if even a single extra chromosome either leaves the cell or remains inside—the effect may be devastating after the cell becomes joined to its partner of the opposite sex and begins developing into an embryo.

Chromosome Errors

Errors in chromosome number are thought to account for 40 percent of miscarriages in the first three months of pregnancy. In some cases, the error is less severe and the fetus survives in spite of a serious handicap. A commonly known condition resulting from an extra chromosome in the twenty-first pair is Down's syndrome. Children born with this affliction are mentally retarded and small in stature and have abnormal fingerprints. Typically, their eyes are somewhat slanted, which is the reason this condition was formerly named mongoloidism.

Another disorder is known as fragile X. This condition, thought to be about half as common as Down's syndrome, is associated with extreme fragility of the X chromosome. It results in mental retardation and affects male children only. Females are not affected, for they have a second X chromosome to fall back on.

Geneticists have discovered that the risk of having children with chromosome abnormalities exists for parents of all ages. In the future, when testing has become more simplified, genetic screening for expectant parents of all ages and both sexes may become routine.

Genetic Disorders

About 2,500 genetic diseases are caused by an abnormality in a single gene. It might be located in any one of the forty-four non-sex chromosomes (autosomal diseases) or in the X chromosome (X-linked). Over 2,000 more hereditary diseases are caused by defects in several genes. Abnormal births may also result from environmental factors such as toxic chemicals that enter through the mother's bloodstream or from viral infections such as German measles contracted by the mother in early pregnancy.

Like other inherited traits, genetic disorders may be dominant or recessive. A person who has inherited a recessive disorder from one parent is a carrier who may be completely free of symptoms. This is true, for instance, of people who carry only one gene for albinism, a defect in the body's ability to form pigment in hair, skin, and eyes. If two carriers of this gene produce a child, however, chances are one in four that their child will be born an albino.

Some common autosomal recessive disorders include phenylketonuria (PKU), Tay-Sachs disease, and sickle-cell anemia. These diseases tend to run in certain population groups and will be discussed in the section on preventive screening.

X-linked disorders are more threatening to males than to females. In a man, a single recessive gene mutation of the X chromosome produces disease because he has no second X to provide a normal, compensating gene. Some of the common X-linked recessive disorders are hemophilia, color blindness, and certain types of muscular dystrophy.

Prenatal Testing

In 1980, a team of surgeons at New York's Mount Sinai Hospital performed a bold and precarious maneuver on a woman pregnant with twins. Prenatal tests had shown that one twin was in good health, while the other carried an extra chromosome twenty-one. Pictures of the chromosomes of each fetus showed that both were male, that they were not genetically identical but were fraternal twins, and that one seemed to be free of abnormalities while the other was afflicted with Down's syndrome. Not only would this child be born retarded, but he was also likely to be physically disabled. Four months before the twins were due to be born, surgeons destroyed the abnormal fetus without harming the normal twin.

Amniocentesis

The prologue to this procedure began a few months earlier with an amniocentesis, which enabled doctors to examine the chromosomes of the two fetuses. The patient was over forty years old, which placed her in a high-risk category for fetal abnormalities. As in all such cases today, her obstetrician advised prenatal testing.

Amniocentesis is usually performed in a hospital operating room. To prevent injury to the fetus, the doctor follows its exact position from moment to moment with a pulsed ultrasound scanning device. The doctor inserts a thin, hollow needle through an anesthetized area in the mother's abdominal wall and into the amniotic sac, then draws out about 20 cubic centimeters (2/3 of an ounce) of amniotic fluid. This clear yellow liquid is the habitat in which the embryo floats until birth. It contains the embryo's urine as well as other body chemicals and cell materials. The proce-

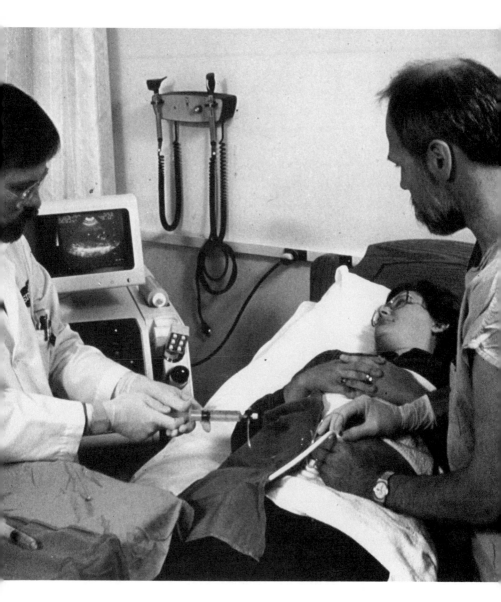

Amniocentesis is a widely used procedure in prenatal testing.

dure takes only a few minutes. The fluid is taken to a genetics laboratory where a karyotype is made.

<table>
<tr><td>Making a
Karyotype</td></tr>
</table>

It is surprisingly easy to see a picture of your own chromosomes. The picture, an enlarged and organized photograph of the chromosomes of a cell, is called a *karyotype*. Such a picture allows experts to count and examine the chromosomes to see if any are duplicated, missing, broken, or misshapen (see Figure 9). Usually, the sample to be examined comes from the patient's white blood cells or from a small patch of skin tissue.

When the patient is an unborn child, however, the cells for examination are cultured from amniotic fluid. A technician takes the fluid in a small, flat-sided bottle from the operating room to the genetics laboratory. The technician puts the bottle in an incubator at 98.6°F (37°C), which is normal human body temperature. The bottle lies on its side. After a while, the fetal cells sink down and attach themselves to the bottom surface. A nutrient solution is added to help the cells multiply quickly. This part of the process is called "planting." Twice a week, the technician feeds the cells by cautiously removing the old solution under a sterile laboratory hood and adding fresh nutrients.

After two weeks, when enough cell colonies have formed, the process of harvesting can begin. A chemical is added to the bottle to loosen the cells from the glass, and the mixture is then centrifuged (spun at

FIGURE 9: A NORMAL HUMAN KARYOTYPE

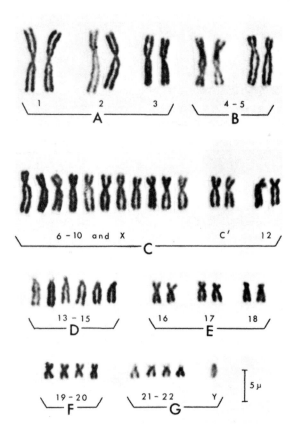

*From an enlarged photograph of the burst cell,
a lab technician has snipped these twenty-three
chromosome pairs and arranged them in order. Each
chromosome can be recognized by its size, shape,
banding pattern, and the position of the indentation
called the centromere. The sex-determining factors
(XX or XY) are always placed last. Here, the X and Y
chromosomes show that the subject is male.*

high speed) to remove the liquid, leaving only the pure cell culture.

Shortly after this, the technician adds a drop of inhibitor, which stops further cell division. Then a special agent is dropped onto the slide, which causes the cells to burst open and spew out their chromosomes. The chromosomes are treated with a fixative, to keep them from decomposing, and stained.

Looking through a powerful microscope, a lab technician chooses three or four burst cells to be photographed by an enlarging camera built into the microscope. Finally, the pictures of individual chromosomes from a single cell are snipped from the photograph and pasted in four rows of numbered pairs onto another sheet of paper. This is the karyotype.

Chorionic Villus Biopsy

A relatively new procedure that permits doctors to examine cells from an unborn child is called a chorionic villus biopsy. The procedure can be performed much earlier than amniocentesis—within eight to ten weeks after conception. At the present time, it can only be performed at a few, specially equipped hospitals.

The chorion is one of the layers of extra tissue that surround the developing embryo as it floats in the womb. The fuzzy surface of the chorion is made of floating, mosslike projections called villi (plural of villus). These will eventually embed themselves in the wall of the uterus.

For the test, doctors carefully withdraw a few chorionic villi through the mother's birth canal. They send this tissue sample to a specially equipped laboratory for analysis.

Genetic Counseling

When a woman becomes pregnant, the doctor who sees her throughout her pregnancy until after the baby is born will want to know many things about her and the baby's father. If there is any concern about the health of the baby, the doctor may refer the couple to a genetic counseling center. The counseling center constructs a more detailed "pedigree" of both sides of the family, taking into account all health problems, major physical abnormalities, lengths of life, and causes of death. Medical examination of both parents may be part of the complete routine, sometimes including X rays, biochemical analyses, and analysis of the chromosomes by karyotype. If the outcome shows that this family is at high risk for some kind of chromosomal abnormality in its descendants, the counselor will probably suggest amniocentesis, so that a karyotype can be made from the fetus's amniotic fluid cells.

Karyotyping is not the only test performed on amniotic fluid, though. Another test investigates the cell-free fluid itself for the presence and amount of alpha-fetoprotein, a substance produced by the fetus until shortly after birth. Too much of this protein may indicate a malformation of the baby's brain and spinal cord. This can result in two serious defects: "open spine" (spina bifida) and anencephaly. Anencephaly denotes the absence of brain and cranium, the "headless baby" syndrome which is always fatal. Victims of spina bifida often do survive but remain handicapped

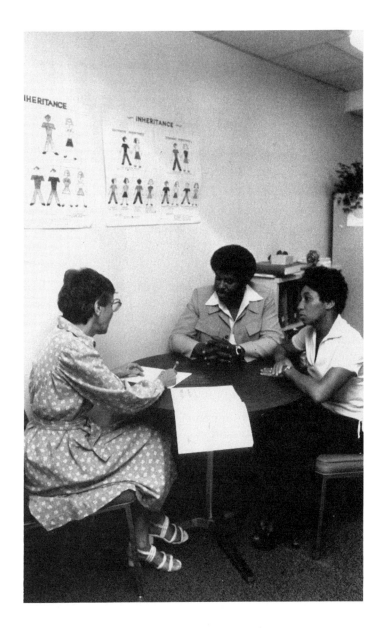

*Prospective parents receive information
at a genetics counseling center.*

by weak or paralyzed legs, curved spine, and lack of bladder and bowel control. Today, a screening test for high levels of alpha-fetoprotein can be done without amniocentesis, simply by using the expectant mother's blood serum.

If the level of alpha-fetoprotein is found to be high, the doctor usually suggests a followup test called a sonogram, an image created by ultrasound and projected on a screen. Ultrasonography is the newest technique for looking at a baby before birth. As the mother lies on a table, painless high-frequency soundwaves are bounced off the fetus, creating a pattern that is translated into visual images on a screen. Not only can doctors and technicians observe a shadowy image of the developing baby as it moves and floats about in the uterus, but the mother can watch it, too, and often the father is invited in to share this fascinating display.

Amniocentesis allows doctors to detect some seventy-five metabolic disorders of the unborn child. If a defect is found, the genetic counselor will tell the parents their options, depending on the severity of the condition. In a few cases prenatal therapy is now possible and can be started immediately. In other cases, the child's disorder can be remedied with drugs or surgery after birth. In cases where the condition leads to untreatable suffering and early death, parents can decide on an abortion.

Testing by Molecular Techniques

First perfected in 1978, techniques of recombinant molecular biology now permit scientists to diagnose sickle-cell anemia and many other genetic blood disorders in the unborn child. The test uses as little as 15 milliliters (half an ounce) of amniotic fluid. A restriction enzyme is used to analyze the genetic structure of the fetal cells. Restriction enzymes can snip out certain segments of DNA. The particular enzyme used to investigate blood disorders recognizes the site on the DNA molecule where the hemoglobin gene is encoded. The size of the fragment the enzyme cleaves from the DNA will vary in size, according to whether the gene is normal or abnormal. The test can be applied to a group of hemoglobin disorders, including sickle-cell anemia, which affects mostly blacks, and thalassemia, which affects mostly people of Mediterranean descent.

Locating Genetic Markers

As researchers improve their techniques in genetic engineering, they are coming closer to discovering the exact location on the chromosomes of markers for many disorders that run in families. Since the chromosomes are inherited in pairs—one from each parent—scientists can compare them and see if any fragment of DNA has been accidentally added, deleted, or modified from one of a pair.

Recently, a group of scientists announced that they had found genetic markers for two mental disorders that have a way of cropping up in several generations of one family: Alzheimer's disease, which deprives people of their memory, and manic-depressive syndrome, which produces extreme and severe mood swings.[1] Another group of scientists announced that they had discovered a gene that predisposed people to one type of intestinal cancer.

Preventive Screening

How can birth defects be prevented in the general population? Some enthusiasts of eugenics—the practice of human stock improvement—suggest storing in a central data bank a karyotype and genetic profile for every citizen. Parents would become statisticians. Every couple wishing to have children would consult the data and get advice on the kind and degree of risk involved for their offspring. Perhaps they would be advised to adopt children rather than producing their own. If they went ahead and gave birth after all, they might be fined or taxed.

But few people want "Big Brother" to watch them quite so closely.[2] Instead, mass screening of certain high-risk populations has recently been carried out in selected areas, as a public service. Three inborn errors of metabolism due to single-gene defects have received wide attention. They are phenylketonuria (PKU), Tay-Sachs disease (TSD), and sickle-cell anemia (SCA).

Mental Retardation Through PKU

In 1934, a Norwegian mother of two retarded children brought them to see a physician because she noticed that they carried a peculiar chemical odor. Chemical tests on their diapers showed the substance to be phenylpyruvic acid, an abnormal metabolic product in the family of chemicals called phenylketones. In writing about the disease that he was the first to identify, the doctor named it phenylketonuria, or PKU.

In the United States, only about one out of ten thousand infants is born with PKU, but about one person in fifty carries the recessive gene. PKU is most often found in people of northern European origin. PKU patients tend to be pale complexioned, light blond, and blue-eyed. Because of their inborn biochemical deficiency, they lack the enzyme to convert the amino acid phenylalanine into other needed compounds. Therefore, if babies are not treated from early infancy, they succumb to increasing mental retardation, seizures, and skin lesions.

Since 1961, a rather simple test and special diet have made PKU retardation preventable. Once detected, the disease is treated with a diet using specially prepared milk protein in place of meat, milk, or cheese. Once rapid brain development is past, at about the age of six, the diet may safely be discontinued. However, the gene remains present and may be passed on to that person's children.

Tay-Sachs Disease

More dreadful than PKU, because it is always fatal, is Tay-Sachs disease, an inherited enzyme deficiency tending to strike Jews of Eastern European descent. It affects about one in three thousand infants born to this population group. The disease is named after the two physicians who first analyzed and described it.

Victims of TSD are born in apparently perfect health. A few months later, though, they become weak, listless, and spastic. Their condition deteriorates over a period of three or four years, until the child dies. Since there is still no cure for affected infants, screening for TSD must begin with future parents. Research has shown that one in twenty-five Jews of Eastern European descent carries this specific genetic defect. Each time two carriers become parents, there is a 25 percent chance that their child will receive the defective gene from both father and mother and thus become a victim of TSD.

When two known carriers of TSD decide to have a child, the mother usually undergoes amniocentesis early in pregnancy. If tests on the amniotic fluid show that the baby has TSD, abortion is the only other option now available.

Sickle-Cell Anemia

Another single-gene deficiency often subject to prenatal screening is sickle-cell anemia (SCA), a disease frequently found in people of African ancestry. SCA is caused by a genetic change in the protein hemoglobin, the body's oxygen-carrying molecule in red blood cells. Under certain low oxygen conditions, the cells cave in at the center and assume a sickle shape instead of their normal doughnut form. Severe anemia is one result. Another result can be blockage of small blood vessels and blood clots in vital organs.

Sickle-cell patients suffer from painful and disabling attacks, which eventually lead to complications and death in early middle age. Mass screening has revealed that approximately one in twelve black Americans carries one gene for the disease and is virtually unaffected. About one in six hundred, though, carries both genes and suffers from sickle-cell symptoms. There is evidence that the disorder, which can also be found in people who live in regions where malaria is common, is actually a defense mechanism that helps block the worst effects of malaria.

Until recently, tests for sickle cells had to be performed on prospective parents rather than on the unborn child. If each parent carried one gene for the disease, the doctor could only say that the expected child had one chance in four of getting the disease. Now, however, genetic engineering techniques allow scientists to diagnose sickle-cell disease by examining the amniotic fluid cells or chorionic villi of the fetus.

Help for the Unborn

Even when a certain defect has previously occurred in the family, expectant mothers and fathers sometimes prefer to hope for the best and await the outcome rather than to subject themselves and the child in the womb to extensive medical procedures. In great part, this is because the number of options for expectant parents of a defective child is still depressingly low. In many cases, abortion is currently the only alternative to the birth of a child with the genetic trait.

Fortunately, this unhappy state of things is changing. More and more, doctors are working on treatments for the unborn in the womb. For instance, certain life-threatening vitamin deficiencies caused by genetic defects can be treated by giving the mother large doses of the needed substance during her pregnancy. Cortisone administered through the mother's bloodstream hastens maturing of the baby's lungs and is used with infants expected to be premature. This helps forestall respiratory disease and possible death.

Yet another technique is to administer digitalis to strengthen an unborn baby's heartbeat.

The major breakthrough, though, would be genetic surgery. Indeed, there is a good chance that disabilities such as those caused by the lack of an enzyme will become curable by genetic engineering. This might be done by placing normal liver cells capable of making the enzyme into the fetal bloodstream. If all went according to plans, these cells would lodge in the fetal liver, multiply there, and take over production of the missing substance. This is possible to consider because the child's immune system is not yet functioning completely.

In a first step toward such a procedure, a group of scientists managed to microinject single genes into single mammalian cells and were pleased to observe that in at least one case the gene caused the cell to function normally.

A team of scientists led by Dr. C. Thomas Caskey at the Baylor College of Medicine in Houston, Texas, is using recombinant technology in an attempt to cure Lesch-Nyhan disease, a rare neurological disturbance. Children who suffer from the disease have a defect in the gene for the enzyme hypoxanthine-guanine phosphoribosyltransferase (HGPT or HGPRT), which is essential for the breakdown of uric acid. This faulty gene causes children to become hyperexcitable and damage themselves by compulsively biting their hands and mouth.

Dr. Caskey and his staff have spliced the HGPT gene into some viral DNA and hope to insert the gene into a group of cells by "infecting" the cells with the virus. The hope is that the gene will replicate itself along with the virus and supply the missing enzyme to the cells.[3]

The next step will be to correct defective cells in live mammals instead of in test tubes. One laboratory has developed a valuable strain of mice carrying the genetic blood defect alpha-thalassemia. The mice will be used to study this disorder so that ways can be found to ameliorate it in humans.

In spite of the progress being made in gene therapy, many scientists still remain pessimistic about the possibility of gene replacement in humans. They feel that although research with animals is valuable, applying genetic engineering to human embryos is both dangerous and morally wrong.[4]

IS IT SAFE, IS IT WISE, IS IT MORAL?

7

"In the hands of the genetic engineer, life forms could become extraordinary Tinkertoys," writes Robert Sinsheimer, a molecular biologist and the chancellor of the University of California at Santa Cruz.[1] Dr. Sinsheimer urges us to consider the dark side of genetic engineering. Three crucial questions must be asked, he continues: "Is it safe, is it wise, is it moral?"

| The Asilomar
| Conference

In July 1974, an unusual event occurred in the American scientific community. A group of ten scientists working mainly in microbiology issued a public letter to biologists everywhere, asking them to put a temporary stop to certain types of recombinant DNA research. A meeting would soon be called to discuss the dangers of the new technique and to safeguard the public.

A few months earlier, two California researchers had taken a crucial step in the history of science when they found a way to remove hereditary information from one organism and insert it into another. Once this was accomplished, it appeared that the technique was simple enough for some irresponsible person to combine the DNA of any two organisms and produce a "monster," such as a new disease-carrying, cancer-causing, or antibiotic-resistant form of life. As in Mary Wollstonecraft Shelley's novel *Frankenstein*, the creation might turn on its creator and become destructive. Were molecular biologists about to unleash a source of plagues? Were they about to change the course of evolution?

One of the scientists who called for an international meeting to discuss biohazards was Dr. Paul Berg, whose own research had involved splicing DNA from a monkey tumor virus into bacterial cells. By this time, though, he had given up certain parts of this research as potentially hazardous. Later on, in 1980, Dr. Berg received a Nobel Prize for his pioneering work.

The most famous international meeting of concerned molecular biologists and biochemists took place in February 1975 at the Asilomar Conference Center in California. One of the first topics discussed was the bacterium *E. coli*, the microbial workhorse of the gene-splicing lab.

There were fears that *E. coli* programmed for antibiotic-resistance, containing cancer-causing viral material, or producing hormones or toxins, might invade the intestinal tract of a laboratory worker and move from there to the general population.

Present at the conference were a number of experienced cancer virologists and microbiologists used to dealing with infectious organisms. Some of them did not think the new experiments unusually dangerous. They felt that as long as standard safety procedures were followed in laboratories, no further official restrictions were necessary. At one point in the conference, James Watson speculated that genetic engineering work was probably no more hazardous than working in a hospital.

Still, one important fact emerged from the discussion. The participants had no way of knowing how dangerous their collective work might prove to be. The subject was so new and had developed so fast that data were not yet available. In spite of this, the scientists agreed on a final document establishing categories of risk for gene-splicing experiments and recommending safety procedures in each category. Moderate- and high-risk experiments were to be done only with special strains of crippled or "disarmed" bacteria, unable to survive in natural surroundings.

These guidelines for academic research laboratories have remained in effect, although they have been changed many times. They were reformulated and made more specific by the National Institutes of Health's Recombinant DNA Advisory Committee, operating under pressure from Congress and the general public. Revisions of the NIH guidelines are published in the Federal Register.

Yet by 1986, the biotechnology field had grown so rapidly that coordination among federal agencies was found to be necessary. By this time, more than two hundred biotechnology companies and dozens of pharmaceutical and chemical firms were seeking licenses to market genetically engineered products ranging from vaccines to pesticides. Investment in the industry ran to $1.5 billion yearly, and profits were expected to mount into tens of billions of dollars by the end of the century.

An updated set of policy statements by federal agencies was approved by President Ronald Reagan on June 16, 1986.[2] Responsibility for overseeing the multiple aspects of biotechnology was now to be shared by six federal agencies: the Department of Agriculture, the Environmental Protection Agency, the Food and Drug Administration, the National Science Foundation, the Occupational Safety and Health Administration, and the National Institutes of Health.

Easing Standards

Since the days of the Asilomar conference, molecular biologists have become more and more reluctant to be restricted in their research. On the whole, the issue of biosafety has receded into the background. As the field has expanded and become familiar, workaday attitudes have replaced the former sense of awe. Projected accidents have not occurred. Researchers have not contracted "doomsday bugs," and no monsters have escaped. Newly patented bacteria are being cautiously tested in outdoor areas. So far, the hybrid plant and animal creations brought to life have been only moderately successful. A transgenic pig, for example, created at a government research facility in Maryland, carries a copy of human genes. But instead of displaying impressive human characteristics, it is a feeble creature, especially weak in the legs.

What About the Future?

But immediate safety is not the only problem that worries critics of the new biotechnology. Other consequences may lie ahead, as yet hidden from view. One of these has to do with the interaction of living creatures as nature has evolved this interaction over millions of years. Dr. Sinsheimer calls it "a delicately balanced, intricate, self-sustaining network." Our understanding of this network is only dim, and Dr. Sinsheimer fears that in trying to improve what we now consider imperfect, we could inadvertently destroy the ecological system that has sheltered humans for so long.

The Specter of Genetic Screening

Some critics of biotechnology, however, expect less drastic but still undesirable effects long before any environmental disasters are likely to occur. Among these effects is the use of genetic screening in the workplace. Genetic screening, as we have seen in Chapter Six, can help to detect and prevent genetic disorders. But it could also be used against people who are found likely to develop certain illnesses.

In 1981 and 1982, the House Committee on Science and Technology held hearings on the applications of genetic screening tests by industries and business organizations. A representative of the Office of Technology Assessment (OTA) presented the results of a survey on genetic screening in business and industry.[3] Of the 366 companies who took part in the survey, 54 said they anticipated using genetic screening tests on their employees in the next five years.

Genetic testing helps employers and insurance companies predict any tendency of an employee to develop certain health problems. In an article on genetic testing in the workplace, Thomas H. Murray, codirector of the Occupational Health Research Group at the Hastings Center, in Hastings-on-Hudson, New York, distinguishes between genetic screening and genetic monitoring.[4] The first is more open to abuse. It could lead to denying people employment, transferring them out of good jobs, and even dismissing them. Genetic monitoring, though, is a way of keeping track of workers' health in order to identify any hazards that need attention and any dangerous conditions that need correction.

Many optimistic predictions have appeared in the medical journals on the use of genetic engineering to determine the likelihood of a person developing diabetes, heart disease, rheumatoid arthritis, or psychological disorders.[5] Should employers use the results of recombinant DNA–based tests to reduce their costs, such as by advocating premature retirement for a risky employee? The temptation to avoid having to pay job-related disability claims and high-risk insurance claims is very great. The employer need only say that the exclusion of certain workers is necessary to protect the safety of the workplace, or that it is a "business necessity." There are few laws regulating the use of genetic information, and many observers now feel that such regulation by the state or federal authorities is absolutely essential.

Reverence for Life

One of the most controversial aspects of humanity's new powers over biology is human reproductive engineering. Some people believe that life is a gift from God. They feel that birth, death, and the lottery of genetic heredity belong forever in the hands of a superior power. To them it seems wrong for humans to interfere with these basic elements of existence.

In 1987 the Vatican, as the chief authority of the Roman Catholic Church, issued a statement entitled "Instruction on Respect for Human Life in Its Origin and on the Dignity of Procreation."[6] This long and detailed document calls on the government leaders of the world to pass laws against the abuses of reproductive technology, which it condemns as unnatural. Included in the list of abuses are surrogate motherhood, artificial insemination involving persons not married to each other, and prenatal diagnosis such as amniocentesis aimed at eliminating fetuses that are malformed or who carry hereditary illnesses. The document stresses the rights of the embryo from its very formation. It forbids any experiments on living embryos unless done with a directly therapeutic aim, and keeping alive human embryos for commercial or experimental purposes as well as the freezing of an embryo even in an attempt to save its life.

Embryo Rights

The rights of embryos present a troubling moral problem, even for people who would otherwise endorse many of the reproductive techniques the Vatican roundly condemns. (The embryo stage of life begins the moment sperm cell and egg cell are joined and continues until the start of the third month of formation. After this, the unborn child is called a fetus.) As doctors delve into the problems of fertility as well as of genetic therapy, human embryos are more and more sought after as subjects of research. Mostly, the embryos available for research are a by-product of in vitro fertilization (IVF). To make sure the IVF procedure will succeed, surgeons collect and fertilize several of the mother's eggs. But of several embryos that are created, only one will be implanted in the womb. Those that are left don't get a chance to go on living, unless they can be frozen and implanted at a later time.

This in itself seems morally undesirable. But further questions arise. Who owns these embryos? Should the parents or the hospital decide their fate? And, if the embryos can't develop normally, is it better to donate them to scientific research than to let them be destroyed? Hospitals and laboratories might even be tempted to create embryos just to sell for research purposes. Should this be permitted or prohibited by law?

A few years ago, a Parliamentary Committee of Inquiry was appointed by the government of England to study the ethics and legal issues arising from the new human reproductive technology and embryology.[7] The Warnock report—named after the committee's chairperson, philosopher Dame Mary Warnock—came out with the results of the inquiry in 1984. By far the most controversial section was the one on embryo research. The majority of committee mem-

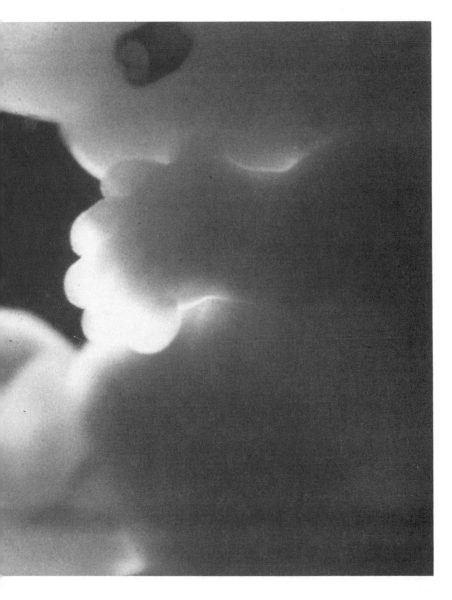

*A human embryo
at about eight weeks.*

bers agreed that human embryos should be treated with greater respect than those of other animal species. But, on the other hand, they felt that research on human embryos is likely to produce great benefit to society and should not be prohibited. They recommended that research and handling of human embryos should be permitted only by special license. And they were sharply divided over the question of whether embryos should ever be produced specifically for research, or whether only those left over from other procedures should be used. In short, even though the people on the committee were wise and thoughtful, they found it hard to come to any definite conclusions on this important topic.

Improving the Species— The New Ethics

There are many scientists who feel that it would be morally wrong to avoid using genetic engineering to cure genetic defects. There are others, however, who agree with the *New York Times* editorial entitled "Whether to Make Perfect Humans."[8] The editorial points out that "there is no discernible line to be drawn between making inheritable repairs of genetic defects, and improving the species." If scientists can repair genetic defects, "it will become much harder to argue against adding genes that confer desired qualities, like better health, looks or brains."

But what is good looks? What if a group of researchers decides that a certain skin color is a genetic disorder? There are sociologists who believe that all human behavior is genetically determined. It follows, then, that we must change our genes in order to eliminate such socially undesirable behavior as aggression and crime. Daniel Callahan, a noted writer on ethics in biology, has observed that "behind the human horror at genetic defectiveness lurks an image of the perfect human being. The very language of defect, abnormality, disease, and risk, presupposes such an image, a kind of proto-type of perfection."[9] Many observers feel that genetic engineering poses the danger that future generations of human beings will be created simply to suit the ideal of some particular group.

Truth Seeking and Profit Making

Science often begins in free inquiry and ends in profitable technology. Some observers regret this change from pure research to practical applications. Others hold that research of any kind is justified only if it leads to something useful. In any case, we should consider the earnest view of Erwin Chargaff, the renowned biochemist who laid some of the groundwork for the discovery of DNA structure. As he once told a group of college students, he prefers to think of science as a way to learn the truth about nature, not as a way to change it.

A few critical science watchers fear that what looks to us now like a harvest of benefits to humanity may end up doing more for large corporations than for large numbers of people. A few giant business empires already control the production of such things as pharmaceutical drugs, chemicals, pesticides, cattle hormones, fertilizers, seeds, and grains. Genetic engineering holds out the promise of huge profits. This may leave little room for small business enterprises.

Other questions come to mind: Will corporations conscientiously maintain genetic diversity of agricultural strains so that an unexpected pest or blight would not create disaster? Will they consider nutrition in their products? Will giant companies attempt to protect the public from biohazards when they have yet to be careful about toxic wastes, air and water pollution, worker safety, and cancer-causing food additives?

In the eyes of some observers, the intensely competitive research and development that now exists in the large new genetic engineering companies is destroying the traditional atmosphere of free inquiry in biological research. Scientific ideas are no longer free to be communicated to other workers in the field but are treated as trade secrets. Universities compete for funds from industrial groups that are dedicated to commercial products rather than the free exchange of ideas.

The availability of industrial money has led many of the most gifted biologists to shift their efforts from basic research to applied biological research. The number of genetic scientists, including several Nobel laureates, who spend large amounts of their time as industrial consultants has grown enormously. Professor Walter Gilbert, for example, who won the Nobel Prize in chemistry in 1980 for his work on the identification of nucleotide sequences, took a leave of absence from Harvard University to serve as chief executive officer of Biogen Corporation.

Gloomy Predictions

A few "worst case" prophecies by critics of genetic engineering sound very much like science fiction scenarios. They range from the possible development of biological warfare organisms that would selectively eliminate young people or members of one sex, to the advent of an ultimate doomsday bug to end all human life. They also raise the old specter of "eugenics"—the effort to improve human hereditary stock as if people were cattle—with all its abhorrent possibilities of abuse and its threat of domination by one racial or ethnic group over others.

Disturbing
the Universe

Are scientists "playing God"? Religious leaders of every faith have debated this question. Some find it arrogant to tamper with life as God created it. But others point to the verse in the Old Testament in which God tells Adam and Eve to "be fruitful and multiply and fill the earth and subdue it, and have dominion over . . . every living thing that moves upon the earth." To them it seems that men and women were put in charge of nature, to use it and change it for their own benefit.

Molecular biologist Robert Sinsheimer voices his concern in scientific terms. He objects to scientists interfering with evolution, upsetting balances that have been set by the trial and error of millions of years, and speeding up the pace of natural development. He thinks humans are not yet wise enough to direct the course of their own evolution.

On the other hand, supporters of biotechnology like to point out that humans began disturbing evolution long ago. Medicine, by saving lives, continually interferes with evolutionary patterns. Even by the simple means of correcting young people's vision with eyeglasses we change the evolutionary rule that people who can't see well enough to hunt and gather food may be eliminated from the gene pool in early youth.

Finally, what some observers call "playing God" seems to others no more than fulfilling our duty to guide our own destiny. Biotechnology gives hope to those who dream of perfecting human beings and the life they lead on earth. This dream is far from simple to put into practice. Technical power must be used with respect and concern. Like all power, it can be beneficial or destructive. Its application lies in the hands of future generations.

GLOSSARY

Amino acids. The chemical "building blocks" that are linked together to form proteins. All proteins are made up from the same set of twenty different amino acids.

Amniocentesis. A medical procedure allowing doctors to examine the amniotic fluid that surrounds the unborn baby in the mother's womb.

Anticodon. The sequence of three bases on the transfer RNA molecule that recognizes a complementary sequence of three bases on the messenger RNA.

Antigen. A foreign molecule that stimulates the production of specific antibodies.

Autosomal disorders. Genetic disorders in any of the twenty-two human autosomes.

Autosomes. The twenty-two pairs of chromosomes that are identical in the cells of both human sexes as distinguished from the twenty-third pair, the sex chromosomes.

Bacteriophage. A virus that infects bacteria. It lives and multiplies inside the bacterium.

Bacterium. A microorganism, such as *E. coli*, with a cell wall and a chromosome not enclosed within a nucleus.

Bases. The set of chemical substances present in DNA and RNA: adenine, guanine, thymine, cytosine, and uracil. Their sequence in DNA contains the genetic information.

Cell. A microscopic structure of plant or animal life, consisting of living matter within a membrane.

Chromosomes. Threadlike structures in the cells. Chromosomes carry hereditary material in the form of genes.

Cleaving. A term applied to the cutting of DNA strands at specific sites by means of restriction enzymes. Also called *cleavage.*

Clone. One of a group of genetically identical cells all descended from a single common parent cell.

Codon. The sequence of three bases on DNA or RNA that codes for a particular amino acid.

Complementary bases. The exact pairing of bases that bind strands of nucleic acid together. In DNA, adenine always pairs with thymine, and guanine always pairs with cytosine; in RNA, adenine always pairs with uracil.

Cytoplasm. The material in the cell outside the nucleus but within the membrane.

DNA. The chemical compound deoxyribonucleic acid, which contains the hereditary information in a cell.

DNA ligase. An enzyme that helps in joining the two DNA strands that make up the double helix. Also aids in repairing damaged DNA.

DNA polymerase. One of the enzymes involved in DNA replication. It helps position the proper nucleotides onto the template and supplies the energy to join them together to form a chain.

Double helix. The 3-D structure of the DNA molecule. The structural model of DNA, first conceived by Francis Crick and James Watson, consists of two long strands of DNA twisted about each other.

E. coli. A common type of bacteria found in the human intestines. Many strains of the *E. coli* bacteria are used in gene splicing.

EcoR1. One of many restriction enzymes used to cleave DNA in unique sequences.

Embryo. An organism in the early stages of formation. The embryonic stage in humans extends through the first eight weeks in the womb.

Enzymes. Proteins that act to speed up the chemical reactions found in all biological systems.

Eukaryotes. A general name for organisms whose cells contain a nucleus and more than one chromosome.

Fetus. An unborn animal in the intermediate and late stages of formation. In humans, the fetal stage lasts from the ninth week until birth.

Gene mapping. Locating the positions of the genes on the chromosomes of a particular organism.

Genes. Molecules of DNA (or, in certain viruses, RNA) that are carried on the chromosomes. Each gene carries the code for synthesis of a specific protein.

Genetic code. The relationship linking the sequence of bases in DNA or RNA to the sequence of amino acids in proteins.

Genome. The section of DNA that carries the complete set of genetic instructions for an organism.

Genotype and phenotype. Terms used to distinguish between the genetic constitution of an organism (genotype) and the observable constitution (phenotype).

Heterozygous. Carrying an unmatched gene for any particular autosomal hereditary trait (except for X-linked traits).

Homozygous. Carrying genes for any particular hereditary trait on each of two chromosomes.

Hybrid. Offspring of genetically diverse parents.

In vitro. The term literally means "in glass." *In vitro* lab experiments are distinguished from those performed directly on animals or humans *(in vivo).*

Karyotype. The organized chart of the chromosomes of a cell. A karyotype is made for the purpose of counting and examination of chromosomes.

Lambda phage. An example of a bacterial virus (bacteriophage) that has two different life cycles. After infecting the bacterium, it can multiply in the usual manner and destroy its host. Under certain conditions, however, it can become integrated with the chromosomes of the host bacterium and remain dormant for a time.

Lyse. To cause cells to dissolve or burst. The process is called *lysis.*

Meiosis. The process by which the human reproductive cells (germ cells) are formed. In meiosis, the cell divides twice, but the chromosomes duplicate only once. As a result, the male and female germ cells are *haploid*, which means that they contain half the usual number of chromosomes, twenty-three instead of forty-six.

Messenger RNA (mRNA). The intermediate RNA molecule that is synthesized in the cell nucleus according to instructions encoded in the DNA. It then moves out into the body of the cell, carrying its "message" to the ribosomes, where the proteins are made.

Microorganisms. General term for microscopic plant or animal life.

Mitochondria. Tiny bodies found in all cells. They contain enzymes that aid in the release of energy from food. Frequently called the "powerhouses" of cells.

Mitosis. The process by which cells usually divide and multiply.

Molecular biology. The study of the molecular structure and chemical reactions of living cells.

Molecule. The smallest subunit of a compound, consisting of two or more atoms.

Monoclonal antibodies. Genetically engineered antibodies derived from hybrid cancer and antibody-producing cells that are cloned and cultured to produce pure, specific antibodies.

Mutation. A change in the genes caused by alteration in the structure of its DNA.

Nucleotide. A chemical compound that consists of a base, a sugar, and one or more phosphate groups. The basic structural unit of DNA and RNA.

Organism. Any form of life having one or more cells, including bacteria, plants, and humans.

Phage. See *Bacteriophage.*

Phenotype. See *Genotype and phenotype.*

Plasmids. Small, circular DNA molecules present in bacteria that are accessories to a bacteria's chromosomes. They reproduce independently and enable bacteria to transfer genetic material among themselves.

Polygenic diseases. Hereditary disorders caused by defects in several genes.

Polynucleotide. A molecule composed of many nucleotide units linked to each other, such as DNA or RNA.

Prokaryotes. Those organisms whose cells have no nuclear membrane and only one chromosome.

Proteins. One of the most important groups of biological molecules. All enzymes are proteins, but not all proteins are enzymes. All proteins are constructed from combinations of the same set of twenty amino acids.

Recombinant DNA. The creation of a new DNA molecule by the process of cleaving and rejoining different DNA strands.

Replication. The process whereby DNA reproduces itself.

Restriction enzyme. An enzyme that recognizes a specific base sequence in DNA and cuts, or cleaves, the DNA chain at a specific site.

Ribosomal RNA (rRNA). The form of RNA that is the major component of ribosomes.

Ribosome. A complex structure found in cells that acts as the site for protein synthesis. It is made up of proteins and ribosomal RNA.

RNA. Ribonucleic acid (RNA) is a chemical relative of DNA. It is usually a single-stranded molecule that differs from DNA in using the sugar ribose in its nucleotide backbone and in substituting the base uracil for thymine.

Sex chromosomes. The chromosomes that determine gender. In humans, females have two X chromosomes (XX). Males have an X and a Y chromosome (XY).

Spina bifida. Defect in which the neural tube containing the spinal cord has failed to close. Also known as "open spine."

Split genes. Genes of higher organisms where the coded sequences of bases are interrupted by noncoding "nonsense" sequences of bases. The function of these discontinuities in the genetic information carried by the gene is not known.

Sticky ends. The ends of a DNA molecule that has been cleaved by certain restriction enzymes. These ends are called sticky because they combine with, or stick to, a complementary sequence of bases on another DNA strand.

Synthesis. The making of a complex chemical substance by combining simpler compounds or elements.

Terminal transferase. An enzyme that adds a tail, consisting of a predetermined sequence of nucleotides, to the end of one of the strands of a DNA molecule.

Transcription. The process by which the genetic information in DNA is copied to form messenger RNA (mRNA) molecules.

Transfer RNA. (tRNA). A form of RNA that is coded to collect the amino acids needed for protein synthesis and "transfer" them to their proper position on messenger RNA at the ribosomes. There is at least one transfer RNA molecule for each kind of amino acid.

Transformation. A process of introducing foreign DNA, such as plasmids, into a bacterial cell.

Translation. The process by means of which the genetic message carried by messenger RNA directs the synthesis of a protein molecule on a ribosome.

Vector. A vehicle for moving DNA from one cell to another, such as a plasmid into which foreign DNA can easily be inserted and which will be efficiently taken up by the host cell.

Virus. A disease-causing agent that consists of a core of DNA or RNA enclosed in a protective coat. Viruses reproduce only in living cells.

X-linked. The term is used in relation to genetic traits or diseases located on the X or sex chromosomes.

X-ray diffraction. The technique of determining the structure of molecules using the visible patterns obtained by the scattering of X rays from crystals.

NOTES

Chapter 1

1. Robert F. Weaver, "Changing Life's Genetic Blueprint," *National Geographic*, 166 (December 1984): 818–47.

Chapter 2

1. James Watson, *The Double Helix* (New York: Atheneum, 1968).
2. Francis Crick, "The Double Helix: A Personal View," *Nature*, 26 April 1974, 768.
3. Horace Freeland Judson, *The Eighth Day of Creation* (New York: Simon & Schuster, 1979), 342.

Chapter 4

1. "New Animal Forms Will Be Patented," *New York Times*, 17 April 1987, sec. A1.
2. "Mouse Patent, a First, Issued at Harvard," *New York Times*, 13 April 1988, sec. A1.
3. "Genetic Engineers Prepare to Create Brand New Proteins," *New York Times*, 20 February 1988, sec. A1.

4. "States Spurring Outlays in Biotechnology Field," *New York Times*, 20 February 1988, sec. A7.
5. "New Weapons Against Rabies," *New York Times*, 5 August 1986, sec. C4.
6. "Powerful Adhesive," *New York Times*, 1 July 1986, sec. C9.
7. "The Genome Project," *New York Times Magazine*, 13 December 1987.
8. "Superior Farm Animals Duplicated by Cloning," *New York Times*, 17 February 1988, sec. D6.

Chapter 5

1. "Scientific Transplant Grain Genes," *New York Times*, 13 January 1987, sec. C1.
2. For an explanation of Mendelian genetics, see Chapter 2 in this book.
3. For more information, see Nina Pedoiroff, "Transposable Genetics Elements in Maize," *Scientific American* (June 1984), 85–86.
4. See Pedoiroff above, 85.
5. "Test Is Due Today on Gene Alterings," *New York Times*, 30 May 1986, sec. A15.
6. Calvin Miller, "Pea Genes to Help Aussie Scientists Increase Wool Production in Sheep," *Genetic Engineering News* (July/August 1986), 41.
7. Robert F. Weaver, "Changing Life's Genetic Blueprint," *National Geographic*, 166 (December 1984), 827.
8. "New Animal Forms Will Be Patented," *New York Times*, 17 April 1987, sec. A1.

Chapter 6

1. "Burst of Discoveries Reveals Genetic Basis for Many Diseases," *New York Times*, 31 March 1987, sec. C1.
2. "Ethics in Embryo," *Harper's Magazine* (September 1987), 37–47.
3. "Gene Therapy: Will It Work," *Technology Review* (April 1983), 82–87.
4. "Genetic Engineering: Life as a Plaything," *Technology Review* (April 1983), 14–15.

Chapter 7

1. "Genetic Engineering: Life as a Plaything," *Technology Review* (April 1983), 14–15.
2. "Biotechnology Regulations Are Signed by Reagan," *New York Times*, 19 June 1986, sec. A25.
3. "Thinking the Unthinkable About Genetic Screening," *Across the Board*, 20 (June 1983), 34–39.
4. "Genetic Testing at Work: How Should It Be Used?" *Technology Review* (May–June 1985), 51–59.
5. Marc Lappe, *Broken Code: The Exploitation of DNA* (San Francisco: Sierra Book Clubs, 1984), 114.
6. Text of Vatican's Doctrinal Statement on Human Reproduction, *New York Times*, 11 March 1987, sec. A14–17.
7. "Research on Human Embryos: The View From England," *Genetic Engineering News* (February 1985), 5.
8. "Whether to Make Perfect Humans," *New York Times*, 22 February 1988, sec. 1, p. 18.
9. Burke K. Zimmerman, *Biofuture: Confronting the Genetic Era* (New York: Plenum Press, 1984), 166.

FOR FURTHER READING

Anderson, W. French, and Elaine G. Diacumakois. "Genetic Engineering in Mammalian Cells." *Scientific American* (July 1981), 106–121.

Baskin, Yvonne. *The Gene Doctors*. New York: Morrow, 1984.

Calder, Nigel. *The Green Machine*. New York: Putnam, 1986.

DeYoung, H. Garrett. *The Cell Builders*. New York: Doubleday, 1986.

Doyle, Jack. *Altered Harvest*. New York: Viking, 1985.

Elkington, John. *The Gene Factory: The Science and Business of Biotechnology*. New York: Carroll & Graf, 1987.

Gilbert, Walter, and Lydia Villa-Komaroff. "Useful Proteins from Recombinant Bacteria." *Scientific American* (April 1980), 74–94.

Goodfield, June. *Playing God*. New York: Random House, 1977.

Gross, Cynthia S. *The New Biotechnology: Putting Microbes to Work* (Discovery Series). New York: Lerner Publications, 1987.

Howard, Ted, and Jeremy Rifkin. *Who Should Play God*. New York: Dell Publishing Co., 1977.

Judson, Horace Freeland. *The Eighth Day of Creation*. New York: Simon & Schuster, 1979.

Lappe, Marc. *Broken Code: The Exploitation of DNA*. San Francisco: Sierra Club Books, 1984.

Milstein, Caesar. "Monoclonal Antibodies." *Scientific American* (October 1980), 66–74.

Milunsky, Aubrey, ed. *Genetic Disorders and the Fetus*. New York: Plenum Press, 1986.

Nossal, G. J. V. *Reshaping Life: Key Issues in Genetic Engineering*. Cambridge: Cambridge University Press, 1985.

Olesky, Walter G. *Miracles of Genetics*. Chicago: Children's Press, 1986.

President's Commission for the Study of Ethical Problems in Biomedical Research. *Splicing Life: A Report on the Social and Ethical Issues of Genetic Engineering*. Washington, D.C.: U.S. Government Printing Office, 1982.

Rifkin, Jeremy. *Algeny*. New York: Viking, 1983.

Sylvester, Edward J., and Lynn Klotz. *The Gene Age: Genetic Engineering and the Next Industrial Revolution*. New York: Scribner, 1987.

United States Congress. House Committee on Science and Technology. *Genetic Engineering, Human Genetics, and Cell Biology*. Washington, D.C.: U.S. Government Printing Office, 1980.

United States Congress. House Committee on Science and Technology. *Genetic Engineering, Human Genetics, and Cell Biology.* Washington, D.C.: U.S. Government Printing Office, 1980.

Watson, James. *The Double Helix.* New York: Atheneum, 1968.

Watson, James, and John Tooze. *The DNA Story.* San Francisco: W. H. Freeman, 1981.

Wheale, P. R., and Ruth McNulty. *Genetic Engineering: Catastrophe or Utopia?* New York: St. Martin's Press, 1987.

Zimmerman, Burke K. *Biofuture: Confronting the Genetic Era.* New York: Plenum Press, 1984.

———, and Raymond A. Zilinkas, eds. *Reflections on the Recombinant DNA Controversy.* New York: Macmillan, 1984.

INDEX

Hitler's
Reich

Titles in the World History Series

WORLD
HISTORY SERIES ■ ■ ■

Hitler's
Reich

by
Gail B. Stewart

Lucent Books, P.O. Box 289011, San Diego, CA 92198-9011

Library of Congress Cataloging-in-Publication Data

Stewart, Gail, 1949–
    Hitler's Reich / by Gail B. Stewart.
        p.   cm.—(World history series)
    Includes bibliographical references and index.
    Summary: Traces the rise to power of Adolf Hitler and dis-
cusses life in Nazi Germany before, during, and after World
War II.
    ISBN 1-56006-235-5 (alk. paper)
    1. Germany—History—1933–1945—Juvenile literature.
2. Hitler, Adolf, 1889–1945—Juvenile literature. [1. Germany—
History—1933–1945. 2. Hitler, Adolf, 1889–1945.] I. Title.
II. Series.
DD256.5.S767   1994
943.086—dc20
                                                                93-17098
                                                                    CIP
                                                                     AC

Contents

Foreword

Each year on the first day of school, nearly every history teacher faces the task of explaining why his or her students should study history. One logical answer to this question is that exploring what happened in our past explains how the things we often take for granted—our customs, ideas, and institutions—came to be. As statesman and historian Winston Churchill put it, "Every nation or group of nations has its own tale to tell. Knowledge of the trials and struggles is necessary to all who would comprehend the problems, perils, challenges, and opportunities which confront us today." Thus, a study of history puts modern ideas and institutions in perspective. For example, though the founders of the United States were talented and creative thinkers, they clearly did not invent the concept of democracy. Instead, they adapted some democratic ideas that had originated in ancient Greece and with which the Romans, the British, and others had experimented. An exploration of these cultures, then, reveals their very real connection to us through institutions that continue to shape our daily lives.

Another reason often given for studying history is the idea that lessons exist in the past from which contemporary societies can benefit and learn. This idea, although controversial, has always been an intriguing one for historians. Those that agree that society can benefit from the past often quote philosopher George Santayana's famous statement, "Those who cannot remember the past are condemned to repeat it." Historians who ascribe to Santayana's philosophy believe that, for

example, studying the events that led up to the major world wars or other significant historical events would allow society to chart a different and more favorable course in the future.

Just as difficult as convincing students to realize the importance of studying history is the search for useful and interesting supplementary materials that present historical events in a context that can be easily understood. The volumes in Lucent Books' World History Series attempt to present a broad, balanced, and penetrating view of the march of history. Ancient Egypt's important wars and rulers, for example, are presented against the rich and colorful backdrop of Egyptian religious, social, and cultural developments. The series engages the reader by enhancing historical events with these cultural contexts. For example, in *Ancient Greece,* the text covers the role of women in that society. Slavery is discussed in *The Roman Empire,* as well as how slaves earned their freedom. The numerous and varied aspects of everyday life in these and other societies are explored in each volume of the series. Additionally, the series covers the major political, cultural, and philosophical ideas as the torch of civilization is passed from ancient Mesopotamia and Egypt, through Greece, Rome, Medieval Europe, and other world cultures, to the modern day.

The material in the series is formatted in a thorough, precise, and organized manner. Each volume offers the reader a comprehensive and clearly written overview of an important historical event or period. The topic under discussion is placed in a

broad, historical context. For example, *The Italian Renaissance* begins with a discussion of the High Middle Ages and the loss of central control that allowed certain Italian cities to develop artistically. The book ends by looking forward to the Reformation and interpreting the societal changes that grew out of the Renaissance. Thus, students are not only involved in an historical era, but also enveloped by the events leading up to that era and the events following it.

One important and unique feature in the World History Series is the primary and secondary source quotations that richly supplement each volume. These quotes are useful in a number of ways. First, they allow students access to sources they would not normally be exposed to because of the difficulty and obscurity of the original source. The quotations range from interesting anecdotes to far-sighted cultural perspectives and are drawn from historical witnesses both past and present. Second, the quotes demonstrate how and where historians themselves derive their information on the past as they strive to reach a consensus on historical events. Lastly, all of the quotes are footnoted, familiarizing students with the citation process and allowing them to verify quotes and/or look up the original source if the quote piques their interest.

Finally, the books in the World History Series provide a detailed launching point for further research. Each book contains a bibliography specifically geared toward student research. A second, annotated bibliography introduces students to all the sources the author consulted when compiling the book. A chronology of important dates gives students an overview, at a glance, of the topic covered. Where applicable, a glossary of terms is included.

In short, the series is designed not only to acquaint readers with the basics of history, but also to make them aware that their lives are a part of an ongoing human saga. Perhaps they will then come to the same realization as famed historian Arnold Toynbee. In his monumental work, *A Study of History,* he wrote about becoming aware of history flowing through him in a mighty current, and of his own life "welling like a wave in the flow of this vast tide."

Hitler's Reich in History

1889
Hitler born in Braunau, Austria.

1908
Leaves home and arrives in Vienna.

1914
World War I begins; Hitler joins 16th Bavarian Reserve Infantry.

1918
(Nov. 11) Armistice ends World War I.

1919
(June 28) Treaty of Versailles signed;
(Sept. 16) Hitler joins German Workers' Party.

1920
Name of German Workers' Party changed to National Socialist German Workers' Party (Nazi, for short).

1921
Hitler becomes president of Nazi party.

1923
(Jan. 11) French forces occupy the Ruhr after Germany defaults on reparations payments;
(Nov. 8–9) Hitler and other Nazis attempt to overthrow German government in the Munich putsch;
(Nov. 11) Hitler arrested for his part in uprising, sentenced to prison.

1925
Publication of Hitler's book *Mein Kampf.*

1929
(Oct. 29) New York stock market crashes.

1930
(Sept. 14) Nazis win 107 seats in the Reichstag in national elections.

1932
(Nov. 8) Franklin D. Roosevelt elected president of the United States.

1933
(Jan. 30) Hitler becomes chancellor of Germany;
(Feb. 27) fire destroys Reichstag in Berlin; Communists blamed although Nazis responsible;
(March 23) Enabling Act passed in Germany, giving Hitler dictatorial powers.

| 1900 | 1910 | 1920 | 1930 |

Hitler (to right of helmeted officers) and his Reichswehr.

1945
(Jan. 26) Auschwitz death camp liberated by Soviet army;
(April 30) Hitler commits suicide;
(May 7) unconditional surrender of Germany to Allies;
(May 23) Himmler captured by British, commits suicide.

Enthusiastic Viennese are restrained by police as they applaud their new leader, Adolf Hitler.

1939
(May 22) Germany and Italy sign Pact of Steel;
(Aug. 23) Germany signs pact with Soviet Union;
(Sept. 1) German forces invade Poland;
(Sept. 3) Allies declare war on Germany.

1943
(Jan. 27) United States launches first bombing attacks on Germany.

1934
(June 29–30) Hitler's Blood Purge, in which many SA leaders are executed;
(Aug. 2) President Hindenburg dies; Hitler becomes sole leader of Germany.

1946
Principal Nazi war criminals executed.

1940

1950

1935
(Sept. 15) Nuremberg laws deprive German Jews of all citizenship rights.

1938
(March 12) German troops invade Austria;
(Oct. 1) Czechoslovakian Sudetenland occupied by German army;
(Nov. 9–10) *Kristallnacht*— tens of thousands of Jews arrested, synagogues and Jewish businesses vandalized.

1940
(April 9) German troops invade Denmark and Norway;
(April 27) Himmler orders building of Auschwitz death camp in Poland;
(May 10) German troops invade the Netherlands, Belgium, Luxembourg, and France;
(August 10) Battle of Britain begins.

1941
(June 22) Germans attack Soviet Union;
(July 31) Göring asks Heydrich to design a "Final Solution" to the Jewish question;
(Dec. 7) Japanese launch surprise attack on Pearl Harbor;
(Dec. 8) United States declares war on Japan;
(Dec. 11) Germany declares war on United States.

1948
State of Israel created in Middle East.

1936
(March 7) German troops march into the Rhineland.

A Thousand-Year Reich

The document is official-looking, nine full pages. At the top of the first page are the words "Secret Reich Business" boxed in a heavy black rectangle. The document is a memorandum to top German officials from a security officer named Jager, stationed in Lithuania. The document is dated December 1, 1941.

It is a detailed list, with scores of dated notations, followed by large numbers, their total carried over onto each succeeding page and ending finally with a grand total of 137,346. To someone glancing at it quickly, the document might look like a tally of military supplies used or troops assigned to various locations. But the large numbers are not counts of troops or sup-

The official portrait of Der Führer *reveals a strong, determined character.*

plies. They are counts of Jewish men, women, and children murdered each day in Lithuania, on orders from the Reich.

Solving "The Problem"

With a chillingly businesslike tone, Jager reports, "Today I can confirm that our objective, to solve the Jewish problem for Lithuania, has been achieved. . . . In Lithuania there are no more Jews, apart from Jewish workers and their families."[1]

In the town of Semiliski, on October 6, Jager reports the executions of "213 Jews, 359 Jewesses, and 390 Jewish children." Three days later, in Svenćiany, Jager enters an additional "1169 Jews, 1840 Jewesses, and 717 Jewish children."[2] Page after page, the numbers of the dead are totaled in neat columns.

Most of the Lithuanian killings—called "actions" by Jager and other Reich officials—were done methodically, by firing squads armed with machine guns. According to Jager's report, dozens of people were lined up on the edges of trenches and shot. The impact of the bullets sent the bodies toppling into the trenches, where they were covered with a thin layer of sand or lime. Then the next batch of prisoners would be led out and shot, their bodies falling on those of the previous group.

According to Jager, it was this system's "efficient use of time" that enabled him

and his men to carry out enough executions that, in his words, "no backlog was allowed to build up."[3]

The mass shooting of more than 137,000 innocent Jews in Lithuania was not an isolated incident, nor was it the most horrible of the crimes committed by Germans in the 1940s. There were other acts, almost unspeakably brutal, carried out by German soldiers during this time.

And although such acts took place during a time of war, they were not the actions that take place in battle. Nor were they the inevitable effects of war. Rather, they were part of a grim plan that formed the very backbone of Germany's Reich.

This Reich, or "empire," was the creation of one man—Adolf Hitler. There had been two previous Reichs in German history, during times when the nation had been a world power. But more recently there had been a time during which Ger-

Surrounded by stirring pageantry and buoyed by overwhelming popular support, Hitler ascends to his place of power.

many had seemed powerless, at the mercy of its enemies. Hitler vowed to ensure that Germany would never again have to answer to another nation. His Reich, Hitler promised, would last for a thousand years.

To be strong, Hitler said, and to achieve world domination, Germany must eliminate the outside influences that had long weakened it. Jews were at the top of his list

---

Jew as Enemy

Hitler's hatred of Jews should have been no surprise to anyone who read his autobiography, Mein Kampf, *written during his time in prison in 1923. In the following passage he describes the Jew as a parasite on society.*

"Wherever he establishes himself the people who grant him hospitality are bound to be bled to death sooner or later. . . . He poisons the blood of others but preserves his own blood unadulterated. . . . The black-haired Jewish youth lies in wait for hours on end, satanically glaring at and spying on the unsuspicious girl whom he plans to seduce, adulterating her blood and removing her from the bosom of her own people. The Jew uses every possible means to undermine the racial foundations of a subjugated people. . . . The Jews were responsible for bringing Negroes into the Rhineland, with the ultimate idea of bastardizing the white race which they hate and thus lowering its cultural and political level so that the Jew might dominate."

Confronting the Evil

Historian Konnilyn Feig, in her book Hitler's Death Camps: The Sanity of Madness, *tackles the problems that arise from studying the Reich's Holocaust. It is not a study without risk, she warns.*

"Many who read about the Holocaust find it the most fascinating and horrible event in history. Yet leaving it at that level evidences ignorance or immorality. One can become wiser by confronting the evil, the madness, and the death, but it is a terrible wisdom that haunts one ceaselessly. It scars. Acquainting oneself with hell is hard work. Initially, it requires studying the history of the Holocaust to cut away the legends surrounding the camps. Then it demands an internal, put-myself-in-their-place confrontation with the killers and challenging the indifferent. However much energy the searcher exerts however, he remains on the outside. How does one respond to the truth that an ordinary man can bash a Jewish child's head against a wall, pick up the child's apple, eat it, and return home to fondle his own children?"

of undesirable influences, although they were by no means alone. Hitler also saw Poles, Slavs, priests, Russians, homosexuals, Communists, and Gypsies as threats to the German Reich's strength. Historians estimate that Hitler's Reich executed 11 million such "undesirables"—including 6 million Jews, about two-thirds of the Jewish population of Europe.

Not a Monster

In what became World War II, Hitler's Reich came frighteningly close to achieving its goals—both of wiping out "undesirable" populations and of conquering Europe. What is more frightening, however, is that Hitler was no homicidal monster who achieved his goals by wrenching political power away from Germany's rightful leaders. Quite the contrary—he was offered power because of his popularity and the popularity of his message.

The Reich lasted not a thousand years, as Hitler had hoped, but merely twelve. But the story of those twelve years is one of the most tragic and interesting in all of history, and raises some fascinating questions. How did a man with such hideous ideas become so powerful? How could the German nation, in a shambles after World War I, become such a formidable military threat so quickly? And even more puzzling, how could Hitler's politics of hate become so popular in Germany that the executions of millions of people and the loss of so many individual rights was considered acceptable? The answers lie among the rubble and ruin of what was once one of the most powerful political forces of the twentieth century—Hitler's Reich.

Chapter

1 "Squeezed . . . Until the Pips Squeak"

The seeds of Adolf Hitler's Reich were planted at the end of World War I. The war was bloody and destructive in a way the world had not seen before: tanks, airplanes, and heavy artillery had been used for the first time. An entire generation of young European men had simply been erased.

The Allied nations of France, England, Belgium, and Italy—with the help of the United States—won the war but suffered tremendous losses. In November 1918,

Allied troops paid dearly for the victory over Germany in World War I. The Allies believed the humiliated Germans would never again threaten the world.

these Allied nations had one main objective: to make sure that Germany would never be able to wage such a war again.

As British politician Sir Eric Geddes remarked at the war's end, "[The Germans] are going to be squeezed, as a lemon is squeezed—until the pips squeak."[4]

"Immeasurably Harsh and Humiliating"

To weaken Germany, the victorious Allies came up with the Treaty of Versailles, in which they set out a vast number of terms—440 in all—to which Germany had to agree. The treaty was so strict that some Americans involved in the making of it were frankly embarrassed. When the treaty's terms were finally written out, U.S. secretary of state Robert Lansing admitted, "The terms of peace appear immeasurably harsh and humiliating."[5]

Some of the terms were obvious attempts to dismember Germany's military might. The treaty drastically reduced the size of the German army. It allowed Germany an armed force of only 100,000—a tiny fraction of what it had had during the war. The German navy was forced to give up its submarines; it could keep only six of

"SQUEEZED . . . UNTIL THE PIPS SQUEAK" ■ 13

Destitute Germans wait in line for food. World War I devastated Germany's economy.

its mighty warships. The treaty also forbade Germany to build tanks, military airplanes, or any other weapons of aggression.

Other terms of the treaty stripped Germany of much of its territory. Colonies in Africa, China, and the Pacific were taken away. The German-speaking province of Alsace-Lorraine, located between France and Germany, was given to France. Large parcels of land once controlled by Germany were sliced off and given to Poland. The Rhineland, a fertile territory west of the Rhine River, was entrusted to the Allies, who would occupy it for the next fifteen years.

The treaty not only decreased Germany's size, population, and military strength, but also affected its economy. Many of the territories seized by the Allies were important industrial, mining, or agricultural areas. As one historian calculated, "The treaty took away from Germany about 13 percent of its prewar territory, 10 percent of its population, 75 percent of its iron ore, and 25 percent of its best-quality coal."[6]

Guilt and Shame

But the most shocking parts of the Treaty of Versailles were what came to be known

as its "guilt clauses." Under these terms, the people of Germany were assigned blame for starting the war. And because the war was Germany's fault, said the treaty, the German people would be held financially responsible for paying for the damage it caused. The "price tag" of World War I, according to the Allies, was about $100 billion (over $600 billion today).

Germany was in no condition to pay, however. The last months of the war had devastated the nation's economy. Although no battles had been fought on German soil, the war had made life hard for the German people. Medical supplies, coal, and fuel for furnaces had been all used up by the soldiers fighting at the front.

Even worse, the Germans had almost no food. The nation's farmers had never been able to grow enough food for its people. Germany had always relied on food obtained by trade with its neighbors. During the war, the Allied nations had put up a blockade, cutting off Germany's trade routes. The lack of food resulted in mass starvation. Millions of "luckier" Germans lived on a steady diet of turnips, pine cones, nettles, and a bitter coffee made from crushed acorns.

"Living skeletons roamed the streets of Germany's cities," writes historian Albert Marrin, "looking for dead horses and

U.S. president Woodrow Wilson (right) assured the German people that America's quarrel was not with them but with their emperor, Wilhelm II (left).

were they angry—they also felt betrayed. All along they had been assured by President Woodrow Wilson that America's quarrel was not with the German people, but with the German emperor, Wilhelm II. And shortly before the war ended, certain that his regime faced defeat, the emperor had fled to Holland, leaving political power in Germany dangerously uncertain.

So why did the Treaty of Versailles blame and punish the German people, who were now without their emperor? Although the Germans knew they would be forced to make some reparations, never in the history of wars and treaties had one nation been assigned such blame, and such responsibility for payment. It made no sense to President Wilson, either, for he privately commented to Secretary of War Newton Baker that "If I were a German, I think I should never sign it."[8]

fighting over a handful of putrid flesh. Starvation claimed hundreds each day. Often there was no wood for coffins and people were buried in mass graves; small children were laid to rest in cardboard boxes."[7]

Because the German people were facing such horrors at home, they were furious at the Allies' insistence that they take the full blame for the war. And not only

No Choice

But Germany had little choice. Without the treaty, the war was not officially over. Allied soldiers could resume their attacks,

At Versailles, France, in 1919, members of the German peace delegation discuss the harsh terms of their country's surrender.

storming past German lines all the way to Berlin, and an Allied government might be set up in Germany. Germany would lose everything, including its status as an independent nation. And being governed by French, British, or American politicians was simply unthinkable to German leaders.

So a delegation of German diplomats—280 of them—traveled to France to sign the treaty. Significantly the Allies had made no place at the negotiating table for the Germans during the writing of the treaty. Only afterwards, when Germany's approval was needed in the form of a signature, were the German delegates invited.

Before they even arrived in Versailles, the Germans knew they were in for trouble. The French leaders had given strict orders that the train carrying the delegates was to crawl along at ten miles per hour through the countryside, so that the Germans could plainly see the damage they had caused. When the delegates arrived at Versailles, French prime minister Georges Clemenceau spoke harshly to them. "The hour has struck," he said, "for the weighty settlement of our account."[9]

"The Gathering of Clouds Before a Storm"

The settlement was indeed weighty. Throughout Germany, writes historian Charles Bracelen Flood, "there arose a cry of humiliated pain and anger."[10] At first the delegates from Berlin refused to sign. One of the senior delegates, Count Brockdorff-Rantzau, finally delivered a bitter speech to the gathering. Historians note that the count's words were "rasping" and "insolent,"[11] and that he did not even bother to rise from his chair. In his speech,

Allied leaders (left to right), David Lloyd George of Britain, Vittorio Orlando of Italy, Georges Clemenceau of France, and Woodrow Wilson of the United States.

Count Brockdorff-Rantzau refused to admit that his country was solely responsible for the war.

"It is demanded that we confess ourselves guilty," he said through clenched teeth. "Such a confession in my mouth would be a lie."[12] He reminded the Allies that they, too, had caused hundreds of thousands of civilian deaths by their blockade of Germany. "Think of that when you speak of guilt and punishment," the count told the gathering.[13]

The Allied nations were angered by the German delegation's response. They wanted the Germans to be more contrite. Witnesses said that French prime minister Clemenceau turned purple, and British prime minister David Lloyd George snapped a wooden letter opener in two.

And although the German delegation filed more than 440 pages of formal objections to the terms of the treaty, the Allies steadfastly refused to change a word. And why should they? Anti-German sentiment was strong, especially in England and France. David Lloyd George had won the 1918 election in England by his promise to

"make Germany pay." More than 750,000 British soldiers had died in the war, and the British people were not ready to forgive Germany.

Georges Clemenceau was in the same position. More than 1.4 million young French soldiers had been killed in the fighting, and much of France's countryside lay in ruins. In addition, both France and Britain owed billions of dollars to the United States for war supplies. Better, they thought, to have Germany pay those bills than the war-weary Allies.

So the treaty was read and signed, and the war pronounced officially over. The angry and humiliated Germans returned home; the Allies congratulated themselves on a job well done. But even though on paper it seemed as if Germany had been put in its place, many people feared that the Allied powers had gone too far, and pushed Germany into a corner.

Count Harry Kessler, a publisher living in Europe, predicted in 1919, "A terrible era begins for Europe, like the gathering of clouds before a storm, and it will end in an explosion probably still more terrible than that of the World War."[14]

A Shaky Government

The Allies' demands upon Germany were not only unfair, they were unrealistic. Germany, like France and England, was in ruin. Its economy was in shambles, its people starving, and its political scene chaotic. Trying to extract billions of dollars from a country in such trouble was like asking for the moon.

In the months before the war ended, Germany's cities had experienced a great deal of unrest and violence. The shortages of food and fuel, together with uncertainty about how long the war would drag on, made people angry at their government. In Berlin and other cities Communists staged uprisings. They had witnessed the Communists' success in overthrowing the Russian government in 1917, and hoped to do the same in Germany.

Penniless men wait for a bowl of soup in post-World War I Berlin. Its people starving, its economy crushed, Germany could not pay the Allied demands.

However, the Communists were unable to gain control. When Emperor Wilhelm finally fled Germany, paving the way for Germany's surrender in 1918, some influential Germans formed a democratic republic—the first such government Germany had ever had. Because the government's founders had met in Weimar, a city 150 miles southwest of the capital (Berlin had been taken over by Communist rebels), the new government was known as the Weimar Republic.

The Weimar Republic seemed doomed from the start. Its leaders saw the militant Communists as the greatest threat to their government, and relied heavily on military forces to maintain order. These forces, whose main task was to fight Communist rebels, were known as the *Freikorps,* or Free Corps.

The Free Corps

The troops who made up the first Free Corps were highly disciplined and well trained. They were volunteers—4,000 of them—selected from the many soldiers arriving home after Germany's defeat. They were enthusiastic, and could march and drill with impressive precision. The government needed more than 4,000 men, however, and put out a call for more.

It was not long before the ranks of the Free Corps swelled to almost half a million men, "drawn from the ranks of demobilized soldiers, fanatical nationalists, military adventurers, and unemployed youths."[15] And although they were paid, armed, and uniformed by the republic, the Free Corps troops had no loyalty to it.

Learning About the Nazis

Hanns Peter Herz was a little boy during the last days of the Weimar Republic. In this excerpt from Voices from the Third Reich: An Oral History, *Herz recalls learning how intimidating the Nazis were to the incumbent democratic party.*

"My first inkling of the Weimar Republic's instability was on May 1, 1932, when I was five years old. The Social Democrats and the [Nazis] met for the 1st of May rally. My father took me to the assembly and said, 'Look at everything very carefully, and tell me later if you see anything odd.' I noticed that they'd rolled up their flags and banners and marched off with them tucked under their arms. When asked if I'd noticed anything, I said, 'Yes, they marched with their flags rolled up, and usually they hold them up high.' 'That's right, son,' my father said. 'Remember that. They're Social Democrats and they don't want to be provoked by the Nazis. That's why they carry their principles rolled up under their arms.' That was one impression of the Weimar Republic I've never forgotten."

The opening of the new German parliament. No longer a monarchy, the post-World War I Weimar Republic elected a governing body called the Reichstag.

Most, in fact, were flat-out angry with the Weimar Republic and all it stood for. They saw the new government's leaders as weak and ineffective, unable to rule without the army's backing. Still, they were united in their belief that the Communists were worse.

Many soldiers who had been at the front during the war felt that the German Communist party had weakened Germany and thus been responsible for the country's surrender to the Allies. These soldiers were bitter, believing they had been betrayed by Communists and their sympathizers while risking their lives in the bloodiest war in history.

And now these Communists were trying to undermine the new German government! To the Free Corps soldiers, it not only made sense to fight the German Communists, it was satisfying to get revenge against them. Free Corps soldiers became a powerful force in peacetime Germany—more powerful than the government they represented.

Because the government was so weak, it was easy for the Free Corps to abuse its power. Within months of the November 1918 cease-fire, roving bands of Free Corps soldiers sought out and murdered suspected Communists and their sympathizers by the hundreds. No trials were necessary, for the government had given the Free Corps full rein. Enemies were simply seized by the Free Corps and shot. In fact, the slogan the Free Corps lived by was "Up against the wall, dirty dog!"

One young officer who created his own Free Corps unit described the attitude of his recruits. "Fighting was the whole content and meaning of their lives," he said. "Nothing else made any sense. It was battle alone that they loved. The battle that was hard, brutal, pitiless."[16]

Dangers in the Versailles Treaty

The Treaty of Versailles was partly responsible for the anger and ultranationalism of the Nazis. Quoted in An Illustrated History of World War II, *one participant in the treaty negotiations foresees trouble.*

"'I cannot conceive of any greater cause of future war,' wrote British premier David Lloyd George during the Paris peace conference, 'than that the German people, who have certainly proved themselves one of the most vigorous and powerful races in the world, should be surrounded by a number of small states, many of them consisting of people who have never previously set up a stable government for themselves, but each of them containing large masses of Germans clamoring for re-union with their native land.'"

Within months of its creation, the Free Corps had achieved its goal. By May 1919, much of the political disorder that had rocked the new republic had been suppressed. But the quiet lasted only a few weeks—until news of the signing of the Treaty of Versailles reached Germany.

That news created a whole new set of enemies for the Weimar Republic. No longer were the Communists the government's only enemies. Right-wing political leaders, who had been against signing the treaty, now blamed the government for bringing shame on Germany. Scores of political factions, many of them extremist, loudly criticized the Weimar Republic and called for its leaders to step down. Rumors began circulating that the exiled emperor might be brought back, or that there might be a military takeover of the government. Republic leaders were threatened; several who had signed the hated treaty were murdered. Germany, it seemed, was embroiled in a new war—this one within its own borders.

Not Paying

As any reasonable person might have predicted, the political chaos that Germany experienced made it impossible for the republic to keep up its scheduled payments to the Allies. Not only was Germany short of money, it was painfully short of ways to *make* money. The Allies had taken over Germany's coal mines and many of its best factories. What goods the Germans could manufacture were banned from Allied markets. It seemed only a matter of time until the Germans would have to default on one of their obligatory payments.

It happened in 1923. Germany stalled on a shipment of 140,000 telephone poles that were supposed to be sent to France. As specified in the Treaty of Versailles, the French army was entitled to intervene. In January the French and their Belgian allies marched into the Ruhr, the rich industrial section of Germany, and took over factories, mines, and railroads.

Germany could not fight back, for its armed forces had been decimated by the treaty's terms. The Free Corps, too, was illegal according to the treaty, and to call attention to those troops by using them would have been dangerous. But an army is only one way to fight. The Germans had an alternative.

The German government chose to resist—peacefully. All reparations payments were cut off, and people were urged not to cooperate with the invaders: "Throughout the Ruhr commerce and industry came to a halt as workers walked off their jobs, officials refused to acknowledge the new French bosses, and saboteurs hit the transport system."[17]

In the face of this resistance, French and Belgian troops retaliated. They hunted down and executed Germans they suspected of the sabotage. They also took over money and goods desperately needed by Germany.

Bringing Germany to Its Knees

The French occupation of the Ruhr had other effects. The Allies began demanding even larger reparations payments, while at the same time, and because of the protest, more than 100,000 German officials and railroad workers were unemployed. To meet the demands of both its own unfortunate people and the Allies, the German government began printing more money. It was a tragic mistake.

Because the French and the other Allies had stolen so much German gold from the national treasury, there was nothing to back up the money being printed. And what amounts of money were being printed! No fewer than 133 government printing offices with 1,783 presses turned out the paper money, called *marks*, night and day.

French troops and tanks take over the Ruhr, Germany's main industrial center, in 1923. According to the Treaty of Versailles, the takeover was legal because Germany had defaulted on its payments to France.

A Brief Interlude

In the time immediately after the armistice ending World War I, people had mixed feelings. There was joy and relief, as Robert Elson mentions in his book Prelude to War, *but there was also pessimism and bitterness.*

"Out of the silence of the battlefield, and the joyous clamor in Paris—and London and New York—there came a great surge of hope that for a brief time seemed to envelop much of the world: perhaps, in the wake of four years of unprecedented destruction, mankind would at long last learn to live in peace, forever. As farmers returned to their fields and refugees to their homes, the leaders of the victorious nations met to hammer out the shape of a world without war.

Reasonably enough, the defeated shared little of this optimism. For them, the long war . . . brought chaos and hunger and despair. Among many returning veterans, especially in Germany, it brought something worse. Looking at the destruction around them, they refused to accept the fact of their battlefield defeat. Almost before the ink was dry on the treaty of peace, they were looking for ways to redress the blow to their warriors' pride."

Since nothing of worth backed up the marks, their value quickly plummeted. Soon many marks were needed to buy what had once cost only one. In 1919, for instance, nine marks equalled one American dollar on the world market. But in 1923, an unbelievable 4 trillion marks equalled a single dollar! Yet still the government continued to print the worthless money.

When paper shortages threatened to curtail mark production, the printing offices began stamping old money with new denominations in red ink. And when that ran out, some German cities began printing their own currency, using leather, linen, silk—anything that would hold ink.

The runaway inflation greatly affected how people in Germany lived. Prices jumped a hundred or more times in a single day. Employees were urged to bring wagons or wheelbarrows to work to carry their pay home, since pockets or wallets were simply not big enough. "Factories paid their workers twice a day, with time off to buy food for their families before prices went even higher," reports historian Warren Morris. "People bought two beers at a time and drank the second warm because, if they waited, the price would double or triple while they enjoyed the first."[18]

No one in Germany—or even in all of Europe—had ever seen inflation anything like this. A newspaper subscription in Berlin jumped from 6 marks a week to over 500 billion marks! And because the paper money was so worthless, people

(Above) A German woman in 1923 uses German marks as fuel for a cookstove. Soaring inflation made it cheaper to burn money than to spend it on wood.

(Below) A man sells German coins for scrap metal. Inflation had made the coins' face value less than its value as a raw material.

used it for insulation, for wallpaper—even as scrap paper to light their kitchen stoves. One woman complained that when she left a large basket of money outside a store for a few minutes, a thief stole the basket—but left the money!

Setting the Stage

As Germany's economic woes worsened by the week, the German people grew more and more troubled. Many watched money they had saved all their lives become worth-less. In some parts of the country, desperate people formed angry mobs and looted stores and attacked trucks carrying food.

Most Germans blamed their government; after all, they said, it was the spineless leaders of the Weimar Republic who had signed away Germany's pride in the Treaty of Versailles and caused the wild inflation. Complaints about the republic were widespread. Many Germans turned to the Communists for leadership, and the violence between Communists and government troops continued.

This chaotic and frightening atmosphere set the stage for a young Austrian ex-corporal to begin his move to power.

2 Waiting in the Wings

Oddly enough, Adolf Hitler, the man who would eventually lead Germany out of its miserable state, who would create a super-power from a shambles, was not born into wealth or power. As one historian writes, Adolf Hitler was, "by origin, a nobody."[19]

Early Years

Adolf Hitler, born on Easter Sunday in 1889, was the fourth child of Klara and Alois Hitler, of Austria. Alois was a customs official for the Austrian government. He made a comfortable living for his family, and urged young Adolf to do well in school so that he might grow up and have a good job, too.

But Adolf, although bright enough, was not a hard worker. In school he did well enough to get by in some of his courses, but had no time for subjects that did not interest him. Years later his former school-mates would remember how Adolf would taunt his teachers and draw unflattering sketches of them in his school notebooks for the enjoyment of the other boys. One

Baby Adolf (left) and Adolf as a schoolboy (circled). Hitler was bright but uninterested in schoolwork.

One of young Hitler's paintings done in Vienna in 1910. When his application to the Vienna School of Fine Arts was rejected, he became a vagrant.

of his teachers in high school classified young Hitler as "notoriously cantankerous, willful, arrogant, and irascible. He had obvious difficulty in fitting in at school."[20]

Adolf saw no real reason to stay in high school. He left school at age sixteen without the leaving certificate that would have made job-seeking easier. That made no difference to him, for he often scoffed at the "drudges" who were satisfied with jobs behind desks, taking orders from other people. That, he insisted, was no life for him.

Leaving Home

Adolf had no real plan after leaving high school. Instead, he spent his unlimited free time living a fairly easy life. One historian notes that he

> sat around at home, enjoying the meals cooked for him by his doting mother and staying up all night absorbing endless books on art, history, and military matters, as well as the wildly inaccurate tales of cowboys and Indians written by Carl May, a German who had never crossed the Atlantic.[21]

Adolf's older sister and brother-in-law thought that he was taking advantage of his mother. They urged her to force Adolf to leave home—or at the very least, to get a job. Instead, Adolf's mother agreed to foot the bill for him to move to Vienna and enroll in art school.

In September 1907, Hitler left home, taking with him all the money left to him by his father, who had died a few years earlier. The trust fund his mother provided would be enough to pay for tuition and board at the art school in Vienna. He would study there, he decided, and would soon become a well-known artist.

The Ill-Fated Artist

The Vienna School of Fine Arts had strict entrance requirements. After taking a preliminary entrance examination, each applicant was asked to submit several drawings or paintings illustrating biblical stories, such as the Flood, the Crucifixion of Jesus, and the Creation. Hitler's drawings were returned to him with comments

saying that they were too wooden, too lifeless. His application was rejected.

He tried again months later; this time he failed even to pass the entrance examination. An advisor at the school suggested that Hitler's talents might be better suited to studying architecture, and told him to apply to that school instead. Unfortunately, the fact that Hitler had no leaving certificate from his high school prevented the school of architecture from even considering his application. His career as an artist, it seemed, was over even before it really began.

The rejection devastated Hitler. He had counted on becoming a famous painter; now he had no hope of that happening. As historian Robert Payne writes, "He had no prospects, no future, and was confronted with an absolutely blank wall."[22]

Down and Out

Instead of being comfortably situated as a student in Vienna, young Adolf Hitler found himself living the life of an unemployed dropout. After a few months, his money ran out, and because he refused to look for regular work, he had no way to obtain more. It was, he would later recall, the bleakest period of his life.

Occasionally he made a few pennies by painting watercolor postcards and peddling them on the streets. He also did several posters advertising soap, cigarettes, and deodorant powders. Such work was a long way from his dream of being a famous artist, but it did allow him to buy a cheap hotel room and a bowl of soup for his supper.

Hate Literature in Vienna

Hitler read a great deal of hate literature, and especially enjoyed that put out by the List Society. As the writers of The Twisted Dream *point out, many of the ideas in List's pamphlets sound eerily like those Hitler later employed.*

"List wrote that it would take a great world war to annihilate what he characterized as the 'mongrelized brood that destroys customs, religion, and society.' The way to prepare for the conflict, he argued, was to build a strong, racially pure state—an Aryan Reich. List outlined the structure of this Reich: It would be divided into . . . districts, each headed by a *gauleiter* bound by secret oath to a supreme leader, or Führer, who would be the 'visible embodiment of the divine Aryan law.' The new Reich would have special marriage laws to prevent the mixing of races, and each household would be required to maintain 'blood charts' . . . detailing racial background that would be available for examination by government authorities on demand."

When he could not sell his art or his postcards, Hitler went without food or a roof over his head. He spent more than five months in Vienna, going from one flophouse to another, sleeping in doorways or on benches. Sometimes he was able to get a bed at the Asylum for the Shelterless in downtown Vienna, where, as one historian reports,

> He was given a bath, his clothing disinfected, and he slept in an iron bed with wire springs covered with two brownish-colored sheets, his own clothes serving as a pillow. . . . The only food supplied was bread and soup, which were distributed in the early morning and evening. Those who entered the Asylum were expected to be out looking for work during the daylight hours.[23]

Identifying Scapegoats

Although Hitler was not interested in looking for a regular job, he kept himself occupied during the day. He spent a great deal of time in museums and attended an occasional opera, when he could afford an inexpensive ticket that would allow him to stand at the back of the theater. The public library, too, was one of his haunts during his Vienna days. It was through his reading during this time that Hitler first came into contact with the radical Pan-Germanic ideas that were popular in that city.

The theory of Pan-Germanism advocated that all the Germanic people of Europe should be united into a single large empire. The theory held that the Germanic people were superior in terms of their physical beauty, intelligence, and nobility. Sometimes referred to as the Aryan race, these Germanic people were thought by Pan-Germanists to be more "pure" than any other people on earth.

People who believed in Pan-Germanism were critical of the current Austrian rulers for allowing non-Germans, such as Italians, Slavs, Czechs, Russians, and Poles to live in the country. And although all of these other groups were viewed with suspicion and dislike by Pan-Germanists, the group most hated were the Jews.

For centuries, Jews had been persecuted throughout much of Europe because their religion was different from that of the Christian majority. Writes one historian, "Jews were said to have killed Christ, worshipped Satan, and used the blood of murdered Christian children in their ceremonies."[24] And although in modern times such charges are considered ridiculous and untrue, in the early twentieth century, many people still held to such beliefs.

While Hitler lived in Vienna, abundant anti-Semitic (anti-Jewish) literature was for sale. In fact, historians agree that Vienna was the most anti-Semitic city in Western Europe. Part of the reason was that many Jews had arrived in Vienna from eastern parts of Europe. In fifty years, the Jewish population of Vienna had risen by 6 percent and some Germanic people felt threatened by those numbers.

"Poor Jews aroused the radical and social contempt of the Viennese," writes historian John Keegan. "Rich Jews provoked their resentment."[25] Jews provided a handy scapegoat, a people who could be blamed for all that was wrong with the world. And to a down-and-out young man like Adolf Hitler, Jews were an easy target for his bitterness and frustration.

An anti-Semitic poster displayed on a German street corner. Hitler made Jews his scapegoat.

In his autobiography, Hitler wrote of his first impression of a Jew in Vienna:

> One day . . . I suddenly encountered a phenomenon in the long caftan and wearing black sidelocks. My first thought was: Is this a Jew? . . . I watched the man stealthily and cautiously, but the longer I gazed at this strange countenance and examined it section by section, the more the question shaped itself in my brain: Is this a German? I turned to books for help in removing my doubts. For the first time in my life I bought myself some anti-Semitic pamphlets for a few pence.[26]

He used such anti-Semitic ideas to explain all that was wrong with his life. It was the Jews, he concluded, who were respon-

sible for his failure to gain admission to art school. It was the wealthy Jews who controlled the money and the banks and kept people such as himself trapped in poverty. It was the radical Jewish intellectuals who caused political unrest throughout the cities of Europe. And the more he thought about this explanation, the more hate-filled anti-Semitic literature he read, the more believable it all seemed.

To Arms

Early in 1913 Hitler moved from Vienna to the German city of Munich. Although Munich was not nearly as large or as colorful as Vienna, Hitler was happier being in Germany. There were, he felt, far too many non-German people in Vienna, and he believed that they were ruining Austria. "He saw Germany," writes Albert Marrin, "as the Aryans' last stronghold, a haven for people like himself."[27]

Although life was no easier for Hitler in Munich, an event occurred that greatly changed his life. In August 1914, the First World War began. While many people were frightened and sad at the thought of a world war, Hitler was delighted. What pleased him especially was that he was able to enlist in the German army. Years later, he wrote,

> For me, those hours came as a deliverance from the distress that weighed upon me during the days of my youth. I am not ashamed to admit that I was carried away with enthusiasm. I fell on my knees and thanked Heaven from the fullness of my heart that it had granted me the favor of being allowed to live in these times.[28]

The Mystery of the Iron Cross

Hitler received the Iron Cross for bravery during the First World War. As Robert Payne writes in his book The Life and Death of Adolf Hitler, *Hitler seemed to have mixed feelings about the medal.*

"He received the Iron Cross, first class, on the recommendation of First Lieutenant Hugo Gutemann, who had ordered him to carry urgent dispatches to the rear commanding the artillerymen to stop shelling the German forward trenches. There had been a breakdown in communications, the artillerymen did not know that there had been a slight German advance, and many German soldiers had already been killed by German shells. . . . The dispatch runner who crossed that patch of ground would have to be a very courageous man, indeed. Lieutenant Gutemann promised Hitler the Iron Cross, first class, if he succeeded.

When Hitler came to power all the circumstances leading to the award were discreetly veiled as though some dark mystery was attached to it. The mystery was very simple. First Lieutenant Hugo Gutemann was a Jew, and by then Hitler preferred not to let it be known that he owed his Iron Cross . . . to the recommendation of a Jewish officer in the German Army."

Even though Hitler had been something of a failure in civilian life, he was a fine soldier. He held the rank of corporal, and in forty-seven battles he served on the Western Front as a dispatch runner, delivering messages back and forth between the front lines and the officers in the rear. As one historian notes, "The patch of ground between [the] dugout and the base artillery was under heavy English machine gun fire, and the dispatch runner who crossed that patch of ground would have to be a very courageous man indeed." [29]

Hitler was extremely brave, often volunteering for highly dangerous missions that other dispatch runners tried to avoid.

His courage during one of these missions earned him the Iron Cross, a highly prized medal for bravery that was rarely awarded to a mere corporal.

But although his daring deeds won him respect, Hitler was still viewed as peculiar by those with whom he served. Some of the soldiers in his company found it odd, for example, that Hitler enjoyed the war so much. One fellow soldier recalled him as "this white crow among us that didn't go along when we damned the war to hell." [30]

Others remembered Hitler as a loner who found gruesome ways to amuse himself during long weeks in the filthy

trenches. "Long after the rest of us had turned in," one recalled, "Hitler was still fooling around with a flashlight in the dark and spitting the rats on his bayonet. Finally someone chucked a boot at his head, and we got a little peace."[31]

"My Eyes Had Turned to Glowing Coals"

For all the dangerous duties he performed, Corporal Hitler was amazingly lucky. He was never injured so seriously that he could not return to his unit at the front—a fact that pleased him very much. However, on October 13, 1918—a month before Germany surrendered to the Allies—his incredible good luck ran out.

While Hitler and his fellow dispatch runners were waiting in line for their food rations, British troops began lobbing high-explosive shells nearby. Some of these shells contained chlorine gas, a deadly poison. Hitler and the others quickly put on their gas masks, but not before they had been exposed to the fumes.

By the next morning some of the men were dead, and others, like Hitler, were suffering from breathing and vision problems. "My eyes," wrote Hitler later, "had turned to glowing coals; it had grown dark around me."[32]

He and other victims of the gas were evacuated to a nearby hospital. They must have made a pathetic picture as, blind and gagging, they walked the whole distance. As one of the men wrote later, "In order not to get lost, we held on to the coattails of the man ahead, and so we went in single file to Linnselle, where we got first aid."[33]

Devastating News

The prognosis for victims of chlorine gas was never certain, so Hitler waited to see if he would regain the use of his eyes. Over

As a young German soldier during World War I, Hitler, pictured here on the far left, distinguished himself by his bravery and his peculiar enjoyment of the war.

Ecstatic Londoners celebrate the Allied victory in 1918. Germany's surrender shattered Hitler. But out of the ashes of his despair arose a burning new purpose—to right the wrongs done to Germany.

the next few weeks, to his great relief, his vision returned and he began making plans to return to his unit. This goal was shattered, however, when on November 10 a pastor from the hospital visited the men. The old man had an announcement to make, the content of which, Hitler recalled, seemed to make the man seem "all a-tremble."

The message was all bad news. The German Empire, the pastor said, was no longer in existence. Rebels and Communists had overtaken the capital, and Kaiser Wilhelm had fled for his life to Holland. A republic had been created in Germany, and the new leaders had surrendered to the Allies. The war was over.

Hitler was devastated. "I could sit there no longer," he later wrote in his autobiog-

raphy. "Once again, everything went black before my eyes, and I tottered and groped my way back to the place where we slept, and buried my burning head in the blankets and pillows."[34]

For Hitler, it was a time of utter despair. He thought about how he and his fellow soldiers had risked their lives—millions had died—only to have Germany betrayed by its own people. The thought filled him with rage, but it also gave him a sense of purpose he had lacked before.

"In these days hatred grew in me," he wrote, "hatred for those responsible for this deed."[35] It was during these days, convalescing in the hospital, that he vowed to fight back. He would somehow right the terrible wrongs that had been done to Germany.

Russian troops gather to hear a Communist revolutionary leader in Austria during World War I. Hitler blamed the Communists for betraying Germany and forcing its surrender to the Allies. He became an ardent anti-Communist and was given the task of spying on subversive groups for the German government.

The Undercover Agent

To Adolf Hitler, twenty-nine years old and fresh from the military, peacetime seemed frightening. The army had been a home to him, and the only thing at which he had ever succeeded. He asked to remain a soldier, and was given a post as a prison guard at a camp sixty miles north of Munich. His duties were to keep watch over Russian and British prisoners until their release. Although the post was boring, he had—at least temporarily—a job, food, and shelter.

When this job ended, Hitler returned to Munich and was shocked by what he saw. Revolutionaries with bright red armbands and signs were everywhere. They had taken control of the banks, the hotels, and other public buildings. Hitler hated them and later referred to them in his autobiography as "wretched and miserable criminals."[36] It was they, he believed, who were responsible for Germany's trouble. It was they who would pay—if only he could find a way.

His chance came in the fall of 1919. Knowing that Hitler's right-wing, anti-Communist views were in tune with the military, his superiors gave him a more challenging assignment. They made him an undercover agent, keeping close tabs on individuals or groups that might be a threat, either to the military or to the infant Weimar Republic.

Hitler enjoyed the assignment, sometimes spying on his fellow soldiers, writing

up daily reports, and informing his superiors whenever he felt that someone was subversive in any way. An additional bonus to this job was special training at the University of Munich. Long bitter about his failure to enter college, there he was at last, attending political philosophy classes with the goal of helping his beloved Germany!

Member Number 55

When he completed his training, Hitler was asked to investigate certain political groups—again, to see if they were potentially harmful. The first one he investigated was a tiny group calling itself the German Workers' Party.

The group was hardly a threat to the right-wing German military. It had only fifty-four members and no organization at all. At the meeting Hitler attended, the treasurer reported that there were only seven marks (about $2.25) in the party's savings. The group's members believed that Communists and Jews were to blame for most of Germany's woes—a belief shared by many in the army. Hitler was scornful when he made his written report, writing that "aside from a few directives, there was nothing, no program, no leaflet, no printed matter at all, no membership cards, not even a miserable rubber stamp." [37]

Even so, Hitler's commanders were interested in the party's philosophy. They urged him to join the German Workers' Party and see whether it could perhaps be formed into something useful later on. And so, three days after attending his first meeting, Adolf Hitler received a blue tag in the mail informing him that he was member #55 of the German Workers' Party.

Could anyone have known then that with a new name, this little group would in a few years become the mightiest political force in Europe?

Chapter

3 Seeds of the Reich

In 1919 Hitler had become a card-carrying member of the German Workers' Party. His work with the little political organization kept him so busy that he was forced to resign from the military. With the same vigor with which he applied himself as a dispatch runner, young Adolf Hitler threw himself into his new role as a party politician.

Getting a Foothold

One of the first to see Hitler's potential as a leader was the founder of the German Workers' Party, Anton Drexler. Drexler was a thirty-five-year-old machinist who shared Hitler's hatred of Communists and Jews. He believed, as Hitler did, that Jews were responsible for many of the revolutionary ideas that had hurt Germany. And the fact that a few prominent Jews had been among the founders of the floundering Weimar Republic led Hitler and Drexler to distrust the Jews in Germany even more.

Although Drexler was dedicated to his party's ideas, he was not an administrator. He had no instinct for publicity or public relations, so his German Workers' Party seemed doomed to remain a tiny fringe group with almost no voice or power. Drexler was pleased to offer Hitler the po-

sition of director of propaganda. And how things changed!

Until then, the party had published no written announcements of its meetings. Instead, Drexler and the others relied on word of mouth, and as a result, most of the group's gatherings had only a small turnout. Hitler set to work, creating striking circulars in black and blood red. He also used most of the treasury's holdings to pay for an announcement in some popular Munich newspapers.

This publicity increased attendance almost immediately. The announcements brought die-hard right-wingers as well as people who were merely curious about what the German Workers' Party had to offer. But what kept people coming back—and they did—had little to do with the advertisements and circulars. It was Hitler himself.

Finding His Voice

Shy, awkward young Adolf Hitler had the ability to transform himself into a powerful speaker, one who could hold audiences spellbound. He had first become aware of his gift for public speaking while taking classes for the military at the University of Munich. The few times he had stood up to

argue a point with a professor or a fellow student, he sensed that the entire class was moved by his words. One who heard him speak in class described Hitler's as "a strangely guttural voice. . . . I had the peculiar feeling that the man was feeding on the excitement which he himself had whipped up."[38]

Now, as a full-time political activist, Hitler began to improve upon that talent. He spoke at almost every meeting on such topics as "The Shame of Versailles," "The Jew—the Aryan Enemy," and "Germany and the World's Future." His speeches were highly emotional, and his voice would range from whispers and high-pitched screams to a thundering baritone. He would clench and unclench his fists and bounce on the balls of his feet. At the

Adolf the orator. Hitler's animated and emotional speaking style held audiences spellbound.

end of a speech, sweat would plaster his limp black hair to his forehead. Indeed, he was so active during his speeches that it was not unusual for him to lose five pounds in a single evening.

His audiences were spellbound. One man who heard him speak at an early political rally joked that Hitler hardly looked like a skilled orator—more "like a waiter in a railway station restaurant." But he seemed to come to life when mounting the podium, especially if the audience was large. He could, said one witness, "send shivers down one's spine."[39]

As he grew more self-assured, Hitler began to refine his talent. Hours before a rally, he would study the room. What was the light like? The acoustics? What would be the best place to stand, or to enter? Historian Robert Payne notes that Hitler's theatrical eye helped him achieve the effect he desired.

> He learned the advantage of arriving late, keeping the audience in suspense for so long that their wits were dulled. . . . He would appear from some totally unexpected direction and then march across the hall with a fixed and frozen expression on his face, with a wedge of bodyguards in front of him and another behind him, like an army.[40]

And instead of fearing hecklers, Hitler sought them out. He purposely used red in his flyers, for that was the color used by the Communists, and he knew it would enrage them. And when he spoke, he thought nothing was as dramatic as having his bodyguards charge into a crowd to violently silence any hecklers. The audience, he felt, seemed to rise to the excitement, for they always responded with cheers and wild yells.

(Left) Hitler announces the founding of the Nazi party at a 1925 meeting. (Above) Nazi party members march at a demonstration. The swastika became the Nazis' most well-known emblem.

Making Changes

Within a few months the membership of the German Workers' Party began to climb, from under one hundred to almost a thousand. Hitler convinced Drexler that the time was right to make some additional changes, the first being the party's name. Hitler was convinced that the name "German Workers' Party" was vague and uninteresting. Hoping to get the support of Germany's nationalists and socialists, Hitler changed it to the National Socialist German Workers' Party. The first word (in German), *Nationalsozialistsche* could be shortened to "Nazi," which Hitler thought a catchier name.

He also believed strongly in the power of symbols to excite and motivate people. He designed a flag for the Nazi party using the same eye-catching red he used for the leaflets. The flag's symbol, black on a white background, was a hooked cross, or

swastika, which came to be the most recognizable symbol of the Nazi party. As the party grew larger, the bold black swastika seemed to be everywhere—on flags, flyers, armbands, helmets, and rings.

Hitler became the Nazi party's most important asset. He demanded complete control of the party, and Drexler had little choice but to agree. By 1920 Hitler began signing his name as "Adolf Hitler, *der Führer*" (the leader.) The future of the Nazi party would be his alone.

"A Wolf Had Been Born"

To solidify the party's goals, Hitler and Drexler collaborated on a list of eleven of the party's most important beliefs. Then they came up with a series of twenty-five demands they felt the German government needed to address. Among these demands were the abolishment of the terms

The Sign of the Swastika

The hooked cross, or swastika, was adopted by Hitler as the symbol for his Nazi party. As Warren Morris notes in The Weimar Republic and Nazi Germany, *the swastika was not a new symbol—even among political organizations.*

"No one knows the origins of this sign, the name of which means 'fortune' in Sanskrit. It apparently was associated with the worship of the sun in ancient times. Forms of it can be found in such diverse places as thousand-year-old Hindu and Buddhist temples and sculpture, and even on the artifacts of the American Indian. The early Christians used the hooked symbol as the symbol for Christ, the son of righteousness. Hitler probably first saw the swastika on the coat of arms of the Abbey school that he attended as a child in Lambach.... *Ostara,* the violently anti-Semitic and nationalistic newspaper that Hitler read in Vienna, prominently bore a swastika on its masthead. The Austrian German Workers' party also adopted the hooked cross. Thus, despite its association with Christian and ancient religions, the swastika had become a symbol of extreme German nationalism and racism by the 1920s."

of the Versailles treaty and the granting of German citizenship to Aryan Germans only—strictly forbidding Jews.

With the party's goals and demands defined, Hitler decided he needed a larger audience to whom he could unveil the party's demands. He persuaded Drexler and the other party executives to rent one of the largest halls in Munich—one that seated at least 2,000 people, with room for another couple of hundred standing along the sides and in the back. It was a risk, for if the hall did not fill, the Nazis would look foolish. The Nazi elite need not have worried, however—the room was filled to bursting half an hour before Hitler was scheduled to speak. The crowd was fifty times larger than the one that had attended Hitler's first meeting almost two years earlier.

As always, Hitler toyed with his audience as he spoke. He whispered and roared, blaming the Jews and other non-Aryans for betraying Germany. And although there were plenty of Communist hecklers in the crowd, their jeers were drowned out by the cheers of the majority. The twenty-five demands were read, and the audience roared its approval.

The meeting that night was an important turning point for both the Nazi party and Hitler himself. Instead of being applauded by a small roomful of supporters, Hitler had won the boisterous approval of

Hitler's Storm Troopers were the Nazi elite guard. Their terrorist methods made them feared by all.

thousands. "When I finally closed the meeting," Hitler recalled later, "I was not alone in thinking that a wolf had been born that was destined to break into the herd of deceivers and misleaders of the people."[41]

"Hard as Krupp Steel"

After that night Hitler's speeches drew larger crowds. Most of the audiences were supportive, but there were occasional hecklers—especially Communists. At Hitler's request, a private Nazi army was formed to provide muscle and protection for himself and other speakers.

A loyal supporter named Ernst Röhm leaped at the chance to serve the führer. A professional soldier and much-decorated veteran of World War I, Röhm organized a squad of tough ex-soldiers he called *Sturm Abteilung*, or "Storm Troopers." They dressed in brown shirts, dark pants, and metal helmets. The SA, as they were sometimes called, trained and drilled like regu-

lar soldiers and were secretly armed by Nazi sympathizers within the German army.

Hitler was proud of his SA troops, boasting that they were "quick as greyhounds, tough as leather, and hard as Krupp steel."[42] As the Nazi movement grew, the SA troops became more and more feared for their tactics. These were no ordinary bouncers, for there was little tact or courtesy in the SA's method of dealing with those who booed the führer or his associates. They quickly streamed into a crowd, cracking heads as they cleared a path to the offenders, who were beaten, sometimes fatally.

"From the very outset," Hitler wrote, "[they] were instructed and trained in the viewpoint that terror can only be broken by terror . . . that as long as reason was silent and violence had the last word, the best weapon of defense lay in attack."[43]

And attack they did, with increasing intensity every day. When there were no hecklers, the SA found others to bully. Jews were a favorite target—one that Hitler branded in every speech as the root

of the evil that plagued Germany: "Jews evoked a special ferocity: Synagogues were desecrated, and Jews were beaten in the streets. Storm Troopers circulated through beer halls with boxes inscribed 'Contribute to the Jew massacre.' "[44]

A Receptive Audience

By the summer of 1923 the Nazis could boast 150,000 members throughout Bavaria. (Almost 11,000 of these were Storm Troopers.) Each new rally was attracting tens of thousands of excited (or, at least, curious) spectators. Hitler's message of national pride—mixed with a dose of racial and ethnic hatred—was received with roars of approval.

Hitler gives the Nazi salute at a 1928 rally in the Bavarian city of Nuremberg.

Genes and the SS

The superiority of the SS was an obsession with its creator, Heinrich Himmler. He spent a great deal of time devising methods for screening applicants, but the process did not always go smoothly, as shown in this passage from The SS.

"Himmler decreed that no one would be admitted to the SS who did not display the outward signs of Nordic, or so-called Aryan ancestry: The men under his command should be tall, blue-eyed, and fair. But since a large proportion of his existing membership failed even this initial test, he made exception for World War I veterans. . . . For the time being, the main test of an applicant was a lengthy examination of his photograph by Himmler himself, wielding a magnifying glass and brooding. 'I used to think: Are there any definite indications of foreign blood in this man—prominent cheek bones, for instance—that might cause people to say, "He has a Mongolian or Slav look about him"?' The ultimate aim [Himmler] explained, was to create 'an order of good blood to serve Germany.'"

Hitler's appeal was especially strong in 1923, for that was the first year that Germany was unable to make its reparations payments. As a result, the French invaded the Ruhr, stripping Germany of much-needed resources. The invasion made Germans angry and reminded them of the shame heaped upon their nation by the Treaty of Versailles.

And when inflation resulted from the French occupation, and the value of the mark went into a free-fall, that angered them even more. An egg sold for a million marks, a cold beer for over three million. What was wrong, when an egg cost what a large house had cost five years before?

People were angry at their country's predicament—and angrier still at the feeble Weimar leaders who allowed their nation to be bullied. The Germans were desperate to hear that they were a proud and important people. They wanted to blame someone for their troubles, and the intense young Nazi from Austria supplied the scapegoats—Communists, Jews, and foreigners. He made sense, in the Germans' view, and the movement grew. Blizzards of red flags with swastikas greeted Hitler wherever he went.

Waiting for the Moment

With the Nazi movement growing so quickly throughout Bavaria, Hitler knew the time was approaching for making his move to power—not just in Bavaria, but in Germany as a whole. His speeches had motivated people—perhaps *too* well. Leaders of some of the SA squads nervously informed Hitler that the troops were begging for a real fight—not merely roughing up a few Jews or smashing the windows of a synagogue. Unless Hitler could lead them into revolution soon, they might start one without him!

To Hitler, November 11, 1923, seemed like an auspicious time to make a grab for power. It was the fifth anniversary of Germany's surrender to the Allies at the end of World War I, and people's national pride might be fueled by a revolt on that date. Besides, it was a Sunday, when government offices would be closed, the military and police at their most relaxed.

At the last minute, however, Hitler changed the date to November 8. He learned that there was to be a large gathering on the outskirts of Munich, and that

The führer, clad in civilian clothes, awaits his chance to seize power in 1923.

three important government leaders would be there. Gustav von Kahl, the Bavarian state commissioner, was to give a speech. Gen. Otto von Lossow, head of the Bavarian army, and Col. Hans von Seisser, head of the state police, would also be present. The support of the army and the police would be all-important to any takeover of the government, so Hitler knew that his move to power would depend on the support of these two men. Besides, more than 3,000 of Kahl's supporters were expected to come—a dramatic moment for Hitler to surprise them by staging a putsch, or revolt.

That evening, on orders from Hitler, 600 Storm Troopers surrounded the building where the rally was taking place. At exactly 8:30 P.M., in the middle of Kahl's speech, Hitler burst into the hall waving a revolver. Witnesses said later that he presented a strange image, dressed in a baggy tuxedo and spiked helmet, with his Iron Cross displayed on his coat.

"As a policeman tried in vain to stop him," writes one historian, "Hitler jumped on a beer-stained table and shot his weapon at the ceiling. . . . His eyes blazing, Hitler cried that the revolution had begun."[45]

Doomed to Failure

While the SA controlled the stunned crowd, Hitler forced Kahl, Lossow, and Seisser into a back room. There he announced that he was proclaiming a new government for Germany, with himself as its dictator, and that Field Marshal Erich Ludendorff, a military hero of World War I, would be chief of the military in his regime. Hitler told the three men he

During the putsch of 1923, Hitler announced that German field marshal and World War I hero Erich Ludendorff would be his military chief.

needed their cooperation and support. Could he count on a loyalty oath from each of them?

Although the men might have agreed with many of Hitler's ideas, they were startled by his impudence. No, they said, they would never agree to such an oath! Hitler waved his gun threateningly, and announced that if they refused to comply, and the putsch failed, he would kill them as well as himself.

But at the moment Ludendorff arrived, uninformed of the revolt but willing to go along with it. Both Lossow and Seisser were impressed—Ludendorff's reputation was honored among military men like themselves. Since Ludendorff supported Hitler and was such a celebrity, Kahl, Lossow, and Seisser agreed (although tentatively) to go along with Hitler's request. They agreed to make a

show of strength to the audience, which was growing more restless with each passing minute.

The five men—Hitler, Ludendorff, Kahl, Lossow, and Seisser—appeared in front of the crowd. Hitler shouted that Germany's revolution had finally occurred, that he—with the support of the police and the army—was going to take over Germany. There were brief speeches and toasts drunk to the new government. "The revolution was over," writes historian Robert Payne. "The new government had been appointed; it remained only to march on Berlin. To resounding 'Heils' for the new leaders, the 3,000 people in the beer hall drifted away."[46]

But the congratulations and rejoicing were premature, for this putsch was doomed to failure. Kahl and his two associates in the Bavarian government began to have doubts hours after they were released. Lossow and Seisser alerted the military and security police about Hitler's march, due to begin the following day. And when Hitler and 3,000 ardent Nazis marched into the heart of the

Nazi leaders and Hitler's conspirators (left to right), Wagner, Pernet, Brückner, and Röhm, after their 1923 acquittal.

city the next morning, with flags flying, the police were there waiting.

No one was certain who fired first, but a volley of shots began the violence. "Everywhere people were going down," remembers one police officer,

> writhing on the ground in agony, dead and dying, while the guns still rattled into their stampeding midst. Dead were trampled under people's feet, throwing the living down; blood flowed everywhere over the gray pavement. Shrieks and cries rent the air, and always that insane firing went on.[47]

When the shooting was over, sixteen Nazis and three policemen lay dead on the street; hundreds more were wounded. Hitler and the rest of the Nazis fled the scene—all, that is, except General Ludendorff. He had dropped to the ground during the shooting, but afterwards continued his march, all by himself. Ramrod straight, glaring, he walked up to the police and presented himself for arrest, telling his captors, "You are all revolting. I want to vomit before you."[48]

Many of those Nazis who had joined in the putsch fled Germany to avoid being captured by the police. Hitler remained in Germany, however, where he was arrested two days after the attempted revolt. Together with General Ludendorff and seven other participants in the putsch, Hitler was brought before the German court. The charge was high treason.

"The Greatest Stroke of Luck in My Life"

Historians agree that the trial of Hitler and his fellow plotters was a total sham.

Hitler seemed to have a strange power over women. In his book Hitler: The Path to Power, *Charles Bracelen Flood describes the scene at the end of the trial at which Hitler was sentenced after the failed putsch of 1923.*

"The handing down of the sentences took place on April 1. Arriving early at the courtroom, Assistant Prosecutor Ehard found dozens of women already there, carrying bouquets for Adolf Hitler. Ehard had the bailiffs remove the flowers. Other women were wearing rosettes made of red, black, and white ribbons, the imperial colors adopted by the nationalists. A number of the women spectators asked Ehard whether, now that the trial was almost over, they could take baths in the tub that Hitler had used in the guardhouse area, where the defendants had been held during the course of the trial. Ehard said he did not think that would be possible."

Many of the judges and prosecutors were themselves Nazi supporters, and gave Hitler every opportunity to defend his actions. The crowds of spectators cheered gustily whenever he spoke; hordes of reporters from all over Europe recorded every word. Hitler was allowed to speak at length—often for several hours at a time. Witnesses said it was a "political circus."

Hitler reminded the court during one of his speeches that he did what he did out of love for Germany, not to break laws. "It is not you who pronounce judgement upon us," said Hitler, "it is the eternal Court of History. . . . That Court will judge us . . . as Germans who wanted the best for their people and their fatherland, who wished us to fight and die. You may pronounce us guilty . . . but the Goddess who presides over the eternal Court of History . . . acquits us."[49]

Hitler was not acquitted, but his sentence was as light as it could possibly be. As ringleader of the rebellion, he was sentenced to the absolute minimum, five years. Ludendorff, the national hero, was acquitted. The other seven were given suspended sentences. The failure of the putsch, said Hitler, was "the greatest stroke of luck in my life."[50] Although the revolt had failed, Hitler himself had been successful. The trial had attracted news reporters from all over Europe, and Hitler had emerged from the event as not merely a regional political organizer, but a national celebrity.

"The Place Looked like a Delicatessen"

Hitler served only nine months of his sentence—and even that was anything but difficult. Landsberg Fortress, where he was incarcerated, was nicer than any of the rooms he had rented in Vienna or Munich.

The Idea of the *Volk*

One of the most cherished ideals set forth in Hitler's Mein Kampf *is his theory of the blood ties of the people, or* Volk. *The sacredness of this bond formed the basis of his dream of an Aryan superrace, as he writes in his autobiography.*

"The . . . state must set race in the center of all life. It must take care to keep it pure. . . . It must see to it that only the healthy beget children; that there is only one disgrace: despite one's own sickness and deficiencies, to bring children into the world; and one highest honor: to renounce doing so. And conversely it must be considered reprehensible to withhold healthy children from the nation. Here the . . . state must act as guardian of a millennial future in the face of which the wishes and the selfishness of the individual must appear as nothing and submit. . . . The *Volk* state must therefore begin by raising marriage from the level of a continuous defilement of the race and give it the consecration of an institution which is called upon to produce images of the Lord and not monstrosities halfway between man and ape."

The guards gave him a suite of several adjoining small rooms. There were no bars on the windows, and no guards to be summoned if he needed to use a bathroom. Guests could come and go as they pleased.

"The place looked like a delicatessen," remembered one Nazi who had visited him in prison. "You could have opened up a flower and fruit and wine shop with all the stuff stacked there. People were sending presents from all over Germany and Hitler had grown visibly fatter on the proceeds."[51]

When he was not enjoying the gifts of his many admirers and well-wishers, Hitler spent his prison time working on a book. It was called *Mein Kampf,* or "My Struggle." In it he laid out his goals for his future Reich—to abolish civil liberties, to declare war on Europe, to kill anyone not necessary or beneficial to the empire. Jews, especially, were singled out in the book, for he claimed that the thousand-year reich could not start until they were all destroyed.

Mein Kampf was published in 1925, two years after the failed putsch. Max Amann, the manager of the Nazi publishing business, was disappointed in the book's sales at first. It was largely ignored—selling only about 9,000 copies the first year, and progressively fewer in the next three years. Those who did buy it found it boring and difficult to read—the angry babbling of a crazed revolutionary. Eerily, however, *Mein Kampf* was a blueprint of what Adolf Hitler would eventually do in Germany. If people had taken the book—and the man—seriously, perhaps some of the horror of the next two decades could have been avoided.

4 Coming to Power

A lot changed during the nine months Hitler was in Landsberg Fortress. Although he emerged from prison anxious to pick up where he had left off before the putsch, he found that impossible. The Nazi party, a rapidly growing political force nine months before, was almost nonexistent.

A More Stable Country

The German government had banned the Nazi party after the Munich putsch. No red flags with swastikas were allowed, no SA troopers could storm through the streets, no one could solicit new members. And although a faithful core of members remained, even they were arguing and divided in their purpose.

Another reason for the lack of Nazi activity was that conditions in Germany were improving. The Allies had loosened their choke hold on the German economy, aware that if Germany's economy failed, their own might collapse as well. The industrialized nations of the world were simply too closely interrelated for such a catastrophe in Germany not to affect them all.

The French had evacuated the Ruhr, leaving Germany's industries and resources intact. Better yet, the United States had agreed to pump millions of dollars into the German economy to get it back on track. As a result, the mark had stabilized and employment had skyrocketed. The German people were happier than they had been since the beginning of World War I. Although things were not perfect, the frightening downward spiral of the last year had been halted. To a more contented nation, the Nazi message of hate and bitterness had lost its strength.

Back to Business

Even so, Hitler was eager to revive his party. Within two weeks of his release, he met with Dr. Heinrich Held, the Bavarian premier. Hitler promised that if the premier reinstated the Nazi party, it would act legally from then on: no more secret revolts, no more breaking heads. Instead, the party would work through the system and try to get Nazis elected to the Reichstag, the German legislature. The premier had no reason to suspect that Hitler would not keep his word, and gave his permission. He later told the Bavarian minister of justice, "The wild beast is checked. We can afford to loosen the chain."[52]

Hitler in 1925 after his release from prison. He lost no time in gathering his Nazi flock together again.

Hitler launched a major campaign to renew interest in the Nazi message. He rented a large hall—the same one, ironically, in which he had launched the 1923 putsch—and scheduled an assembly. Many who attended did so out of curiosity rather than loyalty. But those who witnessed Hitler's comeback speech said that he exhibited a masterful hold over his audience.

"It was like a revival meeting," writes historian Robert Payne.

> He was the preacher calling upon them to submit to a power greater than themselves. Women wept, wrung their hands, and screamed, overcome with excitement. Former party leaders, who had come only to watch, now marched onto the platform, shook his hand, or embraced him. Some wept openly, while others were so shaken with emotion that they shivered uncontrollably.[53]

After that meeting in February 1925, the Nazis picked up where they had left off before the putsch. Many high-level Nazi supporters who had fled Germany two years before, to escape prosecution, were summoned home by party leaders. Ernst Röhm, the SA commander, was given the nod to reinstate his Storm Troopers—although their activities were to be far more restrained. Hitler and other Nazi politicians crisscrossed Germany, making speeches and holding rallies. The elections in Germany scheduled for 1928 were the first chance the Nazis had to come to power by legal means, and Hitler and his cohorts running for seats in the Reichstag intended to make good use of this opportunity.

But the results of the 1928 elections must have been disheartening. Only 3 percent of the voters selected Nazi candidates for the Reichstag, making Hitler's party the weakest in Germany. Even with the führer's astonishing ability to mesmerize his audiences, the Nazi party was unable to gain much ground. Times in Germany were good, people were feeling content and prosperous, and the Nazi message seemed shrill and reactionary.

The Opportunity of Depression

On October 29, 1929, the Nazi party received a boost from an unlikely source—Wall Street, the center of finance in the United States. It was on that day that the stock market crashed. Years of buying on credit, without cash to back up their

*When the Great Depression hit America, loans to Germany were
called in, sinking Germany back into depression as well. Soup lines and
makeshift shelters became daily life for millions of unemployed Germans.*

purchases, had finally caught up with American investors. The prices of stocks plummeted wildly; many people lost entire fortunes in one day.

This event began the Great Depression. Banks closed, businesses folded, and unemployment was at a record high. The event was a catastrophe for the United States, but it affected other countries as well. Frightened American investors called in the loans they had made to the struggling Weimar Republic.

German businesses and industries that had just begun to thrive because of foreign aid were thrown back into chaos. More than half of all German families were seriously affected by the depression—a staggering 6 million people suddenly found themselves without jobs. The government, which had just begun to gather support, found that many of its supporters were spending their days standing in line for free soup and dry bread supplied by charities. Hundreds of families lined up each day to obtain begging licenses from government agencies.

These hard times delighted both Nazi and Communist party leaders, for both sides benefited from the resulting feelings of bitterness and disgust. The Communists told people that the depression was caused by capitalism and the democratic government that supported it. The Nazis blamed Jewish financiers, and hammered home their message that Jews were the enemies of Germany. Both sides agreed that what Germany did *not* need was more democracy; a dictatorship would be a far more appropriate government for the troubled nation.

Due in large part to the depression, both parties increased their representation in the Reichstag during the 1930 elections, although the Nazis got 2 million more votes than the Communists. The Nazis won 107 more seats, making them second only to the democracy-minded Social Democrats as the most popular party in Germany; the Weimar government lost big in the election. Although the Social Democrats still held the majority of votes, their popularity was slipping away quickly. The politics of discontent were on the rise.

Campaign 1932

Hitler wanted to take Germany by storm in the 1932 elections. He himself was running for president against Paul von Hindenburg, the incumbent and a former World War I hero who had great personal popularity—even though his Social Democrat party was losing support. It would be no easy task to defeat Hindenburg.

Hitler and other Nazis campaigned vigorously, organizing rallies in every large and medium-size town in Germany. (Hitler even became the first public figure in the world to use an airplane to get him quickly from one campaign stop to another.) Speeches, songs, and chants all focused on the appeal to nationalism—the idea that Germany would rise again—laced with a large amount of hate.

In addition to the frequent appearances made by Hitler and the other Nazi candidates, Ernst Röhm and his Storm Troopers became a more visible presence. They had been banned after the failed putsch of 1923, and when Hitler had lobbied to get his party legalized again, government officials worried that the SA would return. Hitler had promised that they would be no more than bodyguards, and that the terror would stop. However, those promises had been made to a government that was enjoying great popular support. Now, with the government weakened, Hitler felt he could give Röhm and his troops free rein to create as much terror as possible.

By 1932 the SA troops numbered 400,000. They engaged in bloody street fights with bands of Communists; they bullied their way into the rallies of other parties and created havoc. They seemed to be everywhere—just as Hitler had planned. The SA's job was to make people afraid, and they accomplished that easily.

An easy target for the SA was Germany's Jewish population. Edith Busek, a Jewish girl who lived in Frankfurt during

Hitler (right), his publicity chairman, Joseph Goebbels (foreground), and other Nazi leaders give the characteristic salute at a campaign rally in 1930.

the campaign, remembers hearing the SA and others singing "bloodcurdling songs day and night. I remember the refrain from one of the songs, 'Oh what a glorious day it will be *wenn Judenblut vom messer spritzt*—when Jewish blood spurts from the knife.'"[54] Another graphic chant among the Storm Troopers was

> Sharpen the knives on the sidewalk
> So that they can cut the enemy's
> bodies better
> When the hour of revenge strikes
> We shall be ready for mass murder.[55]

Hindenburg supporters hold up their "Elect Hindenburg" placards at a 1932 campaign rally.

Tin Hitlers and Other Childhood Memories

Peter Herz was a little boy during the last days of the Weimar Republic. In Voices from the Third Reich, *Herz recalls some of his boyhood memories.*

"We lived in a typical workers' district. I spent my free time during the week with my classmates, and I spent Sundays with my father at the local soccer club matches. It was a typical workers' organization. The high point was always Sunday evening, when we got together in the club's small meeting hall and ate sausages and potato salad and drank a big mug of beer.

The SA tavern was only a short distance away. The SA members often left there late and drunk and came over to our clubhouse to raise hell. But they were usually driven off with table and chair legs. My father usually led the counterattack.

I got my first impression of [Nazis] as a child, when I saw SA model soldiers in a store window. There was also a tin Hitler with a moveable arm. A few days later these tin soldiers were parading through the streets in the flesh. They always carried the party flag right up front, and everyone had to greet them with a tip of the hat or a raised arm, just like that tin Hitler in the showcase."

The Birth of the SS

Upon his arrival in Berlin for a campaign speech in 1932, candidate Hitler accepts a welcoming bouquet of flowers from a young boy.

It may seem strange now that such bloodthirsty tactics would help, not hurt, a candidate for election. But many German people supported Hitler and his Nazis, believing they were the only alternative to the present situation. The government seemed too weak and incompetent to solve the nation's economic troubles, and many Germans believed the Nazi party represented a chance to feel pride and hope for their nation. And, they reasoned, if a little head-bashing was necessary to accomplish that, then maybe that was just the way things had to be.

But the head-bashing was worrying Hitler a bit—not because of the violence itself, but because of who was doing the bashing. By 1932 the SA had become unruly and uncontrollable. In one embarrassing incident, for example, rowdy Storm Troopers had attacked the Berlin headquarters of the Nazi party itself, causing a great deal of damage before they were finally called off.

Such actions enraged Hitler and made him even more determined to have a reliable, trimmed-down security force that would be intensely loyal and completely controllable. For this task he chose a quiet, scholarly young aide named Heinrich Himmler. Hitler called this new security force the *Schutzstaffen,* or "SS" for short. As

Heinrich Himmler (left) was named by Hitler to head the new elite guard, the infamous SS.

"We Do Not Waver and We Follow the Führer"

In his book Never to Forget: The Jews of the Holocaust, *Milton Meltzer reprints an essay written by a young girl in Germany. It is obvious that the anti-Semitic message of the Nazi-run educational system was getting through to children in 1935.*

"Unfortunately many people today still say, 'God created the Jews, too. That is why you must respect them also.' We say, however, 'Vermin are also animals, but we still destroy them.' The Jew is a half-caste. He has inherited characteristics of Aryans, Asiatics, Negroes, and Mongols. In a half-caste, the worst characteristics predominate. The only good thing about him is his white color. . . . The Jews have plotted revolts and incited war. They have led Russia into misery. In Germany they gave the Communist Party money and paid their thugs. We were at death's door. Then Adolf Hitler came. Now the Jews are abroad and stir up trouble against us. But we do not waver and we follow the Führer. We do not buy anything from the Jews. Every penny we give them kills one of our own people. Heil, Hitler!"

time went on, the SS would become the most feared branch of the Nazi organization. As Hitler once remarked, Himmler was "training young men that will make the world tremble."[56]

Hitler wanted the SS visibly distinct from the SA, and Himmler accommodated him. Dressed in black from head to toe, each SS member had a helmet with a silver pin in the shape of a skull. Each had to swear total loyalty to Hitler and prove that he had no Jews in his family tree, going back several generations. (Nazi doctors measured facial structure, skin types, and coarseness of hair to be sure that no SS member had characteristics that might be viewed as Jewish.) As Hitler moved closer to power in 1932, he relied far more on the SS than on Röhm's Storm Troopers.

Victory for "The Vulgar Little Corporal"

But even with the sworn loyalty and assistance of Himmler's SS, Hitler was not able to unseat eighty-five-year-old President Hindenburg. The rest of the Nazis running for office, however, enjoyed remarkable success. In the 1932 election Nazi candidates won 230 seats in the Reichstag—with 14 million votes cast in their behalf. They were the most popular of Germany's political parties, no longer second to the Social Democrats.

Hitler, while disappointed that his bid for president had not worked, was anxious to be chancellor. The chancellor controlled the inner workings of the German government and was similar to a prime

Chancellor Hitler (right) sits in the gallery with other government leaders during a 1933 conference in Berlin. German president Hindenburg had reluctantly nominated Hitler for chancellor, knowing that he wanted to take over.

minister in countries such as England. By assuming the position of chancellor, Hitler would be second only to the president in terms of power. But not enough Nazis had been elected to the Reichstag to guarantee him that position if the president did not nominate him. Unfortunately, Hindenburg's aides, believing that Hitler's nomination would help Hindenburg control the Nazis, urged the president to offer Hitler the position of chancellor.

But Hindenburg neither liked nor trusted Hitler. He often referred to him as "the vulgar little corporal"[57] and was sure that Hitler would seize control of the government if given half a chance. He once told an advisor that the only job he would offer Hitler would be "licking stamps with my picture on them."[58] And although he was pressed again and again to appease the powerful Hitler with the post, Hindenburg refused to nominate him as chancellor. Hitler was offered lesser posts in exchange for his support but refused to accept anything less than the chancellorship.

The president underestimated the voting power of the Nazis in the Reichstag, however. Although he submitted names of men he trusted and admired, the large voting block of Nazis refused to ratify those nominations. In the end, President Hindenburg had no choice. After extracting a promise from Hitler that he would act lawfully, Hindenburg offered the post of chancellor to the führer of the Nazi party. On January 30, 1933, a breathlessly excited Adolf Hitler was sworn in to the second most important position in the German government. In eighteen months he would be in complete control.

Planning for Power

Even after Hitler became chancellor, the Nazi party was still not in control. Without a two-thirds majority in the Reichstag, the Nazis were unable to pass the laws Hitler wanted. Their only hope was to dissolve the Reichstag and start over, with new elections. By skillful political maneuvering, Hitler was able to persuade Hindenburg that it would be in Germany's best interest to hold new elections. Hindenburg agreed, somewhat reluctantly, and set the date as March 5.

The Nazi party leaders were ecstatic, for they were convinced that in the new elections their candidates would be far more successful. "Now it will be easy," wrote Hitler's publicity chairman, Joseph Goebbels, "for we can call on all the resources of the State. Radio and press are at our disposal. We shall stage a masterpiece of propaganda. And this time, naturally, there is no lack of money."[59]

The burned Reichstag building. The fire was a Nazi tactic to discredit the Communists and seize more power.

Much of the money needed to run the Nazi campaign came from wealthy German industrialists and bankers. For years they had been nervous about Communists and trade unions and the threats those groups could pose in the event of a revolution. And although many of these wealthy industrialists and bankers disagreed with some of Hitler's rhetoric, they saw him as a positive alternative to the destruction that the political left advocated. So, as Hitler promised to crush the unions and destroy the Communists, the money flowed in to Nazi campaigns.

It was apparent that it would take more than money however, to win the large number of seats in the Reichstag. A critical event must occur—something that would make the German people flock away from the Communists and other parties and straight into the arms of the Nazis. But what?

The answer happened on a snowy night in February, just a week before the election. The dome of the old Reichstag building began glowing, and then the windows burst open, loosing the flames and smoke inside. The Reichstag, the seat and symbol of democratic power in Germany, was burning!

Immediately people were told that the Communists had planned it all in an attempted putsch against the government. The police, under the command of Hitler's trusted aide Hermann Göring, even arrested the supposed culprit, who at the time of his arrest was clutching an oily rag. He was a young retarded Dutchman named Marinus van der Lubbe—an avowed Communist.

The confused young man confessed to Göring and his police squads, and was put on trial for "crimes against the German nation." He was found guilty—not surprisingly, since Nazis controlled the courts—and was beheaded later that year.

As a result of the Reichstag fire, more than 4,000 Communists and their sympathizers were rounded up by police and arrested. In addition, the government quickly outlawed rallies or other political activity by the Communist party.

But although van der Lubbe made an easy scapegoat for the fire, historians agree that Hitler and the Nazis were responsible. Hitler wanted to eliminate his opposition in Germany, including the Communists. The burning of the Reichstag gave Hindenburg visible, concrete proof that the Communists were a menace to Germany.

Nazi leader Hermann Göring's brutal tactics and merciless extermination of "enemies" of the state won him a place at Hitler's right hand.

"My Fist Will Grab Your Heads"

Soon after the fire, Hitler asked Hindenburg to sign a law that he said was for the protection of the people. In reality, it was an emergency measure limiting most of the freedoms of the democracy. Basic freedoms—of speech, of the press, and of assembly—were all abolished. In addition, the government was given the power to open mail and search homes without a warrant. The elderly Hindenburg, alarmed by what he saw as a Communist threat to his government, agreed to sign the law.

And so began an open season on any perceived enemies of the government. People were terrorized and jailed for no reason. Göring, who would eventually become Hitler's second in command, spoke at a Nazi rally before the March 5 election.

> I don't have to worry about justice. . . . My mission is only to destroy and exterminate, nothing more. . . . I shall use the power of the state and the police to the utmost . . . but the struggle to the death, in which my fist will grab your heads, I shall lead with those down there—the Brownshirts [the SA].[60]

But even with such threats of violence to his enemies, the results Hitler had hoped for did not occur. Although the Nazis gained power in the elections, they still did not control the legislature—housed temporarily in a Berlin opera house. Only 44 percent of German voters chose Nazi candidates—288 seats of the 647 possible. Another tactic had to be attempted—but what?

Fire Warning Two Years Ahead

Historians believe the Reichstag fire of 1933 was orchestrated by the Nazis. Historian Robert Payne, in his book The Life and Death of Adolf Hitler, *points to a confidential interview Hitler did in 1931 where he advocates burning the building down.*

"The [Reichstag] is a symbol of our decadence. It is a hotch-potch consisting of four clusters of Parthenon-like columns mixed up with a Roman basilica and a Moorish fortress—the whole thing gives the impression of a vast synagogue. I tell you, the Reichstag is an extraordinarily ugly building, a meeting house, a talking shop for the representatives of the degenerate bourgeoisie and the deluded working class. Both the building and the institution which it houses are a disgrace to the German people, and one day they must go. In my opinion, the sooner this talking shop is burned down, the sooner will the German people be freed from foreign influence."

The Enabling Act

Since Hitler was unable to get the candidates he wanted into the Reichstag, he chose an alternate solution—to dissolve the Reichstag. He proposed a new law, and directed the Nazi legislators to see that it passed. Called the Enabling Act, it gave Hitler the power of a dictator for the next four years. As one historian explains, the act enabled the government "to pass any law, write any decree, perform almost any act it wished to, even if it violated the constitution."[61] Asking the Reichstag to pass such a law was, in effect, asking it to make itself obsolete.

Because the Nazis had no controlling power in the legislature, they had to rely on persuasion to get their colleagues to help pass the bill. A flurry of threats and promises followed. As the Reichstag delib-

erated on its vote, hundreds of SA troopers ringed the building chanting, "We want the bill, or fire and murder!" In the end, such persuasion won out, and the Enabling Act became law. The Weimar Republic was dead; Germany had become a dictatorship.

Crushing the Opposition

One by one, Hitler had been eliminating each roadblock between himself and full and total control of Germany. The Enabling Act was a big step, for it allowed him to keep in check anyone who disagreed with him. No longer were members of opposing parties tolerated—they were jailed or beaten to death.

As the prisons filled, special areas called concentration camps were set up outside Berlin and Munich. These camps

were technically holding areas for opponents of the Nazis. People could be sent to a concentration camp without even being charged with a crime. Communists, trade union members—anyone who might be considered a threat to Hitler or his Nazi party—could be sent to a camp without warning.

By the autumn of 1933, there remained only two obstacles to total power for Hitler. The first was obvious—President Hindenburg. The president would never consent to stepping down and allowing the government to become a complete dictatorship with Hitler at the helm. Since the president was known to be in failing health, however, Hitler quickly moved to deal with the other obstacle—the German military. He knew that the military could easily block any grab he might make for power, and he wanted its support.

But the SA had created hard feelings among the military. The SA behaved as an army itself and threatened to take over the responsibilities of the professional soldiers. Ernst Röhm did not help matters by boasting that after Germany became a Nazi state, the SA, now a dangerously powerful mob of 3 million, would be the new army.

Not so, Hitler assured the ruffled military commanders. The German army, he promised, would remain intact as Germany's fighting force. He needed the commanders' support, and to prove that he was sincere, Hitler ordered a gesture of goodwill—a bloody sacrifice known in history as "The Night of the Long Knives."

Settling Scores

Hitler told Himmler and Göring to draw up lists of key SA commanders. In addition, Hitler compiled his own list of individuals inside and outside the Nazi party who had ever angered him or done him an injustice. The lists were handed over to

As president of the Weimar Republic, Paul von Hindenburg was one of the last obstacles to Hitler's taking total control of Germany. His death in 1933 gave Hitler a timely entrance to the seat of power.

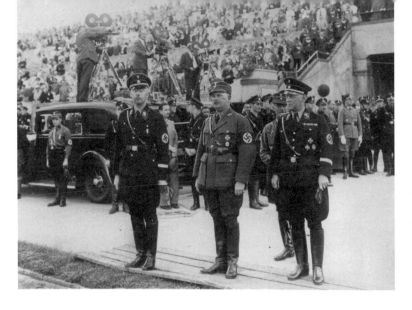

Leaders of Hitler's Storm Troopers (left to right), Heinrich Himmler, leader of the SS; Ernst Röhm, founder of the SA; and Himmler's second in command, Seidel-Dittmarsch.

SS squads. After getting the go-ahead signal from Himmler on the night of June 30, the SS began a massacre.

Throughout Germany SS troops broke into the homes of SA members, forcing them out of their beds and into the street. In Berlin alone, 150 SA leaders were arrested and taken to the basement of an old school outside of the city, where Himmler carefully checked their names against a master list. What followed was a mass execution.

In groups of four, the SA men were brought up from the school basement. They were forced to remove their shirts and coats, and an SS man used charcoal to draw a "target" on each man's chest. Then a firing squad of eight SS men shot the prisoners. The bodies were loaded into a meat truck and taken to a small village a mile away, where they were cremated. When each group of bodies was removed, another group of prisoners was brought up from the basement, and the shooting went on.

Witnesses to the killing said later that many of the prisoners did not understand why they were being killed. Loyal to the führer, many shouted "*Heil Hitler*" as they were gunned down.

Historians disagree on the number of people murdered in the Night of the Long Knives—which actually continued the better part of two days. Estimates range from several hundred to two thousand. Many were shot by firing squad; others were beheaded or strangled by the SS teams.

And so Hitler, together with Himmler and Göring, disposed of the SA by murdering its leaders—those on whom Hitler had depended as he muscled his way to power. The gesture was appreciated by the military, which now felt more secure in its role in the new Reich, and more willing to lend its support.

When old President Hindenburg died two months later, Hitler's last obstacle in his quest for complete power was removed. Using his unlimited (and legally procured) powers, he combined the offices of president and chancellor. To everyone in Germany he was now *Der Führer,* the leader. The Reich that Hitler said would last a thousand years had begun.

5 Life in Nazi Germany

Hitler's Reich depended on the total obedience of all the German people. The views of the führer must be the views of his people. What Hitler decreed must be so, absolutely and without question. But Hitler could not simply declare himself dictator of Germany and leader of the new Reich and expect everyone to accept him, for in the 1932 elections millions of Germans had voted against him and his fellow Nazis. Even though he was the leader of the nation, the battle to win the hearts and minds of its people had just begun.

To win this "battle," Hitler required control of all aspects of German life, not just its politics. For one leader to control so many people demanded not only an iron fist, but a steady stream of persuasive propaganda to convince people that obedience to the führer was correct.

"Nothing to Do with Truth"

To handle the distribution of information, Hitler appointed Joseph Goebbels to the post of Minister of Public Enlightenment and Propaganda. Goebbels had studied to be a writer, but became sidetracked by his work with the Nazi movement. He was a small man (five feet tall, 100 pounds) and was called "the Mouse Doctor" behind his back.

Goebbels was a master of the written word, and could easily fashion believable-sounding statements that were boldfaced lies—anything to further the Nazi cause. To Goebbels, it made no difference whether the information he presented was real or not—as he was fond of saying, "Propaganda has nothing to do with truth."[62] The most important thing was to keep the image of Hitler and the Nazi party positive and pure. It did not matter, therefore, what facts had to be stretched, or how big the lies were.

"The propaganda which produces the desired results," Goebbels wrote in his journal, "is good and all other propaganda

Diminutive Joseph Goebbels was appointed by Hitler to lead the Nazi propaganda machine. He became a master at making lies sound like truth.

The cream of Nazi leadership: (front row, left to right) Hermann Göring, Adolf Hitler, Joseph Goebbels, and Heinrich Himmler. They nearly brought the world to its knees.

about the goodness, the power, and the wisdom of *Der Führer.* Radio stations and newspapers were given stern directives by Goebbels and his staff governing what could be printed, what could be reported. The use, for example, of Hitler's name was only allowed in positive, cheerful contexts. The greetings of "hello" or "good day" were replaced by "*Heil Hitler,*" and the straight-arm salute was substituted for a friendly wave. Radio weather forecasters were urged by Goebbels to use the term "Hitler weather" to refer to a cloudless, sunny day; before long the phrase had crept into nearly every German's vocabulary.

"Cultural Cave Men, Aesthetic Dwarfs"

The arts, too, fell under the thumb of Goebbels and his Propaganda Ministry. Hitler was concerned with the sorts of influences music, art, and literature had on the German people, and he instructed Goebbels to stop any artists he believed were possible enemies of the Reich.

To control such freedom of expression, Goebbels set up the Reich Chamber of Culture. The chamber had a separate section for every part of cultural life: fine arts, films, the press, radio, literature, music, and the theater. Anyone who wanted to paint, or write in a newspaper, or compose music had to register with the chamber. Some, like historian William Shirer, who was in Germany at the time, described the chamber as putting "German culture into a strait jacket."[64]

But Goebbels would have disagreed. According to him, the purpose was "to gather together the creative artists in all

is bad. Therefore, it is beside the point to say your propaganda is too crude, too mean, too brutal, or too unfair, for all this does not matter. . . . Propaganda is always a means to an end."[63]

But who would publish or broadcast such propaganda? When Hitler came to power in 1933, the German media had a free hand; there were more than 7,000 magazines and journals and 4,700 daily and weekly newspapers—more than in any other nation on earth. But Goebbels made it his business to harness the media, so that the Nazi party line was the one voice the German people heard. Through a combination of threats, government intervention, and new laws such as one that put newspaper editors under state control, the German media began to become a servant to Goebbels' brand of "truth."

And so the German people were bombarded from every direction with messages

Hitler attends a showing of modern art. The showing was intended to ridicule art that Hitler despised.

spheres into a unified organization under the leadership of the Reich. The Reich must not only determine the lines of progress, mental and spiritual, but also lead and organize the professions."[65]

What was "good" art to the leaders of the Reich? Hitler had very strong opinions on the characteristics of acceptable painting, for he had been an aspiring artist himself. He instructed Goebbels to be especially ruthless in assessing paintings.

Works by Jewish or Communist artists—or by anyone suspected of being sympathetic to them—were banned from public and private galleries. Hitler especially despised works of modern art, which, he claimed, were done by "cultural cave men, aesthetic dwarfs, and artistic stutterers."[66] He felt that such art was actually a Jewish plot "to demoralize Gentiles by depicting everything in lunatic, distorted fashion."[67]

In the early years of the Reich, Goebbels and his men confiscated more than 16,000 paintings from the walls of public museums and private collections. Among the banned artists were some of

the most famous in the world—Pablo Picasso, Vincent Van Gogh, and Paul Gauguin. Some of these paintings were sold to collectors outside of Germany, and their sale brought in money for the Reich's treasury. But more than 4,000 others were heaped into a pile and burned.

Once the offensive art was gone, Goebbels hoped painters in the Reich would produce art that glorified Nazi ideas. Paintings showing strong, Aryan peasants or soldiers, or especially the führer, were encouraged.

A German newspaper commented on the new attitude towards art in the Reich. "There were times when one went to exhibitions and discussed whether the pictures were rubbish . . . now there are no more discussions—everything on the walls is art and that is that."[68]

Many artists were lucky enough to leave Germany for places that offered more freedom. Some, unwilling to yield to the Nazi edict yet unable to leave Germany, committed suicide. And more than a few artists continued to paint just as they had before,

The Backfiring Experiment

Before getting rid of the art the Reich deemed degenerate, Goebbels organized an exhibit of works selected from the collection. The idea was to show the German people how evil the art was, but as the writers of The New Order *show, the idea backfired.*

"This Exhibit of Degenerate Art, which opened in the city of Munich in July of 1937, featured some 730 pieces created by Germans such as Emil Nolde, Max Beckmann, and others and such non-Germans as Marc Chagall and Piet Mondrian. The paintings were purposely displayed in a jumble without frames, and they were hung under lurid headings such as 'Thus is nature seen by sick minds' and 'The Jewish yearning for desolation comes out.' To the dismay of the National Socialists, the show was the most popular display of paintings ever staged in the Third Reich, attracting two million visitors—five times the number that visited the concurrent exhibit of approved art, which was also held in Munich. It was never clear how many of the visitors came to see the 'degenerate' show as a protest and to take one final look at great art that was earmarked for oblivion, or how many merely wanted to confirm their own prejudices against modern art and demonstrate their agreement with the new cultural establishment."

Goebbels and Hitler at the exhibit of "degenerate" art.

only more secretively, for if an SS agent reported them, they would be sent to a concentration camp or killed outright. One artist who painted in an impressionist style told a suspicious SS man that he was merely experimenting with new methods in camouflage techniques for the army!

A Frightening Bonfire

Painters were not the only artists whose work was judged harshly in Hitler's Reich. Even before the Chamber of Culture's machinery was officially in place, thousands of students in Berlin gathered in what William Shirer notes was "a scene which

Nazi police remove "subversive" books from a library in 1933. Most of the titles removed concerned democracy and freedom or had Jewish authors.

had not been witnessed in the Western world since the late Middle Ages."[69] It was a huge bonfire, fueled by 20,000 books.

Inflamed by Nazi propaganda about "enemies to the German people," the students compiled lists of books they considered subversive. The books were then yanked from libraries (both public and private) throughout Berlin and set ablaze.

A book was considered subversive if it promoted democracy or freedom, peace, or religious tolerance. All books by Jewish authors, too, were considered unfit for the German people. The list of authors whose work was burned that night reads like a recommended-reading list for most high schools and colleges today.

Books by such great German thinkers as Thomas Mann and Albert Einstein were burned. But there were plenty of other authors whose work was considered dangerous, too—Helen Keller, H. G. Wells, Jack London, Upton Sinclair, Sigmund Freud, and Ernest Hemingway, to name but a few.

Although Goebbels was not directly involved in the bonfire, he had nothing but praise for the students responsible. "The soul of the German people can again express itself," he said. "These flames not only illuminate the final end of an old era; they also light up the new."[70]

One might wonder what books *were* acceptable to Goebbels and his staff. The most widely promoted book during Hitler's Reich was *Mein Kampf*, the angry memoirs Hitler had written while in prison in 1923. By a special decree from Hitler, every home had to have at least one copy; a couple applying for a marriage license was required to purchase the book before their marriage was considered legal by the state. Not surprisingly, sales of the book became brisk, making Adolf Hitler a millionaire.

Breeders and Nurturers

People did not have to be involved in the arts to feel their lives changed under Hitler's Reich. Every woman in Germany had to become accustomed to a new status—or lack of one. In pre-Nazi Germany, many women had taken jobs to help their families, but when Hitler came to power they were strongly urged to give those jobs up. Men were providers and warriors, the women were told. Women should serve the Reich by breeding and nurturing.

Hitler harshly criticized "modern" women—slim, dressed in fashionable clothes (including long pants), and using makeup. He viewed these traits as attributes of democratic decadence and urged women to scorn those "trouser wenches with Indian warpaint."[71]

To the Reich's leaders, the ideal woman was "a plump, broad-hipped, fresh-faced, primly gowned, unadorned peasant girl with blond hair pulled into a bun or coiled braid."[72] The highest goal to which she aspired was providing many healthy children for Germany.

The birth rate in Germany had declined in the years after World War I. Widespread poverty and uncertainty about the future had left married couples reluctant to bring children into the world. But if the Reich were to grow strong and take its rightful place among the nations of the world, it needed a larger population.

Because of the need for more children, the government did all it could to

Trying to Keep a Job

Arnold Biegelseisen was a Jewish clerk in a factory in Berlin when Hitler came to power. In Voices from the Third Reich, *he recalls how difficult it was to remain employed then.*

"Our company began making Nazi insignias. One day, one of our customers from Munich showed up and saw me working there. I overheard him talking to the company owner. 'Since you continue to employ Jews, we can no longer do business with you,' he said. After that incident, my colleagues warned me everytime they saw a customer coming, and I would run and hide in the bathroom. This continued until the day in April 1935, when the customer from Munich showed up again. I wasn't able to hide fast enough, and he saw me. He went directly to the management and roared, 'If you think you're pulling the wool over my eyes, you're wrong! You are still allowing Jews to work here!' The company let me stay until December, but then the boss told me, 'I'm sorry, but you will have to go.'"

encourage couples to have large families. The word "family," in fact, became a title of honor—used only for those couples with four or more children. It became the highest calling in the land to bear a child who would grow up to help the Nazis make Germany strong. Pregnant women would proudly say they were "donating a child for the führer." The government would award a bronze medallion, called a "Mother's Cross," to women after the delivery of their fifth child. Silver and gold medallions were awarded after the sixth and seventh child.

There were financial rewards for large families, too. The government provided large, interest-free loans to any couple planning to marry. For each child born to that couple, one-fourth of the loan would be forgiven, so that if they had four children, the entire loan was free. On the other hand, if the wife went against the wishes of the government and got a job, the loan payments would triple.

The Nazi government saw no reason why unmarried women could not also donate children to the führer. They set up several large "breeding homes" for unmarried women. Their children were fathered by SS men (both married and single) who were given the title of "conception assistants."

"Knowledge Is Ruin"

Hitler had plans for all those babies, and a long, carefree childhood was not one of them. It was important, he felt, for children to become strong and independent as soon as possible, for, as the government once reminded a mother who objected to her son's busy schedule of Reich activities, "Your son is not your personal property. . . . He is on loan to you, but he is the property of the German people."[73]

The Reich gained more power over children's upbringing by seizing control of Germany's educational system. Hitler's scorn for intellectualism and scholarship was reflected in the government's new theory of education. Hitler shunned thinkers and philosophers, believing their knowledge useless. "I will have no intellectual training," he stressed. "Knowledge is ruin to my young men. A violently active, dominating, brutal youth—that is what I am after!"[74]

In Hitler's German schools everything had a purpose. Biology teachers taught children to identify Aryan and non-Aryan features in people. History teachers hammered away at the evils of democracy, the betrayal of Germany at Versailles, and the need for Germany to increase its empire. Mathematics, too, had a definite Nazi twist. Children solved word problems such as this: "A modern night bomber can carry 1,800 incendiaries. How long is the path along which it can distribute these bombs, if it drops a bomb every second at a speed of 250 kilometers per hour?"[75]

Hitler Youth

When they were not in school, children were obligated to join clubs. The Nazis had banned all other youth organizations, including church youth groups, so children had no choice of what club to join: *Hitler Jugend,* or Hitler Youth, a way for the Reich to mold young people into the Aryan youth it needed.

(Left) As part of a Hitler Youth program, these girls receive physical training to condition them for the hardships of life in future Nazi colonies around the world. (Right) Little girls learn the Nazi salute.

There were Hitler Youth clubs for both girls and boys. The girls were given extensive training in child care and home economics. Boys were given opportunities to do gymnastics, hike, camp, and climb mountains. There was also heavy emphasis on marching and on shooting guns. "We wish to reach the point," said one Hitler Youth director, "where the gun rests as securely as the pen in the hand of a boy."[76]

Hitler appointed Baldur von Schirach to head the Hitler Youth. Ironically, Schirach had American forebears—two of whom were signers of the Declaration of Independence. As director of Hitler Youth, he maintained strict, military-style discipline with the children. Of the utmost importance were constant reminders that the children owed total allegiance to Adolf Hitler. Each day, in fact, the children were required to stand at attention and recite the sacred Oath of Allegiance: "I promise in the Hitler Youth, to do my duty at all times, in love and faithfulness to the Führer, so help me God."[77]

Prosperity Returns

Surprisingly, most people continued to support Hitler. The führer had done what had seemed impossible—reversed the sickening, downward spiral of the economy. Whereas 6 million Germans had been unemployed in 1933, by 1934 the number had been shaved to 3 million. He was getting the job done.

It was no real secret how Hitler accomplished this. Almost immediately upon gaining control of the government, he had begun a massive program of public works projects. Parks and playgrounds, streets and sewers, schools and government buildings—all got facelifts, and in some cases were completely rebuilt. He designed a huge new network of superhighways, called *autobahns,* to connect the towns and cities of Germany. Such ambitious construction projects required raw materials and plenty of construction workers, resulting in millions of new jobs.

The Third Reich's leaders understood that people would cooperate better with restrictive government programs if they also had some fun. Large festivals and celebrations were often held for this purpose.

Besides the public works projects, Hitler put many more people to work when he began rearming Germany, forbidden under the Treaty of Versailles. But Hitler had made no secret of his intent to build up Germany's armies. And to accomplish this, all factories, foundries, munitions plants, and coal mines had to be working at full staff.

People faced increased restrictions of course, as well as increased employment opportunities. All workers were required to join a Nazi-run organization called the German Labor Front, whose leaders kept close track of any dissidents or trouble-makers. Strikes were not allowed; prices and wages were fixed, so there was no need for bargaining between labor and management. A little more than 35 percent of each worker's wages went back into the German Labor Front as dues.

But even with such restrictions, workers were, for the most part, satisfied. A small paycheck that came regularly was much better than the employment roller-coaster ride they had experienced before the Nazis came to power.

To keep the workers' attention diverted while their freedoms were being whittled away, the government set up a series of programs called Strength Through Joy. These programs provided exciting vacations at prices even the lowest-paid worker could afford. Ocean cruises, ski holidays, weeks at lake resorts—all were available at incredible bargains. And the Reich discovered that these vacations, besides making the workers feel as though they were truly valued, also made them happy and rested—and therefore more productive on the job.

"The Man with the Iron Heart"

But even with $11 mountain vacations and $25 ocean cruises, not everyone in Germany was happy and content. There were many who, while they did not actively protest against Hitler and his Reich, felt strongly that the government was leading Germany down the wrong path.

Because Hitler's dictatorship depended on absolute obedience from every citizen, such critics must be silenced. That was the job of Dachau and the other concentration camps. However, before critics could be silenced, they had to be found—and that job fell to the most secret of secret police, the Gestapo.

The Gestapo differed from other police in that they did not hunt down robbers or solve crimes. Instead, their job was to destroy friendship and trust among Germans. If people learned they could trust no one—not even their families—they would have no strength to revolt against even the most brutal master.

As historian Albert Marrin writes,

> The Gestapo tried to sow suspicion, to build walls of distrust between people. It blanketed the country with thousands of agents and informers. Gestapo men impersonated Roman Catholic priests and heard confessions in church. An informer was stationed in every street and apartment house in every German town and city. He or she could be anyone: the janitor, the maid, or store clerk, or neighbor.[78]

The Gestapo was headed by a tall, blue-eyed blond named Reinhard Heydrich. He was so ruthless and cold that even the SS members were terrified of him, calling him the "Blond Beast." Hitler was proud of Heydrich and invented his own nickname for the Gestapo chief— "The Man with the Iron Heart." Heydrich earned both nicknames.

Spies, Jokes, and "The German Look"

Heydrich hired and trained more than 100,000 part-time informants whose job was to write down the name of anyone who made a critical remark about the government or the führer. The remark might have been casual, or even a joke, but if one of Heydrich's informers heard it, the consequences were terrible.

One man, a concert pianist, commented to a friend before a concert that he thought the Nazis might be losing a little support in Germany. The remark was overheard and reported to the Gestapo. As the pianist left the stage after his concert, he was seized by three Gestapo agents and taken away for questioning. By the next morning he was on his way to a concentration camp.

Even innocent jokes about the Nazis were considered crimes against the state. One teenager who repeated a joke he had heard about Goebbels to a group of friends was overheard and beaten bloody by Gestapo agents. Jokes about the führer were even less funny to the Reich—they were punishable by death. It is no wonder Germans began using what came to be known as "the German look," a sideways glance over their shoulders before speaking to see if anyone was eavesdropping.

Interestingly, the cold-hearted efficiency of Heydrich and his Gestapo was sometimes used by the German people for their own purposes. One woman turned in her good-for-nothing husband to the Gestapo for making fun of Hitler's mustache, although the poor fellow had done nothing of the sort. The man was quickly on his way to Dachau the next day.

In another instance, a woman was shocked when Gestapo agents visited her home and accused her of misusing her radio, listening to such forbidden things as African-American jazz or news programs critical of Germany on foreign radio stations. As it turned out, the man who had reported her was a next-door neighbor who was angry because she disturbed his afternoon nap by cleaning her carpets.

A Storm Trooper stands guard outside a Jewish business to make sure that no Aryan German violated the boycott announced by the sign.

Stepping Up the Terror

But there was another group of people within Germany whose identification did not require the Gestapo or paid informants. These were the Jews, the people Hitler classified as the greatest enemies of the state. And because anti-Semitism had always played a key role in Hitler's politics, it was hardly surprising that once he came to power he increased the mistreatment and terror towards them.

The point Hitler continued to hammer home in his speeches was the importance of building a strong Germany, a strong Aryan race. To accomplish this, he said, it was necessary to weed out the inferior parts of the species. The mentally retarded, the blind, the physically impaired, homosexuals—all were considered "vermin" that had to be eliminated if Germany were to be truly strong. But of all of these "vermin," he said, the Jew was the worst.

> "He [the Jew] stops at nothing," wrote Hitler in *Mein Kampf,* and in his vileness he becomes so gigantic that no one need be surprised if among our people the personification of the devil as the symbol of all evil assumes the living shape of the Jew. . . . It is our duty to arouse, to whip up, and to incite in our people the instinctive repugnance of the Jews.[79]

One might have thought, from the energy Hitler and the Nazis spent vilifying Jews in Germany, that they were a real threat to the Reich. However, Jews were possibly the weakest enemy Hitler could have singled out for his hatred. They were not a sovereign people; they had no central organization that could fight back against

Nazi oppression. They carried no political weight at all. In addition, they were a widely diverse group ranging from wealthy to poor, from conservative to liberal.

Even so, in the Reich's view, Jews were a major obstacle to achieving the grand goal of German supremacy. And as Hitler's influence and power grew in Germany, Jews were singled out for terror. SS and SA thugs accosted Jews on the street and beat them, Jewish shops and businesses were vandalized, and everywhere the signs *Juden verrcke* (Jews perish) were erected. By the middle of 1934, about 7 percent of the nation's Jews had left Germany for other places they hoped would be safer.

A Nazi newspaper vilifies Jewish authors and publishers as pigs. Ridiculed authors included Thomas Mann and Albert Einstein.

"No Jews or Dogs"

In dealing with the 93 percent of Germany's Jews who remained, Hitler leaned heavily on his Minister of Public Enlightenment and Propaganda, Joseph Goebbels. By providing a steady barrage of propaganda, Goebbels was able to keep anti-Semitism in the front of people's minds. The fact that the propaganda was nothing but lies did not matter one bit. Goebbels knew that if a lie was repeated often enough, it would stick.

And so he erected billboards everywhere throughout Germany's cities, reminding people about "Germany's Common Enemy—The Jew." Parks had signs such as "No Jews or Dogs Allowed." Goebbels fabricated press reports of horrible crimes Jews supposedly committed—ritual murders

(Below) Anti-Jewish demonstrators painted the word "Jew" on the windows of this Berlin shop.

A Friend to Animals

Hitler, the man who put millions of innocent people to death, was far more kindhearted to animals, as biographer Robert Payne explains in his book The Life and Death of Adolf Hitler.

"Hans Baur, the pilot, remembered occasions when Hitler saw films given to him by a friendly Maharaja. During the scenes showing men being savagely torn to pieces by animals, he remained calm and alert. When the films showed animals being hunted, he would cover his eyes with his hands and ask to be told when it was all over. Whenever he saw a wounded animal, he wept. He hated people who engaged in blood sports, and several times he said it would give him the greatest pleasure to murder anyone who killed an animal. He had a deep affection for all dumb creatures, but very little for men and women."

and raping little girls. A widely circulated report described a group of Jews who were killing Christian children and drinking their blood.

Schools were fertile breeding grounds for such propaganda, and Goebbels and his staff used every opportunity to teach children that anti-Semitism was not only permitted, but strongly encouraged. Nazi teachers taught first-graders that it was their duty, whenever they saw Jews, to spit on them.

Clara Feldman was a little girl in a small German town at the beginning of Hitler's Reich. She remembers how her teacher singled her out one day. "The first day he came in, he said, 'I understand we have a Jew pig in our classroom.' Then he said, 'Now we will see how much pain a Jewish pig can endure.' He had me put out my hand, and he hit me with a stick. I don't know how many times he hit me. I don't remember the pain. But I do remember the laughter of the other children."[80]

Sometimes the abuse from Nazi teachers was not physical, but emotional. Hanns Herz was a high school student when Hitler came to power. He had vivid memories of his swimming class, taught by a Nazi. "The first day," Herz remembers, "we had to put on our bathing trunks and stand alongside the pool. When we were all lined up, he said, 'Herz, step forward. And you stay there. We won't go into the pool with a half-Jew.' From then on I spent swimming class, two hours every week, standing at the edge of the pool in my trunks."[81]

Not only were teachers encouraged to show hatred toward Jewish children, but schoolbooks and lessons were geared toward anti-Semitism. One primer for beginning readers was entitled *Trust No Fox in the Green Meadow and No Jew on His Oath.* The bright, colorful pictures showed Jewish children being expelled from school as blond German children jeered at them. The pictures were vicious caricatures—

A German school book depicts an Aryan German as strong and beautiful and a Jew as fat and ugly. Schoolchildren in Nazi Germany were taught early to despise Jews.

each Jewish person was fat and ugly, with a large nose and a hideous, drooling mouth. Another popular book for young children was called *The Poisonous Mushroom* and warned children of the dangers of associating with Jews.

Judenrein

As the months passed, anti-Semitism increased, and not just in large cities like Berlin and Munich. Eager to gain the approval of the führer, officials in little villages and towns throughout Germany tried to make life as difficult as possible for their Jewish residents. Their message was: You are worthless. You are unwelcome. If these officials succeeded, their towns would achieve the rank of *Judenrein,* "cleansed of Jews."

Sometimes the message was violent—a brick through a window, a child beaten on the way to school. Often, however, the anti-Semitic message was communicated not in actions, but in nonactions. In many

German citizens read anti-Semitic literature posted outside a Nazi newspaper office.

towns, for example, Jews were refused service in restaurants and could not purchase milk for their children in dairies. Drug stores would not sell them medicine.

Historian William Shirer recalls that some of the ugliest messages of anti-Semitism were found on signs near small towns. He remembers driving along a particularly dangerous stretch of road, along which a sign offered two very different sets of advice, depending on whether a driver was Jew or Gentile: "Drive Carefully! Sharp Curve! Jews 75 miles per hour!"[82] It seemed to make no difference how the message of anti-Semitism was delivered—it was loud and clear. Jews were worthless. Jews were unwelcome.

Nuremberg Laws

Looking back, it might seem foolish for the many thousands of Jews in Germany to have remained in a place where they were unwanted. Why didn't more of them leave?

The answer, apparently, was that few people believed the terror would last. One man who lived in Bavaria told his son to be patient, that the frightening time would not last long. "He told me that the German people would not tolerate the actions of the bullies," remembers Aaron Meier, "and that if we held on, life would return to normal soon."[83]

But life for Gemany's Jews continued to worsen. At a large Nazi rally in Nuremberg in 1935, Hitler introduced two new laws to deal with what he called "the Jewish problem." The first was known as the "Citizenship Law"; the second was called "Protection of German Blood and German Honor." To the Jews, both laws were a sharp tightening of the screws.

The Nuremberg Laws stripped the Jews of all the rights of citizenship. They were no longer German citizens, they were aliens in a foreign land. Jews could not attend German schools, use public transportation, or own telephones. Jewish doctors, lawyers, teachers, writers, and other professionals could not work.

Jews could own automobiles, but they had to have special "Jew numbers" for their license plates. German Jews were required to wear a yellow Star of David, identifying them to the Gestapo. They were also required to change their names—men had to add *Israel* to their first names, and women had to add *Sara* to theirs. It was against the law for any Jew to fly the German flag.

Thousands of Nazi troops gather at a rally in 1935 Nuremberg where Hitler announced laws stripping Jews of their citizenship and forcing their separation from Aryans.

Jews in Nazi Germany had to wear yellow Stars of David on their clothes to identify them as Jews.

Those who broke the laws were shot, or beaten, or publicly humiliated. One young woman whose boyfriend was Jewish was forced to stand on the street with a large sign around her neck stating, "I am a swine that can only have relations with Jews." An elderly Jewish man who had lost his Star of David was forced by SS officers to get down on his hands and knees and pick up thousands of shards of broken glass—with his teeth.

With its new system of hate and abuse written into law, the Reich was striving for a Germany that was *Judenrein*. And contrary to what the Jewish father had told his son, the terror would not end soon. The real horror had not even begun.

Chapter

6 Testing the Waters

As Hitler intensified his persecution of the Jews and other "enemies of the state," he also formulated a foreign-policy plan. It should have surprised no one that it was an aggressive, warlike policy, for he had laid out his ideas for Germany's world domination years before in *Mein Kampf*. "Those who want to fight, let them fight," he wrote, "and those who do not want to fight . . . do not deserve to live."[84]

Germany needed to fight, Hitler explained, because it had been cheated out of territory by the Treaty of Versailles.

Hitler speaks to thousands at a rally. His propaganda, effective in his conquest of Germany, now turned to world conquest.

Lands where German people lived were no longer under the German flag, and that was, he said, "a vicious, brutal crime." Hitler had other reasons why Germany needed to expand her borders, and the most important was the notion of *Lebensraum*, or "living space."

The idea sounded logical enough—simply put, that every group of people needs ample space to be self-sufficient. A nation of people—known to Hitler as the *Volk*—needed enough land to grow its own food and to gather the raw materials needed for a decent life. And because the *Volk* in this case were a superior race of Aryans—"a superrace," as Hitler called them—they needed plenty of *Lebensraum* in which to expand.

Hitler had definite ideas, too, about where this living space should be. While some nations looked overseas to expand their empires, Germany, he felt, needed only to look east, to Poland and Russia. This huge territory, with its vast resources, would be perfect for the expanding Aryan people. Besides, he thought, the Slavs who lived there were an inferior race and deserved to be conquered.

But lands could not be conquered without armies and weapons, and the Treaty of Versailles had very firmly limited Germany's military. With its allotted force

of no more than 100,000 men, and tight controls on weapons, Germany was in no position to expand its borders.

So in 1934 Hitler called his military leaders together and told them that Germany would need a larger army and more weapons in its arsenal. And because he did not wish to anger the Allied nations, Hitler announced that this military rearmament must be secret.

Rearming in Secret

It took only a few months to more than double the size of Germany's army. Hitler passed a new law that reduced the length of a soldier's active service from twelve years to one—but after serving that year, the soldier was placed on reserve duty. So, even though the official tally of those on active duty remained at 100,000—the level acceptable under the Treaty of Versailles—Germany actually had a continually growing pool of trained soldiers, ready to fight. In addition, army officers began to train police and some SS units in combat skills, adding another 300,000 unofficial soldiers to the pool.

Hitler also knew he would need a skilled air force, so he put his assistant, Hermann Göring, a World War I aviation hero, in charge. To keep his actions secret from Allied inspection teams, Göring trained his pilots under the guise of glider clubs and civilian airlines. He also saw to it that Germany's top engineers were kept busy designing new kinds of warplanes.

For his massive rearmament, Hitler counted on the help of wealthy German industrialists. Many were delighted with Hitler's plans for a military buildup, for both political and financial reasons. One of

Hermann Göring, Hitler's SA leader, was assigned the task of secretly building Germany's air force.

the most helpful was the famous steel and munitions maker Gustav Krupp. A strong nationalist, Krupp did not need to be encouraged to resume making weapons; he had long been interested in rearming Germany.

If ever there should be a resurrection for Germany, if ever she were to shake off the chains of Versailles, then [we] would have to be prepared. The machines were demolished; the tools were destroyed; but one thing remained—the men, the men at the drawing boards and in the

Secret Rearmament

Gustav Krupp wasted no time after World War I rearming Germany, even though it was strictly forbidden by the Treaty of Versailles. Because his activity was illegal, he had to keep it secret, as the writers of Fists of Steel *point out.*

"The team [of Krupp military designers] carefully maintained secrecy; even though the treaty did not ban design work, Krupp and his fellow rearmament planners feared a violent Allied reaction should their undertaking become public. In their offices on the tenth floor of 4 Potsdamer Platz, Krupp's designers operated in the guise of a fictitious machine-tool company named Koch and Kinzle. Neither the other tenants in the building nor members of the nearby Reichstag nor even the men's wives had any idea what they were up to. 'Nobody noticed us, nobody bothered us, nobody even knocked on our door,' remarked Fritz Tubbesing, one of the designers. 'There we were, practically on top of the Reichstag, and they didn't know it.'

[Krupp] glorified in code names, covers, and other trappings of secrecy. He loved duping 'snoopers' from the Control Commission and the foreign press. He could even laugh at the rumors making the round. One story had it that the baby carriages Krupp produced could be taken apart and reassembled as machine guns. Another myth held that Krupp had preserved one of his Long Max cannons . . . by propping it upright and camouflaging it with brick so that the gun resembled a factory chimney."

workshops. . . . Their skill would have to be saved, their immense resources of knowledge and experience.[85]

Krupp got around the treaty by taking advantage of loopholes in its wording. For instance, although the Allies had forbidden building weapons, they had not prohibited designing them. So while German engineers designed new, improved submarines, for example, Krupp had his plants in other parts of the world build them for other governments—Turkey, Finland, the Netherlands, Spain. In return, German crews were allowed to make trial runs in the new submarines, gaining valuable experience that would pay off when the time for war approached.

German industrialist Gustav Krupp's international steel and armaments business forwarded the Nazi imperialistic goals.

But most German soldiers had to settle for training with make-believe weapons. No tanks or antiaircraft guns were allowed by Versailles, so for training exercises they were built of cardboard or wood. A car draped in a large sheet, for instance, might represent a tank, and "so-called enemy aircraft were occasionally represented by toy balloons, while an individual soldier might display a placard that proclaimed 'I am a platoon,' or 'This is a machine-gun nest of eight men.'"[86]

Aggression, and a Promise to the World

To the Germans, one of the most irritating terms of the Treaty of Versailles concerned the Rhineland, a valuable industrial area of Germany that bordered France. The Allies had dictated that the Rhineland could not be occupied by Germany; it had to remain a buffer zone between Germany and France.

In early 1936 Hitler announced to his military staff that he wanted the Rhineland back. His generals urged him to wait, telling him that the Reich was not ready for war, that its army and stockpile of weapons could not win against the established armies of the Allies. Hitler ignored their protests and ordered his troops to seize the Rhineland on March 7, 1936.

When the troops marched into the area, Hitler publicly announced that Germany's intentions were not warlike. "We pledge that now, more than ever, we shall strive for an understanding between the European peoples. . . . We have no territorial demands to make in Europe! . . . Germany will never break the peace."[87]

Hitler and his advisors waited to see how the Allies would react. The German invasion of the Rhineland was a direct violation of the treaty—what would the Allies do?

The answer, to the relief of Hitler's military staff, was nothing. Neither France nor Britain wished to go to war over the Rhineland—although Poland, whose leaders did not trust Germany, offered to assist if France did go to war with Hitler. But the horrors of World War I remained vivid in the minds of the European Allies. They recalled all too clearly the millions of dead in the bloody trenches that had snaked across Europe, the enormous expense to their countries. They had no wish to take up arms over a piece of land they cared nothing about. So, although French and British leaders grumbled publicly about Germany's violations of the treaty, they did nothing.

Reich Pet Tricks

There seemed to be no limits to the things loyal Nazis would do to show their adoration of Adolf Hitler. As Richard Grunberger writes in The 12-Year Reich, *there was even said to be a baroness who owned a talking dog who loved Hitler, too.*

"The Baroness prompted my husband to put a difficult question to the dog. My husband asked, 'Who is Adolf Hitler?' We were deeply moved to hear the answer, 'My Führer,' out of the mouth of this creature. At this point, the lecturer was interrupted by an old Party comrade in the audience who shouted, 'This is in abominably bad taste. You are misusing the Führer's name.' To which the lecturer—on the verge of tears—replied, 'This clever animal knows that Adolf Hitler has caused laws to be passed against vivisection and the Jews' ritual slaughter of animals, and out of gratitude his small canine brain recognized Adolf Hitler as *his Führer.*'"

Hitler's gamble had paid off. He admitted later that had France and Britain marched into the Rhineland to fight, Germany would have been beaten easily. "We would have had to withdraw with our tail between our legs," he said. "A retreat on our part would have spelled collapse."[88]

Without Firing a Shot

Having flown his test balloon in the Rhineland, and drawn no unfavorable response, Hitler was eager to have his armies turn to the matter of *Lebensraum* for the German people. He looked east to Austria. In a 1935 speech he had announced, "Germany neither intends nor wishes to interfere in the internal affairs of Austria, to annex Austria or to conclude an *Anschluss* [unification]."[89] And the following year, he

had signed a treaty with Austria, promising the same thing.

But the majority of Austria's people were German, and Hitler strongly favored the unification of all German people—no matter that he had signed the treaty and given his word. In 1937, Hitler announced to his generals that the next military target was Austria.

Austria had a large contingent of Nazis, supported and financed by the German government. The Austrian Nazis had behaved in much the same way as their German counterparts; there had been hundreds of street brawls and violent demonstrations against the democratic government. The chancellor, Kurt von Schuschnigg, strongly opposed the Nazi movement and had arrested and jailed some of its most important leaders.

But Schuschnigg was no match for the führer himself. In a meeting at Hitler's re-

SS troops begin the roundup of Jews in Vienna almost immediately after taking over Austria.

only unopposed, but warmly welcomed by thousands of Austrians who genuinely wanted union with Germany."[90]

However, there were losers in the annexation of Austria. Schuschnigg and other leaders of the republic were arrested and degraded as enemies of what was now called "Greater Germany." Schuschnigg was forced to clean the quarters, slop buckets, toilets, and washbasins of the SS guards. From chancellor to menial slave, Schuschnigg had fallen very far in only a few days.

The Jews of Austria, too, were victims of Hitler's takeover. Within a few days of the German army's triumphant arrival in Vienna, the SS and Gestapo began what Shirer describes as an "orgy of sadism."[91] Tens of thousands of Jews were jailed or sent to concentration camps—for no offense other than being Jewish. Other remained "free" but were treated in demeaning ways by their Nazi overlords. Some were forced to crawl on the ground and bark like dogs, or to run in circles until they became sick.

treat, the Austrian chancellor was given an ultimatum—he must lift the ban on Nazi activities and stop arresting its agents, or the German army would march against Austria that very day. Schuschnigg, fearing the bloodshed that would result, sadly agreed to Hitler's terms. On March 12 the German army streamed across the border, a parade of armored trucks and jeeps "not

Nazi troops march through the streets of Vienna, hailed with the Nazi salute by welcoming Austrians.

One woman remembers vividly how crowds of onlookers would gather and laugh. "As my father went to open his grocery store," she says, "the SA gave him a toothbrush and ordered him to scrub the street. Some of his non-Jewish customers came by, and when they saw my father there, they laughed and jeered. These were customers of long standing," she says sadly. "He considered them to be his friends."[92]

Becoming Bolder

So without firing a shot or spilling a drop of German blood, the Reich annexed Austria, adding 7 million people to Greater Germany. France was in the midst of internal political struggles, and Britain was unwilling to press the issue alone, so the Allies again failed to take a stand against the invasion. Hitler had scored another easy victory and was becoming bolder by the day.

His next target was Czechoslovakia, and it did not take a military strategist to see why. With Austria now part of Germany, the Reich had Czechoslovakia surrounded on three sides. Hitler demanded that the German-speaking section called Sudetenland, a small area on the western border of Czechoslovakia, become part of Germany.

The Czech government was a democracy that was very much against Hitler's demands. Besides, the Czechs had signed treaties with both France and Russia; those nations had pledged to defend Czechoslovakia against any attack. With such powerful allies, the Czechs thought they had little to worry about.

Hitler's generals agreed. They feared that their führer was going too far, that despite his success in the Rhineland and Austria, Czechoslovakia could prove disastrous. But every time they cautioned him, he flew into a rage, screaming that they were fainthearted and of no use to him.

This map shows the territory Germany annexed in the late 1930s before World War II was declared.

War Crocodiles

After successfully invading France, the Nazis tackled the problem of landing their navy ships on British shores. One engineer had an idea that intrigued Hitler, according to Payne's The Life and Death of Adolf Hitler.

"[The engineer] proposed that England be invaded by submarine barges made of concrete, which would crawl along the seabed. These barges, about ninety feet long, could each carry 200 men fully armed with all their equipment, or two tanks, or three or four pieces of artillery. He emphasized the element of surprise: the English would be terrified by the sudden appearances of hundreds of concrete submarines on their shores. Hitler was fascinated by the idea of these 'war crocodiles' and ordered a full inquiry into their practicability by his naval staff. Nothing came of the idea, but for some weeks it was earnestly discussed by the high command."

Some of his generals, angered that Hitler was taking over their territory of military strategy, even went so far as discussing how the führer could be overthrown before he could ruin Germany. They secretly sent a representative to London to meet with a member of the British cabinet, telling him Hitler's exact plans for conquering Czechoslovakia. If only Britain and France could make a public promise to intervene on behalf of Czechoslovakia, pleaded the representative, Hitler would surely back down.

"How Horrible, Fantastic, Incredible"

But high officials in the British government shrugged the warning off. According to one historian, it was "heavily discounted as propaganda from a group of 'outs' against the 'ins.' Thus, at the moment that the German generals needed a real commitment from England, they did not get it."[93]

British prime minister Neville Chamberlain came to Germany to meet with Hitler, and the führer assured him that he only wanted the Sudetenland, nothing more. Hitler also fabricated stories about how the Czechs were persecuting and mistreating the Germans in the Sudetenland, and said that he, as leader of the German Reich, wanted better treatment for those Germans. Yes, Hitler told Chamberlain, he was willing to fight to achieve that goal.

Hitler did a great deal of bluffing in his dealings with Chamberlain, giving the impression that his army was more than ready for a large war. "The British will recoil from confrontation," Hitler told his staff, "as long as the Germans show no signs of weakness."[94] He wanted Chamberlain to

A sullen Neville Chamberlain, Britain's prime minister (center), meets with an equally surly Adolf Hitler in 1938. Neville Henderson, Britain's ambassador to Germany, stands at left.

get an exaggerated impression of how powerful his military was. "All along the route," writes Edwin Hoyt, "Hitler managed to have troop trains passing on the opposite track."[95] In another case, Germany's most modern warplanes were moved from airfield to airfield so that Chamberlain would think there were thousands, rather than just over one hundred.

Hitler would not call off his invasion, and told Chamberlain so. The British prime minister was angered by Hitler's demands, but could see no way out of the dilemma. Neither Britain nor France was ready for war, but Germany would not

back down, and Czechoslovakia refused to have its territory dismantled. War seemed likely. An unhappy Chamberlain reported in a radio speech to the nation, "How horrible, fantastic, incredible it is that we should be digging trenches . . . here because of a quarrel in a faraway country between people of whom we know nothing."[96]

But it seemed not to matter how incredible the situation was, or how frightening the possibilities. Germany seemed bent on aggression, and for the worried Allies, the chances for keeping the peace seemed very slim indeed.

7 The Reich at War

By the early autumn of 1938 keeping the peace seemed an almost impossible task. Hitler was determined to invade Czechoslovakia, and the Allies knew that if he did, they could no longer ignore Germany's aggression. There was one chance left to negotiate peace, and the Allied leaders seized it.

The Failure of Appeasement

Chamberlain set up a meeting in Munich with Italy's dictator, Benito Mussolini, French premier Edouard Daladier, and Hitler. Surely something could be worked out to push Europe back from the brink of war?

Interestingly, the Czechs were not even invited to participate; evidently, appeasing Hitler was the meeting's primary goal. The participants did not need to talk for long. They offered to avoid war by giving Hitler the Sudetenland, and he gladly accepted. In return for this prize, Hitler promised solemnly that he had no further territorial demands. There would be, he said, peace in Europe.

Chamberlain and the other Allies were ecstatic. "I believe," he crowed as he waved the paper known as the Munich Agreement, "it is peace for our time!"[97]

Smiles abound at the 1938 peace conference in Munich. British prime minister Chamberlain (front right) shakes hands with Italian dictator Mussolini as other dignitaries, including Göring (far left) and Hitler (next to Göring) watch.

The Czechs, of course, were furious. They claimed they had been betrayed by the Allies, and they felt the treaties they had signed with the Allies were nothing but a sham. The Czech president, Emil Hacha, warned Britain and France that it would be only a matter of time before Hitler took the rest of Czechoslovakia.

Hacha did not have long to wait. In March 1939 Hitler broke the Munich Agreement and, in an emergency conference in Berlin, informed Hacha that he intended to invade Czechoslovakia. Would the Czech nation fight and risk thousands of unnecessary deaths? Or would Hacha sign the necessary papers and allow the German army to come into Czechoslovakia peacefully?

Hacha eventually signed, but witnesses say that both Hacha and his foreign minis-

Soviet leader Joseph Stalin signed a pact with Germany in 1939 agreeing to share Poland after Hitler invaded it.

ter "sat as though turned to stone. Only their eyes showed that they were alive."[98]

The Allies realized that they had made a terrible, costly mistake. There was no "peace for our time," as Chamberlain had exuberantly proclaimed. There was only the sound of German soldiers, marching into Czechoslovakia. Before the year was out, they would also be marching into Poland, sending the whole world over the abyss into war.

An Alliance with Stalin

Hitler planned to move into Poland, but he was nervous. The Soviet Union loomed threateningly to Poland's east. To attack Poland would be risky—unless Hitler had assurances that Joseph Stalin, the Soviet Union's Communist dictator, would not move to protect the Poles.

So Hitler persuaded Stalin to enter into a nonaggression pact with Germany. Although neither man liked or trusted the other (their politics were as far apart as they could possibly be), the treaty suited them both. Hitler informed Stalin about his plans to invade Poland. In addition to pledging nonaggression toward each other, they secretly agreed to divide Poland between them.

The Nazi-Soviet Pact, as it was called, was signed on August 23, 1939. Eight days later, at 4:45 A.M. the German army invaded. All along the 1,750-mile Polish frontier, German tanks and armed divisions had gathered, and with the go-ahead from Hitler, the Reich's army showed the stunned Poles a new, lightning-fast kind of war.

Blitzkrieg

The Germans, like the Allies, remembered the slow, bloody conflicts of World War I, during which both armies were entrenched in mud, fighting for months over a few yards of territory. Hitler and his generals were determined to find a better way of waging war. They believed the answer was the blitzkrieg, or lightning war. The idea behind the blitzkrieg was to strike quickly, smashing enemies before they could prepare their defenses. The most important principle was to always keep moving.

The weapons the Nazis had developed were well suited to a lightning war. The Germans had built thousands of heavily armored tanks, called panzers, that could roll through muddy terrain. They had developed strange

After a devastating blitzkrieg that left the Poles stunned, German troops controlled Poland within two weeks.

"We Could Do Nothing"

Rafael Loc was a Polish lieutenant in 1939 when the German army invaded Poland. In an interview years later in Time *magazine, he recalled the opening moments of the invasion.*

"The stillness was shattered by the howling and screeching and booming of German bombers and artillery. . . . We could do nothing. We had no antiaircraft guns. We had nothing to return fire at their long-range artillery. Two hours after it began we were panic stricken, and our entire battalion jumped out of the trenches and ran toward our regimental headquarters.

Only half the battalion made it. We continued running and walking, but wherever we turned we met German artillery and tank fire. They were in back of us and in front of us. To the right was automatic fire; to the left we were shot at by artillery. One shell hit a mine 300 yards from us and set off a long line of Polish-laid mines; they exploded in domino fashion. We ran, we lay on the ground, we ran. We didn't know which way to go."

A Child's View of the Polish Invasion

Ryszard Kapuscinski was only seven when he and his family experienced firsthand the blitzkrieg of the German army in Poland. In a special World War II Remembrance issue of Time *magazine, he remembers certain frightening images.*

"I remember walking with my sister next to a horse-drawn cart. High up on the hay my grandfather was lying on a linen sheet. He was paralyzed. When the air raid started, the whole patiently marching crowd was suddenly filled with panic. People sought safety in ditches, in bushes, in the potato fields. On the now empty road there was only the cart on which my grandfather was lying. He could see planes coming at him, how suddenly they dived down. When the planes disappeared, we returned to the cart and my mother wiped the sweat off Grandfather's face. After each raid sweat rolled down Grandfather's tired, emaciated face.

We encountered the corpses of horses everywhere. Poor horses, big defenseless animals that don't know how to hide. They stand motionless, waiting for death. It was always the corpses of horses—black, bay, pied, chestnut—lying upside down with the legs pointing into the air, their hooves admonishing the world. It was as if it were a war not between people but between horses, as if they were the only victims of the strife."

new planes, called Stukas, to divebomb roads and railroad lines. The Stukas were equipped with screaming devices that terrified people on the ground. As one historian writes,

The world had not seen anything like this: tanks lunging 40 miles a day, self-propelled guns keeping right up with them. The army of 1.5 million men was almost completely motorized, moving according to orders by radio, telephone, and telegraph, orders transmitted with what had to seem to the Poles to be lightning speed.[99]

Although the Polish army was large, its weapons were hopelessly outdated. In some cases, the best the Poles could do was to take up lances and charge the huge tanks on horseback, a bloody scene that one writer describes as "medieval knights lost in a time warp."[100]

Success for the German army took less than two weeks. Although the Poles fought bravely, they had no chance. As Robert Payne writes, "It was as easy as cutting the throat of a child."[101] The final punch was delivered by the Soviet army attacking from the east. Two days later, Poland fell.

The Phony War

Like the carcass of an animal, Poland was divided between the victors. The eastern third of Poland went to the Soviets, and the remaining territory, including Warsaw, the capital, increased the size of the German Reich.

But what about Poland's allies? France and Britain, this time honoring their alliances, had declared war on Germany immediately after Hitler's attack. However, there was really nothing they could do to help the Poles. To help the Polish army, the Allies would have had to cross Germany, which was impossible with their limited weapons and armies. Although they were officially at war, until they could get close enough to their enemy to fight, they could do nothing.

After the blitzkrieg against Poland, the armies of France and Britain continued to wait along the border between France and Germany. They waged no offensives, instead hiding behind the Maginot Line, a concrete and steel fortress the French had built along the border after World War I. As the German troops returned from their battles in Poland, they gathered opposite the Allies, on German soil, in a similar fortress called the Siegfried Line.

The two armies sat, poised and ready, but nothing happened. Civilians in Germany, France, and England waited nervously. Weren't their nations at war? All the signs of war were evident—the food rationing, the shortages of fuel and other materials, even the blacking out of city lights at night. But who was fighting? When would the bombing begin? People in Germany began joking about the *sitzkrieg*—the "sit-down war." Journalists in the West started referring to it as the Phony War.

Various reasons prevented the enemies from fighting. France and Britain were not yet prepared for war, both nations believing they were better off huddled behind fortifications than attacking the German forces. And the winter of 1939–40 was one of the worst anyone could recall. The cold rains and strong, icy winds would have made any military maneuvers difficult.

On the German side, differences of opinion between the führer and his generals caused delays. Most of his military aides were very much opposed to Hitler's plan to attack Belgium and the Netherlands. For one thing, the generals said, the German people were not willing to go to war. Although enthusiastic about the military actions thus far, the generals argued, the people would not support a war with the neutral nations. As one general wrote in a memorandum to Hitler, the world would surely turn against Germany, "which for the second time within 25 years assaults neutral Belgium! Germany, whose government solemnly vouched for and promised the preservation of and respect for this neutrality only a few weeks ago!"[102]

While Hitler fumed at his military staff, and the Allies tried to hasten their preparations for war, and the cold European winter raged , the sit-down war continued.

Storming Through Europe

The wait was not a long one, however. In April 1940 the German army continued their blitzkrieg, this time crushing Denmark and Norway. Soon after that, ignoring the protests of his generals, Hitler stormed across Belgium, Luxembourg, and the Netherlands, and then marched into France.

The Allied forces, though better prepared than they had been during the winter, were still no match for the Germans' lightning-fast attacks. By skirting north around the Maginot Line and surprising the French and British forces, the Germans drove the Allies backward, pounding at them from the sky and from the land. The Allies were finally backed up to Dunkirk, on the French coast on the English Channel. Only a heroic evacuation of more than 330,000 troops across the Channel to England allowed the army to survive. They had retreated—but they had also survived to fight another day.

With the Allied army in retreat, it did not take long for the German army to overrun France. The surrender of France on June 22, 1940, was especially sweet for Hitler, who despised the French for their major role in the Treaty of Versailles. There is even a very famous photograph of Hitler doing a little two-step in pleasure, as his aides look on. It is one of the rare photographs of the führer smiling.

A German newsreel photographer films Hitler and his officers in Paris after Germany's successful invasion of France in 1940.

Hitler dances a jig upon hearing of France's surrender to Germany.

After the fall of France, Hitler was certain that Britain would be eager to negotiate a peace settlement. After all, Britain would be fighting alone and seemed no match for the German army. Hitler sent envoys to Britain with messages that he would consider proposals for peace—and would deal with the British less harshly if they surrendered immediately.

He was furious when he received a rebuke from Winston Churchill, the new prime minister. Britain would not surrender; Britain would fight. "Since England, in spite of her hopeless military situation, shows no signs of being ready to come to an understanding," Hitler wrote soon afterwards, "I have decided to prepare a landing operation against England and, if necessary, to carry it out. . . . The aim of this operation will be to eliminate the English

homeland as a base for the prosecution of the war against Germany."[103]

In August 1940 Hitler ordered Hermann Göring to begin a bombing campaign against the British. According to Hitler's plans, called Operation Sea Lion, the merciless bombing of Britain's airfields would remove the threat of the nation's mighty air force. Then, without having to fear British warplanes, the German navy could deliver the German army to the English shore, and the invasion would begin. Göring boasted to Hitler that in four weeks the British Royal Air Force (RAF) would be wiped from the skies. But the results were far different, for the British handed Hitler his first defeat since he began his show of force in the Rhineland.

At first Göring and his air force went after only military targets. Sometimes flying more than 1,000 missions a day, the German air force bombed British airfields, factories, and radar stations. But the bombardment was not as easy as Göring had boasted it would be. The RAF pilots were highly skilled and were helped by radar, a

British prime minister Winston Churchill defied Hitler's proposal to surrender peaceably to the Nazis.

new technology with which the Germans were not yet familiar.

Göring changed his strategy in early September 1940. Frantic because of the heavy losses his air force was suffering at the hands of the RAF, he diverted German bombers from the military targets. Instead, the bombers began flying night missions, dropping their loads on the busy city of London. More than 2,000 people were killed or wounded the first night alone, as buildings and bridges caved in on unsuspecting civilians.

"Bombs began to fall," remembers Len Jones, who was a London teenager during the bombing, "and shrapnel was going along King Street, dancing off the cobbles . . . the suction and compression from the high explosive blasts just pulled and pushed you . . . you could actually feel your eyeballs being sucked out. . . . The suction was so vast, it ripped my shirt. . . . I couldn't get my breath, the smoke was like acid. . . . And these bombers just kept on and on; the whole road was moving, rising and falling."[104]

But Londoners coped, and as it turned out, Göring lost the chance of wiping out the RAF planes. He had no idea how close to total destruction the RAF had been before he ceased bombing its airfields—historians say that had he continued another few days, the British surely would have lost the air war. But by turning his attention to London, he gave workers valuable time to repair runways and airplanes. Göring's decision also backfired in another way: bombing defenseless citizens increased support for the British around the world, particularly in the United States. Even though the United States had not yet entered the war, in 1940 the American government became more involved in sending military aid and money to help the Allies.

By October, Hitler called off Operation Sea Lion. He realized that the German air force could not defeat the British, and that without air superiority, his plan of invading Britain from the sea was doomed. For the moment, the leader of the Reich decided to switch his sights from the losing battle against Britain to the pursuit of a bigger prize—one that had eluded even the mighty Napoleon.

The Attack on Russia

Hitler wanted to conquer the Soviet Union. Its vast wheat fields and unlimited supplies of oil and other minerals would be invaluable to the Reich. Besides, the sheer size of the land would be all the *Lebensraum* the German race could hope for. And what better victims for German aggression than the hated Slavic Communists—subhumans, according to the Nazis.

Again Hitler's generals were hesitant. They begged the führer to think of the alliance he had just signed with the Soviets to keep the war confined to one front, to avoid overextending his armies. But Hitler would not listen. Although he still had divisions of his army at the western front, he would switch the main force of his attack to the Soviet Union. Victory would make Germany the most powerful nation on earth.

Anyone who had read *Mein Kampf* should have found Hitler's actions predictable. In that book he had written, "We stop the endless German movement toward the south and the west of Europe and turn our gaze toward the land of the East. . . . This colossal empire in the East is ripe for dissolution, and the end of Jewish domination in Russia will also be the end of the Russian state."[105]

What did he mean by "the end of the Russian state"? Simply put, he meant the destruction of all Soviet cities and the annihilation of the nation's people. Anyone

---

"The Invasion Was Nonsense"

Hitler's Operation Sea Lion was criticized by his own generals. As quoted in William Shirer's The Rise and Fall of the Third Reich, *German general Gerd von Rundstedt voiced his concerns after the war about the failed operation.*

"The proposed invasion of England was nonsense, because adequate ships were not available. . . . We looked upon the whole thing as a sort of game because it was obvious that no invasion was possible when our navy was not in a position to cover a crossing of the Channel or carry reinforcements. Nor was the German Air Force capable of taking on these functions if the navy failed. . . . I was always very skeptical about the whole affair. . . . I have a feeling that the Führer never really wanted to invade England. He never had sufficient courage. . . . He definitely hoped that the English would make peace."

---

not killed in battle, he directed, would starve, for when the Germans began using the Soviet food supply, there would be nothing left for the Soviet people. According to Alfred Rosenberg, one of the chief Nazi planners, "We see absolutely no reason for any obligation on our part to feed also the Russian people."[106] In Rosenberg's view, millions of people would be starved in this manner. Hitler agreed with the plan, saying, "Wiping out Russia's very power to exist—that is the goal!"[107]

With this plan firmly in mind, the German army astonished the Soviets on June 22, 1941, when an army of more than 3 million burst across the border, beginning another blitzkrieg. The Soviets were so surprised, in fact, that they failed to return fire for four hours after the attack, because of long-standing orders from Stalin's generals never to fire at German soldiers. As far as the Soviets knew, they were German allies. When one soldier called Soviet military headquarters to ask for instructions as the Germans attacked, he was told, "Comrade Stalin has forbidden the opening of artillery fire against the Germans."[108]

Saved by Winter

Hitler's plan was for his armies to reach the Soviet capital of Moscow by late summer. With the fall of Moscow, which was not only the capital but also the Soviet Union's chief railroad and manufacturing center, victory would be assured.

At first it seemed as though conquering the Soviet Union would be as effortless as invading Poland had been. In the first five days, Germany's huge army advanced

Three English children sit dejectedly on a pile of rubble that was once their home. Nazi bombers had destroyed it in a raid.

more than 150 miles into Soviet territory. The Soviet people were fighting bravely, but were clearly unprepared for war with Germany. Nothing appeared to stand in the way of the Nazis' swift march into Moscow. *Life* magazine wrote in July, "This war proves once again what nearly everybody has long known: that the German army of 1941 is the greatest fighting outfit ever assembled. . . . The only remaining doubts were how much of an army the Russians would still have east of Moscow and how long they would trouble to fight there."[109]

But as had happened so often before, there were differences of opinion in the high levels of the Reich. The military experts wanted to continue their push towards Moscow, but the führer had changed his mind. He wanted his armies instead to attack Leningrad, to the north, believing that city's loss would be more devastating to the Soviets. His generals protested bitterly, but Hitler would tolerate no disobedience. Leningrad it would be.

A German soldier lobs a grenade before advancing during the Nazi invasion of Russia in 1941. Though typically devastating, the German invasion was stopped by the harsh Russian winter.

Hitler's decision to delay the capture of Moscow would prove to be a critical error. By diverting many of his divisions to the north, he gave the Soviets almost eight weeks to rally their armies and dig in for a long war. In addition, winter was fast approaching, and the Germans were ill-equipped for the brutal weather they would encounter—one of the coldest winters on record.

As the fall rains turned to mud, and the rains quickly changed to snow, the Germans found themselves in a totally new situation. Having anticipated a summer victory, the Germans had not winterized their tanks or other vehicles, and as the subzero temperatures hit, the machines sat useless in the snow. The German soldiers lacked warm gloves, hats, and coats. As Albert Marrin writes, the German soldier "wrapped his head in women's handkerchiefs, wore woolen dresses, and was glad to get a raggedy cloth coat. His feet froze in boots that fit exactly, making it impossible to wear more than one pair of socks. The flesh of gloveless hands peeled off in strips on ice-cold gun barrels and triggers."[110]

With his plans for a swift victory mired like his tanks in the Russian snow, Hitler busied himself with another problem—how to deal with the millions of unwanted people for whom the Reich had little use. Hitler's answer to this problem remains the most grisly, inhuman aspect of his Reich.

Chapter

8 A Descent into Hell

Since even before the Reich's beginning, one of Hitler's main goals had been the domination of the Aryan race over all others, especially the Jews, who he considered subhuman "vermin." And though the Nazi treatment of Jews in Germany had been harsh and abusive from the beginning, it took a sharp turn for the worse in 1938, shortly after Hitler's diplomatic victory at the Munich summit. In a sense, war was declared on German Jews.

Kristallnacht

It began with a seventeen-year-old Jewish boy, distraught over the forced deportation of his parents to Poland. The boy, a student in Paris, walked into the German embassy there and shot a minor Nazi official. The act touched off an explosion of outrage in Berlin.

Hitler, eager to teach Germany a lesson as to what would happen should a Jew dare to fight back, ordered Heydrich and Goebbels to plan the Nazis' revenge. Government officials throughout Germany were given teletyped orders to destroy all Jewish stores, businesses, homes, and synagogues. There was to be no local police interference in this pogrom, or reign of terror.

On the nights of November 9 and 10, the Nazis unleashed terrible and unprece-dented violence on the Jewish community. Homes were ransacked, Jewish men and boys were murdered, and Jewish stores were looted and burned. More than 30,000 Jewish men were arrested and sent to concentration camps. So much glass from windows littered the streets that night, that the event came to be known as *Kristallnacht,* or "the night of broken glass."

Police kept the store owners from interfering as looters scooped valuable merchandise from window displays. Although firefighters were standing by, they were not there to put out the fires started in Jewish homes and stores—only to see that the fires did not spread to nearby German stores.

Synagogues were singled out for the most vandalism. Thousands were looted and burned in the two-night pogrom. In Berlin, a rabbi was forced to stand in his synagogue and read anti-Semitic passages from *Mein Kampf* before the temple was burned. One young boy was horrified when he visited his synagogue the following afternoon. "Because it was in a house where other people lived," he remembered later, "it hadn't been burned down. But I was shocked when I saw our synagogue from the inside. The thing most sacred to all Jews, the Torah Scrolls, were rolled out all over the floor and had been peed on."[111]

Jews are arrested and searched by Nazi police. Hitler's hatred for the Jews vented itself in greater and greater violence toward them, finally leading to the Holocaust.

Goebbels, handling the touchy propaganda issue, let it be known that the actions were not planned or directed by the government. Instead, he claimed, they were spontaneous outbursts of anger from German citizens over the murder of the Nazi official in Paris.

"The Jewish Question"

The day after the pogrom stopped, Hitler had a conference with Göring. There must, he said, be a better way to get rid of the Jews in Germany. The violence of the pogroms was fine for revenge, but to the world it made Germany seem evil. The Jewish question had to be solved in a more orderly, systematic way.

Forced emigration was slow and difficult, for many countries—including Britain and the United States—had refused to increase the numbers of Jewish immigrants they would accept. At one time, Nazi officials had

begun planning a huge concentration camp on the island of Madagascar, off the eastern coast of Africa. There, under the watchful eyes of Nazi guards, Jews were to engage in mining, farming, and other industries that would benefit the Reich. But the idea seemed more and more farfetched as time went on. And still the question remained—how could Germany rid itself and the rest of Europe of the hated Jews?

The answer seemed to present itself the moment war began in 1939, after Germany invaded Poland. The eyes of the world had been focused on Germany, for people were interested in the political events happening there. A full-scale slaughter of Germany's Jews would have been both visible and repugnant to outsiders, Hitler knew. But now, behind battle lines and shut off from the eyes of the world, the German army had access to millions of Jews—about one-third of the Jewish population of Europe. They could be killed systematically—annihilated—and no one need ever know.

To Hitler, the plan seemed no more immoral than the process of evolution, the survival of the fittest. "Nature is cruel," he said in 1940. "Therefore, we, too, may be cruel. If I don't mind sending the pick of the German people into the hell of war without regret for the shedding of valuable German blood, then I have naturally the right to destroy millions of men of inferior races who increase like vermin."[112]

The answer to the "Jewish question" seemed clear. It began with hand-picking soldiers and organizing them into *Einsatzgruppen*, or "special action groups." These were mobile firing squads, whose job it was to move into an area after the army had secured it, locate all the Jews, and murder them.

Mass Executions

There were four of these special action groups, each consisting of 3,000 men. However, they were nearly always assisted willingly by local civilians, who in some areas were as anti-Semitic as the Nazis.

The victims were escorted out of each village after being told they were being relocated to another area. Men, women, and children followed, one after another, in a slow procession to a remote spot. There,

A moment before an Einsatzgruppen *soldier executes him, a Jewish man is seated at the edge of a mass grave into which many of his fellows have preceded him.*

anywhere from ten to thirty at a time were taken to the edge of a ditch or bomb crater, and told to remove all their clothing. The sharpshooters in the *Einsatzgruppen* would then shoot them in the back of the head, and the next group would step up.

An eyewitness to an execution in Poland remembers it vividly:

> The people, completely naked, went down some steps and clambered over the heads of the people lying there to the place to which the man directed them. They lay down in front of the dead or wounded people; some caressed those who were still alive and spoke to them in a low voice. Then I heard a series of shots. I looked into the pit and saw that the bodies were twitching. . . . Blood was running from their necks.[113]

The *Einsatzgruppen,* by official estimates, killed about 2 million Jews in Poland and Russia. However, that was not nearly enough for Hitler. Killing the Jews was taking far too long and was wasting ammunition badly needed by soldiers at the front. There had to be a better way.

"The Final Solution"

It was Reinhard Heydrich, "The Blond Beast," who came up with the system eventually called "the Final Solution." The Jews would be sent to a new kind of camp—not a concentration camp, in which prisoners might remain for years, but a death camp, where they would be killed in a matter of days. Large-scale murder, done predominantly by gassing, could be accomplished efficiently in these death camps. Under the watchful eye of Adolf Eichmann, head

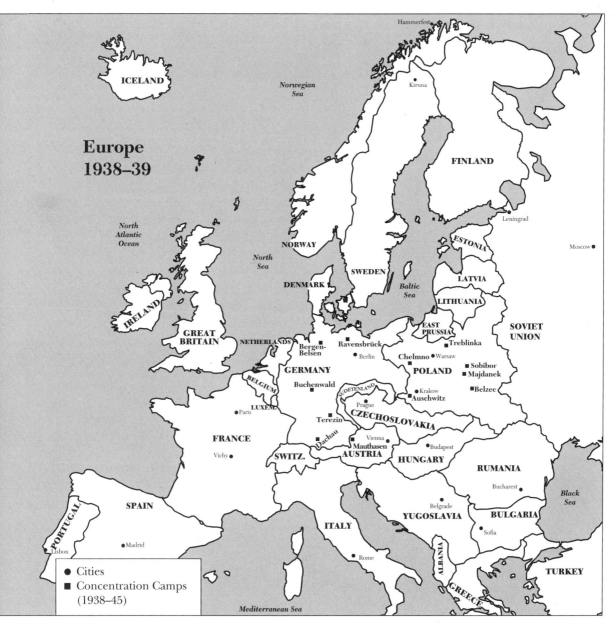

**Europe
1938–39**

ICELAND

*Norwegian
Sea*

Hammerfest

Kiruna

FINLAND

Leningrad

*North
Atlantic
Ocean*

NORWAY

*North
Sea*

SWEDEN

ESTONIA

Moscow ●

DENMARK

*Baltic
Sea*

LATVIA

LITHUANIA

IRELAND

GREAT
BRITAIN

NETHERLANDS

Bergen-
Belsen ■

Ravensbrück ■

● Berlin

Chelmno ■

EAST
PRUSSIA

● Warsaw

Treblinka ■

■ Sobibor

SOVIET
UNION

BELGIUM

GERMANY

POLAND

■ Majdanek

LUXEM.

Buchenwald ■

SUDETENLAND

● Krakow

■ Belzec

● Paris

Prague ●

Auschwitz ■

Terezin ■

CZECHOSLOVAKIA

FRANCE

Dachau ■

Vienna ●

Vichy ●

SWITZ.

Mauthasen ■

AUSTRIA

● Budapest

HUNGARY

RUMANIA

Bucharest ●

*Black
Sea*

SPAIN

PORTUGAL

Lisbon

● Madrid

ITALY

YUGOSLAVIA

Belgrade ●

BULGARIA

Sofia ●

Rome ●

ALBANIA

TURKEY

GREECE

Mediterranean Sea

● Cities
■ Concentration Camps
(1938–45)

*The Nazis operated more than a dozen death camps in Germany and Poland.
The names of some—Auschwitz, Buchenwald, Treblinka—live on in infamy.*

of the SS Department of Jewish Affairs, Jews from every part of Europe would be gathered into holding areas until they could be shipped to these camps and exterminated.

Heydrich and other Nazi officials agreed that the death camps should be located in eastern Europe, far from the eyes of German citizens who might be offended at death on such a gigantic scale. They also

"No Complaint or Plea for Mercy"

A German civilian happened to be on the scene when the Jewish population of a town in the Ukraine was shot by the Einsatzgruppen. *His testimony of what he saw after the Jews were ordered to undress and stand near an open pit is recorded in Milton Meltzer's* Never to Forget: The Jews of the Holocaust.

"During the fifteen minutes that I stood near the pit, I heard no complaint or plea for mercy. I watched a family of about eight persons, a man and woman, both about fifty, with their children of about one, eight, and ten, and two grown-up daughters of about twenty and twenty-four. An old woman with snow-white hair was holding the one-year-old child in her arms and singing to it and tickling it. The child was cooing with delight. The couple were looking on with tears in their eyes. The father was holding the hand of a boy about ten years old and speaking to him softly; the boy was fighting his tears. The father pointed toward the sky, stroked his head, and seemed to explain something to him.

At that moment the SS man at the pit shouted something to his comrade. The latter counted off about twenty persons and instructed them to go behind the earth mound. . . . I walked around the mound, and found myself confronted by a tremendous grave. People were closely wedged together and lying on top of each other so that only their heads were visible. Nearly all had blood running over their shoulders from their heads."

decided to couch the murders in pleasant language, lest civilians or outsiders get an unfavorable impression. The gas chambers would be called "bath establishments," transport to the death camps called "resettlement." The Jews themselves would be labeled, ironically, "the Chosen People."

From the Ghettos

From villages and little towns throughout eastern Europe, Jews were marched to larger cities and into special places known as ghettos. They were a living nightmare. Old, rundown buildings, like those of the worst modern slums, were cut off from the rest of the city by high brick walls, razor-sharp glass jutting out from concrete, and barbed wire. Around each ghetto stood Nazi guards with machine guns. No one was allowed out; the only ones allowed in had to show special passes to the guards.

Most of the inhabitants of the ghettos were children whose parents had been either murdered or sent to concentration camps. Heart-wrenching photographs bear witness to the horrible existence they

endured—tiny boys and girls, so thin they appeared skeletal, lying too weak to move, on crowded sidewalks. Their cries were a constant background to ghetto life. One Polish doctor remembered later how eerie the sound was. "These were not human cries, nor human weeping," he said, "but the haunted baying of creatures facing death."[114]

The living quarters were overcrowded—sometimes 100 people were crammed into a tiny apartment. Heat was nonexistent; food and water were scarce. The Nazis hoped that many of the Jews would die of disease or starvation, sparing the Reich the effort of transporting them to the death camps.

Within a few months of the decision to go ahead with the Final Solution, six death camps had been built—Chelmno, Treblinka, Sobibor, Majdanek, Belzec, and the largest, Auschwitz. Once the camps were ready, a steady stream of thousands of Jews was sent by train each day.

The Jews were told they were being resettled, sent to the country where they would have jobs on farms. They would have more space, more food, clean air. But the journey must have given many of them second thoughts about their true destination.

They were packed like cattle in railroad cars without windows. The cars, which had once been used to transport forty soldiers or eight horses, were now used to transport between 100 and 130 Jews. A survivor who was then seventeen years old remembers, "One hundred people standing in a locked railroad car, no food, no water, people dying, the smell of the dead, and we had no toilets. We did it right where we were standing, and we couldn't move away from it."[115]

Right or Left

Those who survived the journey were shoved off the cars and marched into the camp. As the prisoners filed in the entrance, two doctors quickly determined who had some value to the Reich as slave

(Above) The ghetto in Warsaw, Poland, was in a bombed out section of the city.
(Right) A homeless family languishes on the street in a Jewish ghetto.

Jews are herded toward waiting trains by Nazi soldiers. The trains took them to death camps for extermination.

labor, and who should be exterminated immediately. To the right meant a few days or weeks more of life; to the left meant death in an hour or two.

One survivor of Auschwitz recalls the casual, unfeeling way in which one doctor made his decisions—just a flick of his finger determined the fate of each person marched before him. "Like a metronome this finger swayed from side to side as each victim appeared before him, with a face molded in ice, without a flicker of an eyelash. Only the finger was alive, an organism itself, possessed of a strange power; it spelled out its ghastly message."[116]

Children were immediately sentenced to death, for they could do no real work.

The dead bodies of Jews who did not survive the nightmare journey to the death camp lie in a railroad car.

Pregnant women were also moved quickly to the left, as were crippled people, the elderly, or anyone who looked sick. Families were wrenched apart; children from their mothers, husbands from wives.

Lies to Calm

Although some of the prisoners had been in the ghettos and had seen Nazi abuse firsthand, many others arriving at the death camps believed the talk of resettlement. These Jews, especially those from Western Europe, had not seen the pogroms and the hideous conditions of the ghettos, and to them the stories seemed plausible. How could anyone truly

The entrance to this death camp promises freedom as the wages of labor. But the inmates' only freedom came by death.

believe that millions of innocent women and children were about to be systematically exterminated? The idea was staggering and defied logic. Even those prisoners who suspected, or who had heard rumors, did not always believe.

The Nazis at the death camps kept up an illusion that all would be well. The gas chambers and adjoining crematoria where the bodies would be burned were surrounded by lush green lawns and beautiful gardens. Each camp had its own particular disguise for the buildings; sometimes the gas chambers were labeled "Baths" or "Washing and Inhalation Equipment." At Treblinka, those judged too sick or too old to live were escorted to a building labeled "Infirmary." Camp officials even went so far as to have a Red Cross flag flying. As one historian writes, as the prisoners walked in, "they entered a waiting room with upholstered chairs, went through another door to the outside, were shot in the neck and thrown in a ditch."[117]

The lies were to keep the Jews calm and submissive. Just before the prisoners entered the gas chamber, guards instructed them to remove their clothing, because they were going to take a shower. Numbered hooks outside the chamber were even provided, ostensibly so that the prisoners' clothing would not get mixed up.

This, too, was a ruse. After the guards packed as many of the prisoners as possible into the chamber, the doors were sealed and locked from the outside. As some prisoners waited for water to run out of the false shower heads, others began to panic. By the time they realized they were trapped, it was only seconds before the chemical poison was dropped through a vent in the ceiling.

Zyklon-B created the lethal gas. Originally manufactured as a powerful insect-and rat-killer, it had found another use in the death camps. The dark blue crystals of Zyklon-B were poured into the vent, and ten to forty minutes later, everyone in the chamber was dead.

Special squads of prisoners then came into the chamber and removed the corpses. The bodies were hauled to the crematorium, where they were incinerated. The chambers were washed, cleaned, and made ready for the next group of prisoners.

Because of the thousands of Jews incinerated each day, the skies above the camps were always dark with clouds of smoke and ash. And everywhere was the same strangely sweet, sickening smell that prisoners soon learned was the smell of burning bodies.

One little girl was frightened and in tears after being separated from her mother. As she remembered years later, "Someone said to me, 'You know where your mother is? There.' And she pointed to smoke rising from the chimney."[118] Through the chimney, said the prisoners to one another, was the only way out of the death camps.

For Profit

Adolf Eichmann and his fellow planners had also schemed to make the mass annihilation of the Jews profitable for the Reich. In addition to seizing the clothing and belongings the Jews brought to the camps, the Nazis collected their glasses, shoes, and wedding rings. After the bodies were removed from the gas chambers, their mouths were pried open and their gold teeth yanked out, to be melted down and added to the Reich's treasury. Even the fat from corpses was boiled down and made into soap.

"Full Satisfaction in Practice"

In The Rise and Fall of the Third Reich, *historian William Shirer recounts "a lively competition" among several German businesses to get orders from the Nazis for gas chambers, Zyklon-B poison, and crematoria. To one-up its competitors, one firm emphasized its extensive experience in building the death machinery.*

"Another firm, C. H. Kori, also sought the Belgrade business, emphasizing its great experience in this field since it had already constructed four furnaces for Dachau and five for Lublin, which, it said, had given 'full satisfaction in practice:

'Following our verbal discussion regarding the delivery of equipment of simple construction for the burning of bodies, we are submitting plans for our perfected cremation ovens which operate with coal and which have hitherto given full satisfaction.

'We suggest two crematoria furnaces for the building planned, but we advise you to make further inquiries to make sure that two ovens will be sufficient for your requirements.

'We guarantee the effectiveness of the cremation ovens as well as their durability, the use of the best material and our faultless workmanship.

'Awaiting your further word, we will be at your service.
'Heil Hitler!'"

Canisters of deadly Zyklon-B, the poison used for the Holocaust.

A mountain of clothing and a drawerful of gold wedding rings were all that remained of thousands of lives snuffed out in one Nazi death camp.

Women's hair was shaved, too, and then cleaned, combed, and used to fill mattresses and pillows for Germans. One manufacturer even turned the hair into felt to make slippers for German sailors on submarines.

Unbelievably, there was even a demand for human skin. Frau Ilse Koch, the wife of a German commandant, made lamp shades from the skin. She especially liked skin with interesting tattoos. One historian reports that "one piece of skin that struck her fancy had the words 'Hansel and Gretel' tattooed on it. Frau Koch's table lamp was made of human bones and had a . . . human skin shade. Decorators pleaded for tattooed skin for their customers."[119]

Life on the Left

For those who had been deemed healthy enough or old enough to be of use to the Reich, life was unspeakably brutal. Even though they were temporarily spared being gassed and burned, these prisoners were abused and demeaned constantly, dying a little each day.

They lived in the most appalling conditions imaginable, from the crowded, vermin-infested bunks on which they were packed to the constant threat of death for misbehaving. Food was provided only in starvation rations, and survivors remember soups that contained buttons, mice, keys, rags, and tufts of hair. The black bread fed to them twice each day was made mostly of sawdust.

Hunger was so severe that prisoners would eat what was provided—and worse. One survivor remembers that she and others in her section found a barrel with rotting bones to which clung bits of raw meat and yellow fat. "Avariciously we gnawed these bones clean, like starved wolves, not even thinking of the poison such food might contain. Nothing happened to us. On the contrary, it tasted so good that when several days later . . . we thought regretfully of the bones and the greenish meat, and our mouths watered."[120]

It is not surprising that hundreds of prisoners died each week of hunger, diarrhea, and disease. Rats were a hated part of life in the camps. They lived among the prisoners, in the filthy straw of their bedding. They nibbled on the skin of those who died in the night, and became bold enough to attack the living. They grew fat and sleek, and were as big as cats.

There was no thought to treating the Jews better, for the Nazis were well aware that there was no shortage of labor. More trains arrived each day.

More than 400 prisoners were murdered every day by the Nazi guards in ways other than by the scheduled gassing. Savage, cruel behavior was common among the guards. Some organized games of tag among the prisoners; the losers were shot dead. Some guards amused themselves with a sadistic form of target practice, shooting the ears and noses off prisoners while they worked.

Strangely enough, young children seemed to arouse the most inhuman behavior in the guards. Babies born in the camps were often drowned in the presence of the mothers. According to historian Konnilyn Feig, a guard at Sobibor delighted in "ripping children out of their mothers' arms and tossing them into the air until they died."[121] There seemed no end to the way the camps could kill people.

In the Name of Medicine

The medical profession, usually so determined to save lives, was part of the Reich's camps as well. Himmler and other Nazi officials were interested in finding ways to increase the Aryan population, and encouraged doctors to use the Jews in the death camps as subjects. It was not long before the Reich command had given doctors the

Jewish slave laborers are stuffed into filthy bunks in a Nazi death camp. Many died from disease, maltreatment, and starvation.

Not Just Jews

The Jews were not the only group chosen for extermination by the Nazi government. As Barbara Rogasky writes in Smoke and Ashes, *the Reich also marked Gypsies, Poles, Russian prisoners of war, and the incurable sick for death. The following excerpt deals with the latter group.*

"Hitler signed an order . . . that called for the start of Operation T4. Doctors were allowed to select the incurable sick so that they could be killed. The order described them as 'life unworthy of life.' The 'mercy killing . . .' was carried out on the following: the senile; the mentally retarded; all Jews in mental hospitals; individuals who had been treated in any hospital, asylum, nursing home and so on for at least five years; deformed newborn babies; epileptics; invalids unable to work; victims of any incurable disease. . . .

For the purity of Aryan blood, these sick people had to die. Keeping them alive was also uneconomical, because they produced nothing and were examples, the Nazis said, of the 'useless eaters' in the nation."

go-ahead to use human guinea pigs for their experiments. Few of the "patients" survived.

Some doctors experimented with changing eye color, injecting dyes into the eyes of brown-eyed children to see if they would change to blue. Other prisoners were given high doses of X rays, or were operated on without anesthetic to see how much pain they could endure. Teenaged

A small part of the numbing horrors perpetrated by Hitler's Reich are depicted in these photos of corpses of death camp inmates.

Time is on the side of these concentration camp inmates; they survived long enough for the victorious Allied troops to find them.

girls were injected with poisons to study the effects on their reproductive organs. To see how much water a human could ingest, water was pumped through hoses forced down prisoners' throats until their lungs burst.

One test that was often repeated in the camps was to find out how long humans could stand cold temperatures. According

A row of ovens used to cremate death-camp victims reveals their ghastly contents of bones and ashes. The ovens burned continuously trying to keep up with the carnage.

to one account, 1,700 sick prisoners were stripped naked and forced to stand outside all night. "That night the temperature dropped below freezing. The prisoners stood in the square for four hours as they were sprayed alternately with hot and cold water. The groans of the dying rang through the camp as icicles formed all over their bodies."[122]

Not Fast Enough

From systematic gassing and shooting, from the horrible medical experiments and savage brutality, and from the inhuman conditions, more than 6 million Jews—and countless other Russians, Gypsies, and others—were murdered in the Reich's death camps. But not all the "undesirables" were killed, much to Hitler's great displeasure. And by 1945, time was rapidly running out for the Thousand-Year Reich.

9 The Fall of Hitler's Reich

In 1941 Adolf Hitler seemed to be riding a crest of triumph. Following the bloodless victories in the Rhineland, Austria, and Czechoslovakia and an easy march through Western Europe, by autumn of 1941 the führer and his armies seemed well on their way to total victory over the Allies.

With the defeat of each new country, there were fewer places from which the Allies could launch attacks at Germany. Hitler sent Gen. Erwin Rommel to North

Nazi general Erwin Rommel conquered North Africa for Hitler's Reich. His cunning earned him the title "The Desert Fox."

Africa to make certain that British forces there could not use Egypt or nearby countries as a base from which to attack the Nazis. Called "The Desert Fox" because of his cunning in battle, Rommel was as successful as the other Nazi military leaders. Each week seemed to bring good news from the war's fronts, and Hitler was confident that the fighting would be over very soon.

"This Winter of Our Misery"

The only setback for Hitler's army thus far was the stalemate in the Soviet Union. Cold, wet weather—combined with a new set of orders from the führer himself that split the German advance into three separate fronts—stalled what had been a fairly easy march toward Moscow. As the winter snows blasted the Russian countryside, the Germans were in deep trouble. Without proper winter clothing (and handicapped by their metal helmets, which conducted the icy cold) and with frozen weapons and machinery, the German army was forced to halt. The Soviets, on the other hand, were better prepared for the weather and fought on in spite of it.

German general Heinz Guderian was depressed by his army's plight and mourned

Soviet soldiers dressed in special winter gear are camouflaged amid the snow-covered trees. Unlike the unprepared Nazis, they could continue to fight in the cold.

the fact that he had been stopped so close to Moscow, his target. He wrote in his journal,

> Only he who saw the endless expanse of Russian snow during this winter of our misery and felt the icy wind that blew across it, burying in snow every object in its path; who drove for hour after hour through that no-man's land only at last to find too thin shelter with insufficiently clothed, half-starved men; and who also saw by contrast the well-fed, warmly clad and fresh Siberians, fully equipped for winter fighting . . . can truly judge the events which now occurred.[123]

When the thaw came the following spring, it was very clear that the momentum had shifted from the Germans to the

Soviets. With renewed energy and zeal, the Soviets pushed the German army back 100 miles. Although the Germans would win other battles on Russian soil, they would never get as close to Moscow as they had been that winter. The days of the easy victories were over.

As Hitler remained engrossed in his stalled offensive in the Soviet Union, another emergency arose halfway around the globe. The United States, neutral throughout the war, had changed from observer to participant. And Hitler was to make a serious political error that many historians believe cost him the war.

America First

Up until December 7, 1941, the United States had chosen to stay out of the war. Most Americans were isolationists—they wanted to stay clear of any trouble beyond U.S. borders. The last time Americans had fought someone else's war was in World War I—and it had been terribly costly both financially and in terms of human life. There seemed no good reason to repeat that mistake, isolationists believed.

President Franklin Roosevelt did not believe in isolationism. He had begun speaking out on the Nazi threat in 1937 and had urged Congress to begin appropriating money to prepare for war. But Roosevelt and others like him were in the minority, so in 1941 the United States still had not joined the fighting.

Hitler was thankful that the United States had kept its state of neutrality. America was a wealthy industrial nation, capable of supplying its soldiers with a

The Mountain Retreat

When not at the Chancellery residence in Berlin, Hitler spent a great deal of time at his mountain retreat, called Berghof. As biographer Robert Payne writes in The Life and Death of Adolf Hitler, *Berghof received a facelift by order of the führer.*

"The landscape, too, began to change its character. Forest paths became paved roads, all the villas and votive chapels in the neighborhood were torn down, and a score of ugly concrete buildings were built to house his guards, his guests, and his fleet of automobiles. Originally he had owned about three acres of land. Now he decreed that the whole slope . . . was *Führer* property, and the whole vast area was accordingly surrounded with barbed-wire fences. It occurred to him that the [mountain] itself could be tunneled in such a way that he could be propelled up to the summit in an elevator, thus permitting him to survey the surrounding landscape. . . . Workmen labored for three years at a cost of more than 30 million marks to carve a passage into the heart of the mountain and then to build a vertical shaft to the summit. The work was . . . completed just in time for his fiftieth birthday, April 20, 1939."

The Berghof, Hitler's retreat in the Bavarian Alps, was about ten miles south of Salzburg, Austria.

Smoke billows from the U.S. naval base at Pearl Harbor, Hawaii, on December 7, 1941, after a surprise air attack by Japan. The attack forced the United States into World War II.

huge arsenal of weapons. With its vast resources and large, well-equipped factories, America would be a frightening opponent. For that reason, the Nazi government did more than hope for American neutrality—it actively worked to keep the United States neutral. Hitler ordered his navy not to attack U.S. ships, even those suspected of carrying supplies to the Allies. In addition, German embassies in large American cities gave financial support to various political organizations urging neutrality.

A Costly Mistake

On December 7, 1941, Germany's ally, Japan, made an unexpected air strike against the American naval base at Pearl Harbor, Hawaii. Like Germany, Japan was interested in expanding its empire. The United States was an obstacle to Japan's territorial expansion, and the Japanese knew that sooner or later the two nations would enter into a war. The Japanese leaders decided to make the first move, when America least expected it.

The U.S. Congress moved quickly to declare war on Japan, and to fulfill the terms of his agreement with his ally, Hitler declared war on the United States just three days later. He did not believe that Germany would have to fight the American forces—in fact, he was more than a little relieved that it was Japan taking on the Americans, not Germany.

"I gained the impression," wrote German field marshal Wilhelm, "that the *Führer* felt that the war between Japan and America had suddenly relieved him of a nightmare burden; it certainly brought us some relief from the consequences of America's undeclared state of war with us."[124]

But Hitler's war declaration proved to be a mistake. Britain's prime minister Winston Churchill urged Roosevelt to delay a massive strike in the Pacific against the Japanese. Instead, Churchill argued, the Allies should concern themselves more with the combined European threats of Italy (another German ally) and Hitler. With the added support the Americans could bring to that front, he said, the Allies would gain the upper hand quickly.

So instead of fighting Japan in the Pacific, fresh, eager U.S. troops were bound for war against the Nazis in both Europe and North Africa. Hitler, with the cream of his army bogged down in the snow and mud of Russia, and his forces in Europe facing a heavily armed Allied attack, had a new worry. The war that Germany had expected to win quickly now seemed without end.

Shortages, Mumbling, and "Politeness Weeks"

The most telling signs that the war was not going well for Germany were the bombings. Berlin and other large German cities had been lightly bombed every so often by RAF fliers, but the raids were getting more frequent, and the damage more severe. Bombers were hitting German railroad lines and factories, crippling both production and transportation of badly needed goods.

The result was drastic shortages of food, fuel, and other necessities. Without sugar, eggs, milk, or gasoline—or even needles and thread for repairing clothing—the German people were reminded daily that the Reich's promises were not

Only rubble remains in a bombed out section of Munich, Germany, after RAF bombers relentlessly pummel it from the air. Later, American bombers added to the destruction. The continual bombing of German cities and supply routes eventually crippled Hitler's Reich and brought it to its knees.

(Above) A young German lad and his mother tow their belongings in a cart as they flee the destruction.

Punishing Conspirators

More than once during Hitler's years as leader of the Reich, members of his staff tried unsuccessfully to kill him. After one such attempt, the führer ordered all eight of the conspirators killed. He then enjoyed the film of the occasion, as described by William Shirer.

"The punishment was meted out as soon as the trial had ended on August 8. 'They must all be hanged like cattle,' Hitler had ordered, and they were. Out at Ploetzensee prison the eight condemned men were herded into a small room in which eight meathooks hung from the ceiling. One by one, after being stripped to the waist, they were strung up, a noose of piano wire being placed around their necks and attached to the meathooks. A movie camera whirled and the men dangled and strangled, their beltless trousers finally dropping off as they struggled, leaving them naked in their death agony. The developed film, as ordered, was rushed to Hitler so that he could view it, as well as the pictures of the trial, the same evening. Goebbels is said to have kept himself from fainting by holding both hands over his eyes."

being kept. Grumbling and complaining were common, although those who dared to criticize Hitler aloud continued to receive the harshest punishments.

To try to rally support for the government and the war effort, Goebbels and his staff unleashed a blizzard of propaganda, reminding Germans of the need for sacrifice. Goebbels even devised "Politeness Weeks," during which people were supposed to work together without the usual grumbling. Members of the Nazi party were urged to wear their armbands and uniforms at all times, to try to maintain enthusiasm for the war.

But there seemed to be a common mood of anxiety among the German people as the war entered its fourth year. The prevailing emotion of the German people was summed up in a report issued by Goebbels's office: "Who would have thought, after the great victories at the beginning, that the war would take this course and drag on so long?"[125]

"Rivers of Unquenchable Flame"

However, the vague feelings of nervousness gave way to panic in the months ahead. The bombing raids became incessant, with American and British fliers attacking German cities around the clock. Bomb shelters became a regular part of daily life.

(Left) Smoke rises in the distance from bombs just dropped by an American bomber on a German target in 1943. (Right) A German woman carrying all she can flees for her life as bomb blasts and fires destroy everything around her.

German families came to rely on a *Drahtfunk*, or "cable radio," for early warning. The device was attached to a regular radio and emitted a *ping-ping* sound when an Allied plane came close. As one historian writes, "families and neighbors divided the night into watches of '*Drahtfunk* duty,' taking turns sitting by the radio on alert for the *ping-ping* to start."[126]

But there were times when the early-warning devices did not help. Although every bomb was a threat, the Germans learned to fear one type more than any other: phosphorus bombs, which created firestorms that heated the air to an astonishing 1,800 degrees Fahrenheit. The damage they did was beyond belief.

One man who lived through a Berlin air raid says that his most vivid memory is of "phosphorus bombs that burst and glowed green and emptied themselves down the walls and along the streets in flaming rivers of unquenchable flame, seeping down cellar stairs and sealing the exits to the air raid shelters."[127] Another witness simply wrote, "No imagination will ever be able to comprehend the scenes of terror."[128]

But besides the obvious physical danger, the incessant bombings caused severe emotional stress. That the country could be continually invaded from the skies signalled to some German civilians that they should not trust Hitler's talk of a "superrace" and an easy victory over lesser humans. After all, weren't German cities being destroyed, centuries-old architecture being reduced to rubble and dust? Why was Hitler doing nothing to stop the destruction?

Even Nazi officials like Göring and Goebbels were nervous about the ongoing damage to important German cities. It was no longer possible to pretend that Germany was winning the war, that Germany could not be stopped in its quest for superiority.

At the beginning of the war, Göring had said in his speeches that the German fighting force was so mighty, there was no danger to civilians. He told people he was so confident that the Allies would never be able to drop a bomb on Berlin, the people could call him by the Jewish name "Meyer" if it ever happened. Now, German citizens, frightened and angry because of the bombing, muttered about it being "Meyer's fault."

Withdrawing

Hitler's strategy had depended on a quick defeat of the Soviet Union. The blitzkrieg that had served him well at the war's beginning, however, had stalled. As the Soviet army pushed in from the east, the British

An American tank passes under the Arc de Triomphe as the Allies liberate Paris in the summer of 1944.

Disguising Berlin

One of the ways in which Hermann Göring hoped to keep Berlin safe from Allied bombers was to make the city "invisible," as Charles Whiting writes in The Home Front: Germany.

"One stratagem . . . was to disguise the city's landmarks as forests, black out almost all its lights, and decoy night-flying British bombers into hitting faintly illuminated dummy structures erected several miles away. Just in case, however, the city fathers began to sheathe Berlin's museums, murals, and monuments with bricks and sandbags. Portable treasures—eventually including paintings looted from conquered France and Holland—were packed away in crates to be stored in vaults underground. As they watched workmen shroud the broad boulevards in camouflage netting and paint blackout markers on the curbs, few Berliners could avoid pangs of foreboding."

After routing the Germans from Chambois, France, in 1944, American infantrymen hold up a captured Nazi flag while posing before a wrecked German tank.

and Americans stormed in from the west and south. Paris was liberated, and other Nazi-dominated areas were falling.

Hitler himself had grown quiet and aloof as the war's momentum changed. He had aged considerably in the preceding three years; many people believed him to be on the verge of insanity. He continued to distrust his generals, not allowing them to make decisions that might have saved lives. Instead, he gave garbled and confused battle orders, sometimes to divisions that had been wiped out weeks before.

"He often lied without hesitation," recalled one of his generals later, "and assumed that others lied to him. He believed no one anymore. It had already been difficult enough dealing with him; it now became a torture that grew steadily worse from month to month. He frequently lost all self-control and his language grew increasingly violent."[129]

Hitler seemed to have little interest in maintaining his position of all-wise führer to the German people. He rarely made public appearances. As historian Albert Marrin writes,

> There were no speeches to frenzied crowds, no more rallies with a million people marching by torchlight and chanting his name. Once he could draw on the mood and passion of his audience to rally them to his side. Now he didn't want to know *what* the German people felt.[130]

The Death of the Reich

When in 1945 it became clear even to Hitler that the war was hopeless, he moved into a bunker below his Berlin headquarters. Beneath six feet of earth, and isolated

Hitler's personal bomb shelter (square building in foreground), by his own doing, became his tomb.

Göring, had approached the Allies about peace negotiations.

According to a witness, Hitler lost all composure. "Nothing is spared me," Hitler raved. "No allegiances are kept, no honor lived up to, no disappointments that I have not had, no betrayals that I have not experienced, and now this above all else! Nothing remains. Every wrong has already been done me."[131]

Despairing that all was lost, and fearing what would become of him if he were captured by the Russians storming Berlin, Hitler shot himself on April 30, 1945. By previous order, SS officers soaked his body in gasoline and burned it in the garden of the Chancellery. Following his master's lead, Goebbels administered cyanide to his wife and children before taking the poison himself.

A week after the suicides of Hitler and Goebbels, the German forces surrendered. The war was officially over; however, the world was only beginning to realize the extent of its horror.

from the world by sixteen feet of solid concrete, he grew more and more despondent. He shared the bunker with his trusted aide Goebbels, Goebbels's wife and six children, and a few trusted SS officers. There the führer monitored his troops' last-ditch efforts to save Berlin. He was furious when he learned that two of his most devoted assistants, Himmler and

A Disturbing Legacy

One of the last efforts made by the Nazis before the Allies overtook Germany was to hide the evidence of the "Final Solution." Many prisoners were forced by death-camp guards to march into territory still held by German troops. Any who could not keep up—and thousands could not—were shot. But as Soviet troops invaded Poland, they found Auschwitz, Treblinka, and the other death camps. And the Allies moving into Germany from the west were shocked to see the Nazis' answer to the "Jewish question."

Fighting off the stench from death camp corpses discovered by U.S. troops, a German woman searches among them for a lost relative.

One American soldier who helped to liberate a death camp was appalled:

> The barracks were inhabited by pitiful starving prisoners . . . living skeletons, and many already dead. . . . Outside were heaps of naked bodies like stacks of logs. . . . I had witnessed many battlefield deaths. . . . However, at this sight, I just cried and cried. I lay down my pistols, carbine, and grenades out of respect for the dead.[132]

"Following Orders"

As the Allies liberated the death camps and concentration camps throughout Germany and Poland, people everywhere were horrified. Photographs showing heaps of dead bodies the Nazis had not had time to cremate or bury were published in newspapers all over the world. Stories of atrocities were told and retold by skeleton-thin survivors, too weak to stand.

Between 1945 and 1949 many Nazi leaders who had taken part in the atrocities were put on trial for their actions. The most widely publicized trials were held in the German city of Nuremberg. Writer William Shirer attended some of the trials

and was surprised at the change in the men who had once been so powerful:

> I had often watched them in their hour of glory and power at the annual party rallies in this town. In the dock before the International Military Tribunal they looked different. . . . Attired in rather shabby clothes, slumped in their seats fidgeting nervously, they no longer resembled the arrogant leaders of old. They seemed to be a drab assortment of mediocrities. It seemed difficult to grasp that such men, when last you had seen them, had wielded such monstrous power, that such as they could conquer a great nation and most of Europe.[133]

Most of those on trial used the defense that they were "merely following orders." But the judges—French, American, and British—were unsympathetic. Many of

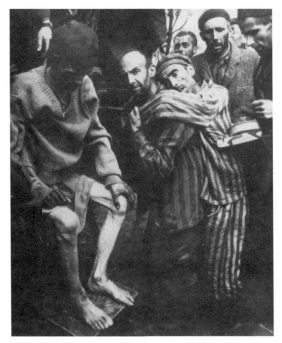

Barely alive, concentration camp survivors are liberated by American troops in 1945. Only then did the world realize the details of Hitler's "Final Solution."

Nazi leaders sit passively at their trial in Nuremberg. Some were sentenced to death; others to life imprisonment. Göring and Himmler cheated the hangman by taking cyanide.

those tried at Nuremberg were sentenced to death by hanging or to life imprisonment for their part in Nazi activities. A few, such as Himmler and Göring, decided to kill themselves by taking cyanide rather than face the consequences of their actions.

A Country Divided, a Country Born

The fall of Hitler's Reich changed people's lives just as dramatically as had its rise just twelve years before. Those who had been its most abused victims, the Jews, were eagerly seeking a homeland, one far from the discrimination and hatred they had experienced in Europe.

No matter where Europe's Jews settled—in Europe, in the United States, or in Israel—people everywhere felt an urgent need to keep the memory of Hitler's Holocaust alive, so that such horrors could never happen again.

Hundreds of thousands of Jews who survived the Reich went to the Holy Land, to Palestine, to which other Jews had fled when Hitler came to power. The majority of Palestine's people were Arabs alarmed by the influx of Jews into their land; even so, in 1947 the United Nations agreed to divide Palestine into two parts—an Arab state and a Jewish state, the latter called Israel. The plan was acceptable to the Jews, but not to the Arabs, and fighting between the two groups broke out almost immediately.

The Reich's end changed the world map not only in the Middle East, but in Germany as well. The victorious Allies were reluctant to repeat the mistakes of the Treaty of Versailles by punishing Germany so harshly that the country could never stand on its feet again. But at the same time, they wanted guarantees that there would never be another Reich like Hitler's.

European Jews leave Germany for Israel in hopes of escaping their horrible memories of persecution.

The Allies decided to divide the military occupation of Germany among the four Allied nations—the Soviet Union, France, Britain, and the United States. Eventually France, Britain, and the United States combined their zones into what became known as the Federal Republic of Germany. The Soviet Union set up a Communist government in its zone, which became known as the German Democratic Republic. Thus, Germany was split into two very separate countries, which were not reunited until 1989.

Troubling Questions

Despite the restructuring of Germany's politics and the changing of its boundaries, and despite the punishment of some of the Nazi leaders, Hitler's Reich left behind some troubling questions. In the months and years after the end of World War II, as the layers of deception were peeled away, the world was shocked at what it saw—the horrors of the death camps, the injustices done to all who opposed the führer, the abridgement of people's rights. And quite rightly, the world asked questions: How could this have happened? Why did no one—anywhere—do anything to stop it? In a country that had been humiliated and degraded after one world war, how could another war have been so eagerly embraced?

Truthful answers cannot put the responsibility on Hitler alone. He led the Reich, but millions of people followed him eagerly—and many others chose to stand and watch in frightened silence.

Notes

Introduction: A Thousand-Year Reich

1. Ernst Klee, Willi Dressen, and Volker Riess, eds., *The Good Old Days: The Holocaust as Seen by Its Perpetrators and Bystanders*. New York: Free Press, 1988.

2. Klee et al., *The Good Old Days*.

3. Klee et al., *The Good Old Days*.

Chapter 1: "Squeezed . . . Until the Pips Squeak"

4. Ronald Gray, *Hitler and the Germans*. Cambridge: Cambridge University Press, 1981.

5. Charles Bracelen Flood, *Hitler: The Path to Power*. Boston: Houghton Mifflin, 1989.

6. Michael Wright, *Illustrated History of World War II*. London: Reader's Digest Association, 1989.

7. Albert Marrin, *Hitler*. New York: Viking, 1987.

8. Flood, *Hitler: The Path to Power*.

9. "The Road to War," *Time*, August 28, 1989.

10. Flood, *Hitler: The Path to Power*.

11. Wright, *Illustrated History of World War II*.

12. Robert T. Elson, *Prelude to War*. Alexandria, VA: Time-Life Books, 1977.

13. Elson, *Prelude to War*.

14. Flood, *Hitler: The Path to Power*.

15. Time-Life Books Editors, *The Twisted Dream*, Alexandria, VA: Time-Life Books, 1990.

16. Heinz Oskar Hauenstein, quoted in Time-Life Books Editors, *The Twisted Dream*.

17. Time-Life Books Editors, *The Twisted Dream*.

18. Warren B. Morris, *The Weimar Republic and Nazi Germany*. Chicago: Nelson-Hall, 1982.

Chapter 2: Waiting in the Wings

19. John Keegan, "Hitler's Grab for World Power," *U.S. News & World Report*, August 28, 1989.

20. Time-Life Books Editors, *The Twisted Dream*.

21. Flood, *Hitler: The Path to Power*.

22. Robert Payne, *The Life and Death of Adolf Hitler*. New York: Praeger, 1973.

23. Payne, *The Life and Death of Adolf Hitler*.

24. Marrin, *Hitler*.

25. Keegan, "Hitler's Grab for World Power."

26. Quoted in Keegan, "Hitler's Grab for World Power."

27. Marrin, *Hitler*.

28. Marrin, *Hitler*.

29. Payne, *The Life and Death of Adolf Hitler*.

30. Quoted in Elson, *Prelude to War*.

31. Quoted in Payne, *The Life and Death of Adolf Hitler*.

32. Flood, *Hitler: The Path to Power*.

33. Flood, *Hitler: The Path to Power*.

34. Quoted in Payne, *The Life and Death of Adolf Hitler*.

35. Time-Life Books Editors, *The Twisted Dream*.

36. Quoted in Time-Life Books Editors, *The Twisted Dream*.

37. Flood, *Hitler: The Path to Power*.

Chapter 3: Seeds of the Reich

38. Quoted in Time-Life Books Editors, *The Twisted Dream*.

39. Quoted in Flood, *Hitler: The Path to Power*.

40. Payne, *The Life and Death of Adolf Hitler*.

41. Time-Life Books Editors, *The Twisted Dream.*

42. Payne, *The Life and Death of Adolf Hitler.*

43. Flood, *Hitler: The Path to Power.*

44. Time-Life Books Editors, *The Twisted Dream.*

45. Morris, *The Weimar Republic and Nazi Germany.*

46. Payne, *The Life and Death of Adolf Hitler.*

47. Quoted in Time-Life Books Editors, *The Twisted Dream.*

48. Marrin, *Hitler.*

49. David Williamson, *The Third Reich.* New York: Bookwright, 1989.

50. Elson, *Prelude to War.*

51. Quoted in Flood, *Hitler: The Path to Power.*

Chapter 4: Coming to Power

52. William Shirer, *The Rise and Fall of the Third Reich.* New York: Simon and Schuster, 1959.

53. Payne, *The Life and Death of Adolf Hitler.*

54. David Adler, *We Remember the Holocaust.* New York: Henry Holt, 1989.

55. Marrin, *Hitler.*

56. Time-Life Books Editors, *The Center of the Web.* Alexandria, VA: Time-Life Books, 1990.

57. William Loren Katz, *An Album of Nazism.* New York: Franklin Watts, 1979.

58. Robert Leckie, *The Story of World War II.* New York: Random House, 1964.

59. Edwin Hoyt, *Hitler's War.* New York: McGraw-Hill, 1988.

60. Wright, *Illustrated History of World War II.*

61. Barbara Rogasky, *Smoke and Ashes: The Story of the Holocaust.* New York: Holiday House, 1988.

Chapter 5: Life in Nazi Germany

62. Time-Life Books Editors, *The New Order.* Alexandria, VA: Time-Life Books, 1989.

63. Milton Meltzer, *Never to Forget: The Jews of the Holocaust.* New York: Harper, 1976.

64. Shirer, *The Rise and Fall of the Third Reich.*

65. Shirer, *The Rise and Fall of the Third Reich.*

66. Time-Life Books Editors, *The New Order.*

67. Thomas Fuchs, *The Hitler Fact Book.* Los Angeles: Fountain Books, 1990.

68. Quoted in Williamson, *The Third Reich.*

69. Shirer, *The Rise and Fall of the Third Reich.*

70. Time-Life Books Editors, *The New Order.*

71. Time-Life Books Editors, *The New Order.*

72. Time-Life Books Editors, *The New Order.*

73. R. Conrad Stein, *Hitler Youth.* Chicago: Children's Press, 1985.

74. Time-Life Books Editors, *The New Order.*

75. Williamson, *The Third Reich.*

76. Quoted in Stein, *Hitler Youth.*

77. Stein, *Hitler Youth.*

78. Marrin, *Hitler.*

79. Adolf Hitler, *Mein Kampf.* New York: Reynal and Hitchcock, 1939.

80. Adler, *We Remember the Holocaust.*

81. Johannes Steinhoff, Peter Pechel, and Dennis Showalter, eds., *Voices from the Third Reich: An Oral History.* Washington, DC: Regnery Gateway, 1989.

82. Shirer, *The Rise and Fall of the Third Reich.*

83. Adler, *We Remember the Holocaust.*

Chapter 6: Testing the Waters

84. Hitler, *Mein Kampf.*

85. Time-Life Books Editors, *Fists of Steel.* Alexandria, VA: Time-Life Books, 1988.

86. Time-Life Books Editors, *Fists of Steel.*

87. Shirer, *The Rise and Fall of the Third Reich.*

88. "The Road to War," *Time.*

89. "The Road to War," *Time.*

90. "The Road to War," *Time.*

91. Shirer, *The Rise and Fall of the Third Reich*.

92. Adler, *We Remember the Holocaust*.

93. Hoyt, *Hitler's War*.

94. Payne, *The Life and Death of Adolf Hitler*.

95. Hoyt, *Hitler's War*.

96. "The Road to War," *Time*.

Chapter 7: The Reich at War

97. "The Road to War," *Time*.

98. "The Road to War," *Time*.

99. Hoyt, *Hitler's War*.

100. "The Road to War," *Time*.

101. Payne, *The Life and Death of Adolf Hitler*.

102. Quoted in Shirer, *The Rise and Fall of the Third Reich*.

103. Wright, *Illustrated History of World War II*.

104. Wright, *Illustrated History of World War II*.

105. Hitler, *Mein Kampf*.

106. Shirer, *The Rise and Fall of the Third Reich*.

107. Payne, *The Life and Death of Adolf Hitler*.

108. Wright, *Illustrated History of World War II*.

109. Quoted in R. Conrad Stein, *The Invasion of Russia*. Chicago: Children's Press, 1985.

110. Marrin, *Hitler*.

Chapter 8: A Descent into Hell

111. Steinhoff et al., *Voices from the Third Reich*.

112. Meltzer, *Never to Forget*.

113. Quoted in Shirer, *The Rise and Fall of the Third Reich*.

114. Quoted in Miriam Chaikin, *A Nightmare in History: The Holocaust 1933–1945*. New York: Clarion Books, 1987.

115. Quoted in Adler, *We Remember the Holocaust*.

116. Quoted in Rogasky, *Smoke and Ashes*.

117. Rogasky, *Smoke and Ashes*.

118. Quoted in Adler, *We Remember the Holocaust*.

119. Konnilyn G. Feig, *Hitler's Death Camps: The Sanity of Madness*. New York: Holmes and Meier, 1979.

120. Quoted in Feig, *Hitler's Death Camps*.

121. Feig, *Hitler's Death Camps*.

122. Feig, *Hitler's Death Camps*.

Chapter 9: The Fall of Hitler's Reich

123. Shirer, *The Rise and Fall of the Third Reich*.

124. Hoyt, *Hitler's War*.

125. Charles Whiting, *The Home Front: Germany*. Alexandria, VA: Time-Life Books, 1982.

126. Whiting, *The Home Front*.

127. Quoted in Whiting, *The Home Front*.

128. Quoted in Whiting, *The Home Front*.

129. Quoted in Shirer, *The Rise and Fall of the Third Reich*.

130. Marrin, *Hitler*.

131. Shirer, *The Rise and Fall of the Third Reich*.

Epilogue: A Disturbing Legacy

132. Quoted in Adler, *We Remember the Holocaust*.

133. Shirer, *The Rise and Fall of the Third Reich*.

For Further Reading

David A. Adler, *We Remember the Holocaust.* New York: Henry Holt, 1989.

Robert T. Elson, *Prelude to War.* Alexandria, VA: Time-Life Books, 1977.

Bernt Engelmann, *In Hitler's Germany.* New York: Schocken Books, 1982.

Ina R. Friedman, *The Other Victims: First-Person Stories of Non-Jews Persecuted by the Nazis.* New York: Houghton Mifflin, 1990.

Richard Grunberger, *The 12-Year Reich.* New York: Holt, Rinehart and Winston, 1971.

Edwin Hoyt, *Hitler's War.* New York: McGraw-Hill, 1988.

John Keegan, "Hitler's Grab for World Power," *U.S. News & World Report.* August 28, 1989.

Robert Leckie, *The Story of World War II.* New York: Random House, 1964.

Albert Marrin, *Hitler.* New York: Viking, 1987.

Milton Meltzer, *Never to Forget: The Jews of the Holocaust.* New York: Harper, 1976.

Abraham Resnick, *The Holocaust.* San Diego: Lucent Books, 1991.

Barbara Rogasky, *Smoke and Ashes: The Story of the Holocaust.* New York: Holiday House, 1988.

William Shirer, *20th Century Journal*, Vol. 2, The Nightmare Years. New York: Bantam, 1984.

R. Conrad Stein, *Hitler's Youth.* Chicago: Children's Press, 1985.

Time, "The Road to War," August 28, 1989.

Time-Life Books Editors, *Third Reich Series.* Alexandria, VA: Time-Life Books.

The Apparatus of Death (1991)

The Center of the Web (1990)

Fists of Steel (1988)

The Heel of the Conqueror (1991)

The New Order (1989)

The SS (1988)

Storming to Power (1989)

The Twisted Dream (1990)

Philip Warner, *World War II: The Untold Story.* London: Bodley Head, 1988.

Charles Whiting, *The Home Front: Germany.* Alexandria, VA: Time-Life Books, 1982.

David Williamson, *The Third Reich.* New York: Bookwright, 1989.

Works Consulted

Joseph Bendersky, *A History of Nazi Germany.* Chicago: Nelson-Hall, 1985. A good look at the factors that helped Hitler rise to power.

John Bradley, *The Illustrated History of the Third Reich.* New York: Grossett and Dunlap, 1978. An interesting source with excellent photographs, especially of the war.

Miriam Chaikin, *A Nightmare in History: The Holocaust 1933–1945.* New York: Clarion Books, 1987. Provides good background information on the anti-Semitism in Hitler's Reich.

Eugene Davidson, *The Making of Adolf Hitler: The Birth and Rise of Nazism.* New York: Macmillan, 1977. A well-documented account of the Nazi party's rise to power.

Konnilyn G. Feig, *Hitler's Death Camps: The Sanity of Madness.* New York: Holmes and Meier, 1979. A graphic account of life in the death camps. Excellent primary quotations.

Charles Bracelen Flood, *Hitler: The Path to Power.* Boston: Houghton Mifflin, 1989. A very readable account of Hitler's life up to the time he came to power.

Thomas Fuchs, *The Hitler Fact Book.* Los Angeles: Fountain Books, 1990. Fascinating, little-known facts about various aspects of Hitler's life.

Ronald Gray, *Hitler and the Germans.* Cambridge: Cambridge University Press, 1981. Short and concise, this book gives a good overview of the Weimar Republic's fall from power.

William Loren Katz, *An Album of Nazism.* New York: Franklin Watts, 1979. Good photographs in a readable, concise text.

Ernst Klee, Willi Dressen, and Volker Riess, eds., *The Good Old Days: The Holocaust as Seen by Its Perpetrators and Bystanders.* New York: Free Press, 1988. A collection of chilling eyewitness accounts of the activities of the *Einsatzgruppen.* Graphic photographs.

Lawrence L. Langer, *Holocaust Testimonies: The Ruins of Memory.* New Haven, CT: Yale University Press, 1991. Painful accounts of the Holocaust's psychological effects on its survivors.

Warren B. Morris, *The Weimar Republic and Nazi Germany.* Chicago: Nelson-Hall, 1982. Excellent bibliography.

Robert Payne, *The Life and Death of Adolf Hitler.* New York: Praeger, 1973. A thoroughly readable account of Hitler's life. Letters and photographs are included.

Detlev J. K. Peukert, *Inside Nazi Germany.* New Haven, CT: Yale University Press, 1982. A thoroughly documented account of life in Germany during the years of Hitler's Reich.

Anthony Read and David Fisher, *Kristallnacht: The Unleashing of the Holocaust.* New York: Peter Bedrick Books, 1989. Excellent quotations from witnesses to the beginning of the Holocaust.

William Shirer, *The Rise and Fall of the Third Reich.* New York: Simon and Schuster, 1959. One of the most thorough accounts of Hitler's Reich. Excellent source notes and quotations.

Johannes Steinhoff, Peter Pechel, and Dennis Showalter, eds., *Voices from the Third Reich: An Oral History.* Washington, DC: Regnery Gateway, 1989. A helpful collection of testimonies of participants in and victims of Hitler's Reich.

David Williamson, *The Third Reich.* New York: Bookwright, 1989. Excellent glossary of terms; helpful thumbnail sketches of important Nazi leaders.

Index

Picasso, Pablo, 60
Poland
    as target of *Lebensraum,* 74
    invaded by Nazi Gemany,
        84–87
    Kristallnacht in, 93–94
propaganda
    employed in Nazi Germany,
        58–62

Reich Chamber of Culture, 59,
    62
Rhineland
    Hitler invades, 77–78
Rogasky, Barbara, 104
Röhm, Ernst, 38, 46, 48, 51, 56
Rommel, General Erwin, 106
Roosevelt, President Franklin,
    107
Rosenberg, Alfred, 91

SA corps (*Sturm Abteilung*). *See*
    Storm Troopers
Schutzstaffen. See SS forces
Shirer, William
    on anti-Semitism, 72
    on gas chambers, 101
    on German propaganda, 59, 62
    reports on Nuremberg trials,
        116–117
Siegfried Line, 87
Sinclair, Upton, 62
sitzkrieg, 87
Sobibor death camp, 98, 103
Soviet Union
    invasion of Poland and, 84, 86,
        87
    Nazi Germany invades, 90–92
        winter stalemate, 106–107,
        110
    retaliates against Germany, 114
    target of *Lebensraum,* 74
    troops liberate death camps,
        116
SS forces (*Schutzstaffen*)
    creation of, 50–51
    destruction of Storm Troopers
        and, 57
    military training of, 75
    terrorize Jews, 69
Stalin, Joseph
    Nazi-Soviet Pact and, 84
Storm Troopers (*Sturm Abteilung,*
    SA)

campaign of fear, 48–50, 54, 55
creation of, 38–39, 46
Hitler orders Night of the
    Long Knives, 56–57
terrorize Jews, 69
Strength Through Joy programs,
    66
Stukas planes, 86
Sturm Abteilung. See Storm Troopers
swastika
    use as Nazi symbol, 36, 37

Treaty of Versailles
    harsh terms of, 13–18, 20, 74
        Germany fails to make pay-
            ments on, 20–21, 40,
            45
    Hitler's beliefs on, 35, 36–37,
        74
Treblinka death camp, 98, 100,
    116
Tubbesing, Fritz, 76

"undesirables", 12
United States
    bombing raids on Germany,
        112
    declares war on Japan, 109
    Great Depression, 47
    helps German economy, 45
    isolationist policy, 107
    Jewish immigrants and, 94
    military aid to Great Britain,
        89
    stock market crash, 46–47

van der Lubbe, Marinus, 53–54
Van Gogh, Vincent, 60
Vienna, Austria
    anti-Semitism in, 27
Vienna School of Fine Arts, 25–26
von Hindenburg, President Paul
    death of, 57
    manipulated by Hitler, 52–55
    popularity of, 48, 51
von Kahl, Gustav, 41, 42
von Lossow, General Otto, 41, 42
von Rundstedt, Gerd, 90
von Schirach, Baldur, 65
von Schuschnigg, Kurt, 78–79
von Seisser, Colonel Hans, 41, 42

Weimar Republic
    economics in, 21–23, 40, 45

effect of U.S. stock market
    crash on, 47
formation of, 18
instability of, 19–21
Jews blamed for problems of,
    34
Wells, H. G., 62
Wilhelm II
    flees Germany, 15, 18, 31
Wilson, Woodrow, 15
women
    treatment in Nazi Germany,
        63–64
World War I, 13–18, 20
World War II
    Allies declare war, 87
    blitzkrieg, 85–87, 91
    failure of appeasement, 81–82,
        83–84
    France
        liberation of, 114
        surrenders to Germany,
            88
    Great Britain and
        bombing of, 89–90
        refusal to surrender, 88
    Japan bombs Pearl Harbor,
        109
    Nazi Germany
        attack on Soviet Union,
            90–92, 106–107
        bombing in, 110–113
        declares war on United
            States, 109
        France surrenders to, 88
        invades Poland, 84–87
        surrender of, 115
        takes Belgium, Luxem-
            bourg, and Nether-
            lands, 87
        takes Denmark and Norway,
            87
    Soviet Union
        Germany invades, 90–92,
            106–107
        pushing Germany out, 107,
            113
    United States
        declaration of war, 109
        fights in Europe, 110
        Hitler wants neutrality of,
            107, 109
        Pearl Harbor, 109–110

Zyklon-B, 100, 101

Picture Credits

Cover photo: Library of Congress

Adolf Hitler: Bilder aus dem Leben des Fuhrers, Hamburg: Herausgegeben Vom Cigaretten, 1936/ Simon Wiesenthal Center Archives, Los Angeles, CA, 11, 65 (right)

AP/Wide World Photos, 9, 14, 23 (right), 25, 38, 50 (both), 52, 65 (left), 66 (both), 69 (right), 75, 77, 82, 83, 88 (bottom), 115

Auschwitz Memorial Museum/Bildarchiv Preussischer Kulturbesitz/Simon Wiesenthal Center Archives, Los Angeles, CA, 101

© Barnaby's Picture Library, 60, 61

Bet Lohame Ha - Geta'ot/Simon Wiesenthal Center Archives, Los Angeles, CA, 28

The Bettmann Archive, 8, 15 (top, left), 17, 19, 24 (right), 36 (left), 40, 47 (both), 53, 57

Bildarchiv Preussischer Kulturbesitz/Simon Wiesenthal Center Archives, Los Angeles, CA, 62, 79 (top), 95, 99 (bottom, right)

Bundesarchiv/Simon Wiesenthal Center Archives, Los Angeles, CA, 98 (right)

Bundesarchiv Koblenz/Simon Wiesenthal Center Archives, Los Angeles, CA, 71 (bottom), 98 (left)

Der Stuermer, January 1934/Simon Wiesenthal Center Archives, Los Angeles, CA, 69 (left)

Deutschland Erwacht/Simon Wiesenthal Center Archives, Los Angeles, CA, 54, 58, 74

Ein Bilderbuch fuer Gross und Klein, Nuremberg, 1936/ Simon Wiesenthal Center Archives, Los Angeles, CA, 71 (top)

Hebrew Immigrant Aid Society/Simon Wiesenthal Center Archives, Los Angeles, CA, 118

Library of Congress, 15 (top, right), 36 (right), 41, 84

National Archives, 10, 13, 16, 30, 31, 39, 68, 72, 79 (bottom), 85, 88 (top), 89, 91, 92, 99 (top), 99 (bottom, left), 102 (both), 103, 104 (both), 105 (both), 106, 107, 108, 109, 110 (both), 112 (both), 113, 114, 116, 117 (both)

Simon Wiesenthal Center Archives, Los Angeles, CA, 73

Stichting Nederlands Foto & Grafisch Centrum/ Simon Wiesenthal Center Archives, Los Angeles, CA, 94

UPI/Bettmann, 15 (bottom), 21 (both), 23 (left), 24 (left), 32, 35, 42, 46, 48, 49, 56, 59

About the Author

Gail B. Stewart received her undergraduate degree from Gustavus Adolphus College in St. Peter, Minnesota. She did her graduate work in English, linguistics, and curriculum study at the College of St. Thomas and the University of Minnesota. Stewart taught English and reading for more than ten years.

She has written over forty-eight books for young people, including a six-part series called *Living Spaces.* She has written several books for Lucent Books including *Drug Trafficking* and *Acid Rain.*

Stewart and her husband live in Minneapolis with their three sons, two dogs, and a cat. She enjoys reading (especially children's books) and playing tennis.

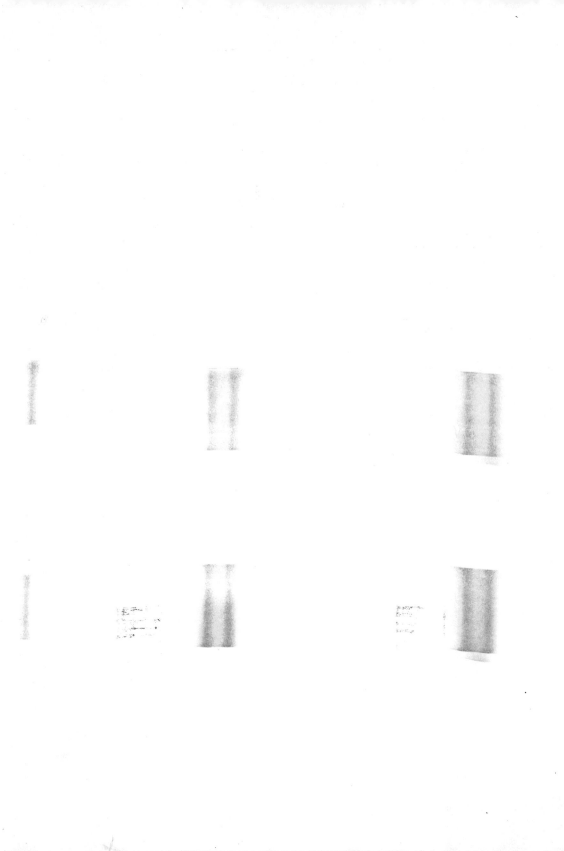

943.086   Stewart, Gail.
STE
          Hitler's Reich.

$19.92   2171

DATE			
MAY 3			

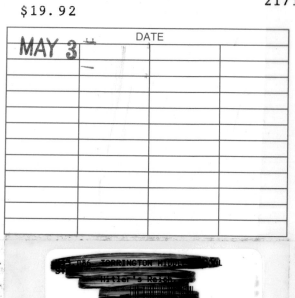